NUMBER 96

Yale French Studies

50 Years of *Yale French Studies:* A Commemorative Anthology Part 1: 1948–1979

Prologues

I. 1948–1959

II. 1960–1969

III. 1970–1979

D1566212

Yale French Studies

Charles A. Porter and Alyson Waters, *Special editors
for this issue*
Alyson Waters, *Managing editor*
Editorial board: Christopher Miller (Chair), Ora Avni,
Jeremy Billetdeaux, R. Howard Bloch, Peter Brooks,
Unity Dienes, Shoshana Felman, Françoise Jaouën,
Charles A. Porter, Susan Weiner
Editorial assistant: James F. Austin
Editorial office: 82-90 Wall Street, Room 308.
Mailing address: P.O. Box 208251, New Haven,
Connecticut 06520-8251
Sales and subscription office:
Yale University Press, P.O. Box 209040
New Haven, Connecticut 06520-9040
Published twice annually by Yale University Press

Designed by James J. Johnson and set in Trump
Medieval Roman by The Composing Room of
Michigan, Inc. Printed in the United States of
America by the Vail-Ballou Press, Binghamton, N.Y.

ISSN 044-0078
ISBN for this issue 0-300-08139-1

Prologues

CHARLES A. PORTER

Yale French Studies:
A Short, Tendentious History

The first issue of *Yale French Studies* bore the date Spring-Summer 1948. The present publication marks, therefore (with only a slight delay), the golden anniversary of a journal that has reflected—and maybe occasionally influenced—the evolution of French literary studies over a half century. In selecting articles to be included in this two-volume anthology, five members of the Editorial Board have looked for scholars and themes that reflect (or subvert, or disrupt) the trends and interests of a vibrant cultural and scholarly tradition going through a period of intellectual ferment. The overview that arises from the introductory essays to each decade and the selections reprinted is by no means meant to present a comprehensive, or even objective, notion of what *Yale French Studies* has accomplished, however. The two volumes, together with the author and title index that is included in the second volume, aim rather at giving today's reader a chance to take a directed stroll through the archives of *Yale French Studies.*

In the age of electronic media, with the appearance of so many journals in easily accessible digital form (*Yale French Studies,* not to be left behind, is now accessible on JSTOR, a not-for-profit organization founded in 1995 by the Andrew W. Mellon Foundation, dedicated to creating a trusted archive of the back files of core scholarly journals), this anthology iterates *Yale French Studies'* love of the book—the one you carry around with you, the one you dog-ear, the one that belongs, rather than to cyberspace, to Blanchot's famous *espace littéraire.*

The nature and the particularity of *Yale French Studies* are admirably captured by the phrase that for years appeared on the cover of all issues: "All articles in English." The journal was directed primarily to American readers; since many of them did not read French, it was as-

YFS 96, *50 Years of Yale French Studies: A Commemorative Anthology,* eds. Porter and Waters, © 1999 by Yale University.

sumed that they could use fresh information about what was going on in contemporary French literature and culture. Such an intention indicated also a certain desire on the part of the inventors of the journal—one might think of it as "benevolent propaganda"—to allow Americans to benefit from the pathbreaking developments occurring in France in those early post-War years. In French Departments in America in that same period, moreover, a rather large number of distinguished literary critics were non-English speaking, or at least non-English writing, scholars: thus even American French scholarship needed to be presented to non-French reading Americans. The new journal would, for reasons such as these, concentrate at first to a large extent on contemporary French writing, and then gradually open itself more and more to other fields of interest to French and other literature teachers at Yale and elsewhere in America. Naturally, *Yale* French *Studies* would devote itself to "French" literature and culture, that is, the literature and culture of the hexagon.

In the first couple of decades of publication all of the statements mentioned in the previous paragraph applied. By the end of the 1960s, however, the changing nature of literary study in both countries, and the difference of style and the differing rhythms of that change in France and the United States, led to a change in the substance of many of the journal's biannual issues. There was still a desire to present what was going on in France, but now what the journal's editors and contributors saw in France was less the old-style philological study of authors and texts than the development of new theoretical and critical approaches to the study of literature. French culture, as it was presented in *Yale French Studies*, was now less exclusively novels and poems and plays and film and painting; criticism of criticism, the applications of several of the *sciences humaines* to the old and the new literary canon, and finally literary theory came to dominate the journal's pages. In many of these areas France was becoming less exclusively French, and thus *Yale French Studies* now often published essays by writers who were not members of French Departments at all. Furthermore, "French" could no longer refer only to France: the journal began to take cognizance of French-speaking culture in other countries and continents.

A second founding principle of the journal, however, continued to apply: each issue was devoted to a specific topic. Certain of these topics turned out to be so new and of such great interest that they were soon republished as books—Jacques Ehrmann's *Structuralism* (Nos.

36–37), republished by Anchor Books, in 1970, and his *Literature and Revolution* (No. 39) and *Game, Play, and Literature* (No. 41), republished by Beacon Press, in 1970 and 1971; Peter Brooks's *The Child's Part* (No. 43), republished by Beacon Press, in 1972; Shoshana Felman's *Literature and Psychoanalysis* (Nos. 55–56) and Joan DeJean and Nancy K. Miller's *The Politics of Tradition: Placing Women in French Literature* (No. 75), republished by Johns Hopkins University Press, in 1982 and 1991, respectively.

However the newer outlook was to be no more the final definition of *Yale French Studies* than was its predecessor. As of the late 90s we are moving more and more toward "Cultural Studies." One is inclined to say that *plus ça change, plus c'est la même chose,* for if *Yale French Studies* is today interesting itself more and more in literature written in French outside France, it is still representing to its American readers a "non-French" literature more and more published and thought about in France. If it has evolved from philology, through theory, toward cultural studies, it has done so reflecting what was going on in leading French intellectual circles. And if sometimes we Americans got ahead of the French for a few years, that became a problem only on those few occasions when they failed to move in the expected (not to say the right) direction!

The operations of *Yale French Studies* were from the beginning directed—rather firmly—by an editorial board chaired by the current Chairperson of the Yale French Department and including other members of the department, both faculty and graduate students. Among the board chairmen who exercised, each in his own way, a particularly strong influence on the shape and direction the journal took, must be singled out Henri Peyre, Victor Brombert, Paul de Man, Peter Brooks, and Denis Hollier. There was always, also, an Editor of the journal, or an editorial junta, or eventually a Managing Editor working with a Special Editor for each issue: this latter plan has been in place now since 1971. The Editors of the journal—Robert Greer Cohn, Kenneth Douglas, Kenneth Cornell, Joseph McMahon, Liliane Greene, Alyson Waters, plus several others who served briefly in that capacity—have all had strong but strikingly different interests and intellectual profiles, affecting in various ways the elaboration and composition of each issue. The appointment of Liliane Greene in 1980 signaled a major change in the journal's operations: she was to be a continuing Managing Editor, and a subject editor would now be designated for each issue. Liliane Greene served as Managing Editor until 1993, at which time she was succeeded by Alyson Waters. From the time of Liliane Greene's appointment, the Editorial Board would no longer take the active role in formulating each issue's contents and approach but rather, with the Managing Editor, would typically evaluate, modify, and eventually accept or reject proposals received from "special editors" who had made known their desire to prepare an issue.

The editorial direction of the journal has always been and continues to be set by the editorial board. Editorial matters that have from the beginning represented a particular concern of the board include, first of all, the interest and timeliness of the topic and the list of potential contributors to be invited (unsolicited articles having never been accepted); then the number of original (as opposed to previously published in French or English) articles, the number of translations (as opposed to articles originally written in English), and, since the time of "special editors," the location of those editors (whether at Yale or not). In general an effort has been made to use as few previously published articles or chapters, as few translated articles, and as few "outside Yale" special editors as possible, though number by number there has been a wide variety of practice on all these matters.

Finally, *Yale French Studies* has always been sold more to subscribers (including libraries) than in bookstores, and the number of issues printed (characteristically 1,500–2,000) continues to be high for a journal of its type. At first a number of different printers were used to produce the journal: Payne and Lane in New Haven printed it during many of the early years; Eastern Press in New Haven printed it during most of the 1960s, during which a handsome new format came into being. The journal was printed for several years in Spain by Artes Gráficas Solar. A major change occurred in 1982, when, at the suggestion of its new director, John Ryden, Yale University Press took up the production of *Yale French Studies*, in a much handsomer version yet.

I would like in conclusion to speak for both the French Department and myself in thanking Liliane Greene and Alyson Waters for the extraordinary efforts they have taken to assure that a journal with as few imperfections as possible appears regularly; personally I have had the great pleasure of working several times under their vigilant guidance and broad cultural expertise. I wish also to thank my colleague, Peter Brooks, for his help with these reminiscences.

ALYSON WATERS

Acknowledgments from the Managing Editor

To Liliane Greene, who so generously gave of her time to make the transition from her management of the journal to mine much smoother than it would have been without her experience, guidance, and wisdom; to those who have served as editorial assistants during my tenure: Noah Guynn, Allison Tait, and James F. Austin, who with tremendous dedication made the journal better and the editorial office a warm, fun place to be; and to those at Yale University Press with whom I work: to Otto Bohlmann, Associate Editor, for keeping the journal's appearance on time in the face of the considerable obstacles I've managed to place in his path; to James J. Johnson, *YFS'* designer, for making our volumes beautiful to look at and to hold; and especially to Lawrence Kenney, the best Senior Manuscript Editor ever, who has made difficult work so pleasant that it seems "a sport and a pastime" (well, almost)—my heartfelt thanks.

YFS 96, *50 Years of Yale French Studies: A Commemorative Anthology,* eds. Porter and Waters, © 1999 by Yale University.

GEORGES MAY

Why A Fez?

The fact that I happen to have witnessed the birth of *Yale French Studies* is presumably the reason I was invited to write these few lines on the occasion of its fiftieth birthday. "Hardly a man is still alive . . ." However, the extent of my participation in this event was a strictly limited one. It consisted in no more than discussions with those who were actively engaged in bringing it about. As the record shows, I didn't begin writing for *YFS* until its third issue.

At the time of its foundation, I had recently received my Ph.D., and held a one-year appointment as Instructor in the Department of French, whereas the new journal was exclusively the creation of a small group of graduate students in the Department. Their leader was Robert Greer Cohn, who, at the time, was completing his doctoral dissertation on Mallarmé's *Coup de dés,* a first step toward what was to be a distinguished scholarly career as perhaps the leading *mallarmisant* of his generation. He recalls in his memoirs, published in 1992, that Henri Peyre, the legendary chairman of the Department for a quarter century, had actively encouraged and supported him in his efforts to create the new journal, whose title echoed that of *French Studies,* the quarterly started at Oxford two years before: "In 1948, largely to please him [Peyre], I conceived of and, in association with others, launched *Yale French Studies.*"[1]

The climate at the time, in our Graduate School as in the country at large, bore little resemblance to what it has become since. Most of us, graduate students and junior faculty members, were former GIs; the war was over; the cold war had not yet started; Senator McCarthy's notoriety was still to come; the academic job market was wide open. No

1. Robert Greer Cohn, *Buttercups, and So Forth* (Lantern Editions, 1992), 118.

YFS 96, *50 Years of Yale French Studies: A Commemorative Anthology,* eds. Porter and Waters, © 1999 by Yale University.

wonder optimism and idealism prevailed. The new enterprise, a product of this environment, was thoroughly amateurish, or, rather, *artisanale*. There was no office, no bureaucracy, no professionals: just a group of enthusiastic students of French literature confident that their generation was in for a bright future.

As an illustration of this, I remember an occasion in those early days when a carload of us drove over, in a prewar and asthmatic car, to Middletown, where the journal's printer was then located. There we read proofs in an open courtyard, where we sat around as for a picnic, passing galleys from hand to hand, like mustard or ketchup.

In his memoirs, Bob Cohn writes: "In 1948, with myself as Editor-in-Chief—Dorrit [Bob's young bride and fellow graduate student, eventually to become a Harvard professor], Ted Morris (a lifetime friend) and Reed Law assisted—we got out the first issue of *Yale French Studies*, on Existentialism, which was the hot topic of the day. I lugged a heavy suitcase full of fresh copies to a Modern Language Association convention in New York and set up a display on a random table. At a dollar a copy, which seemed expensive then, I sold the lot. We signed up hundreds of subscribers. We were on our way" (123).

After Cohn and his founding friends had departed from New Haven with their diplomas and their first faculty appointments, they left among fellow-students no successors to take over. By default, the journal fell into the hands of the faculty. Kenneth Douglas, an assistant professor of French, whom Cohn calls "a bosom pal" in his memoirs, succeeded him as Editor-in-Chief, assisted by a handful of colleagues and graduate students as editorial committee. We met in Henri Peyre's office to discuss topics of future issues and possible contributors. Invariably Peyre called on some of us around the table to write articles, not infrequently on subjects or authors on which we had never worked before. This maintained the initial amateur status of the enterprise; but the élan of the founders was not replicated. After the few issues edited by Cohn, articles by graduate students became the exception, unless we take into account the role they played as translators of manuscripts in French, for Cohn's motto "all articles in English" always remained the rule. Over time, a number of members of the faculty, usually of junior rank, devoted a few years of their careers acting as Editors-in-Chief, until the present system was put in place many years later: a "permanent" managing editor, and "special editors" for each issue.

Following the lines of his memoirs quoted above, Cohn writes of the fledgling journal he had founded: "It has gone on for more than forty years, but it has become Byzantine, politically correct, abstract and unliterary, and Henri Peyre, who witnessed that perversion and decay, expressed his sorrow to me" (123).

Many of the members of Bob Cohn's generation, now backward-looking septuagenarian emeriti like myself—pre-structuralists, premodernists, and in general confirmed arrière-gardistes—would echo these feelings, if not perhaps the words chosen to express them. Yet, given what Cohn had had to say about existentialism—the subject of the initial issue—that it was "the hot topic of the day," one may wonder about the vocation and tradition of *YFS*. To be sure, political correctness had not yet been invented fifty years ago, but trendiness, abstraction, hermetism, and metaphysics had.

Be that as it may, the image of the pendulum comes to mind, as well as—at least for those who still recognize the name of Maurice Barrès, even if they have less respect for the politician than for the writer—the initial pages of *Le jardin de Bérénice*, where the author purportedly reports a wholly imaginary conversation between Ernest Renan and Charles Chincolle, in which the former states sapiently: "If young people fully approved what their elders have put together, would they not implicitly acknowledge that their coming into this world was useless? . . . It is necessary that, half-way in his development, a writer or a politician stop prowling after his predecessor, in order to bash over the head as many of his successors as possible. This is called becoming a moderate, and it is eminently appropriate when one reaches the heyday of life."[2]

Since the succession of generations is not about to cease, it seems safe to foresee that *YFS* will, in future years, keep on changing and thriving. As we blow out the fifty candles on its birthday cake, this should be at any rate the silent wish of all who at one time or another had anything to do with it.

---

2. Maurice Barrès, *Le jardin de Bérénice* (Paris: Plon, 1936), 8–10.

I. 1948–1959

CHARLES A. PORTER

Celebratory Criticism: The First Dozen Years

The first dozen years of *Yale French Studies* set the style and range of subjects for years to come; not until the rampant theoretization of French literary studies began would the journal change notably in its manner of conceiving its subjects. The two persons who seem to have dominated the direction the new journal took in those years were the already long-time Chairman of the Yale French Department, Henri Peyre, and the man who would edit the journal from 1949 until 1950 and from 1954 until 1962, Kenneth Douglas. With both of them in the late 40s greatly interested in the new, popular French philosophy, it is only logical that issue No. 1 was *Existentialism*, a collection of critical and descriptive articles that examined that very visible and somewhat scandalous philosophy cum lifestyle of Paris in the post-War period.

Among the twenty-four issues of *Yale French Studies* in the late 40s through the 50s there are six that deal with literary genres (equitably distributed with two each on the novel, poetry, and theater), four whose subjects involve literary or intellectual movements (two on existentialism, one each on symbolism and romanticism), only two devoted to individual authors (Gide and Malraux), a double issue on contemporary art and a single issue on film, several issues dealing with literary criticism and French in relationship to other literatures, two dealing with French society (*Social and Political France, French Education*), and finally three issues that resist classification (*Eros, God and the Writer, Humor*). The by-and-large general nature of these topics indicates this period's notion of the journal's principal function: to present what was going on in France, particularly in French literature, to those who were not well informed (often because they did not read French or French-language publications). There tended to be a bias in these issues, delightfully in favor of France. *Yale French Studies* was

YFS 96, *50 Years of Yale French Studies: A Commemorative Anthology,* eds. Porter and Waters, © 1999 by Yale University.

not yet principally interested in critical methodology, much less theory, but was eager, rather, to point to the wonders out there in the French cultural world. It was celebratory, descriptive, and evaluative.

The selected articles that follow, from Nos. 3 (*Criticism and Creation*), 13 (*Romanticism Revisited*), 16 (*Foray through Existentialism*), and 21 (*Poetry since the Liberation*), are characteristic of these early years of the journal in that three of the four deal with the twentieth century; they are, also characteristically (but less so), very Yale-related, since three of them were written by Yale French Department faculty members and one by a former graduate student. Three of them deal with questions that were probably not greatly familiar to the journal's readers: Giraudoux—but as a critic; still new existentialism; a new poetic voice. The fourth is intended to reopen debate on a major part of Romanticism that seemed to have slid irretrievably into the past. These articles manifest a notion of the new journal as a teaching tool, from a department committed to its pedagogical mission.

The three Yale faculty authors represented in this section served at Yale for an astonishing total of more than 125 years. It was they who, not surprisingly, represented the department to outsiders. The articles representing them here are intended to be characteristic of their contributions. The first of the three to arrive at Yale was Henri Peyre, who taught at Yale from 1928–33; he then was brought back to Yale in 1939 by President Seymour to be the head of the French Department and Sterling Professor of French. He served as Department Chairman for a quarter century, took his mandatory retirement in 1969—and then went on to head the French Ph.D. program at the Graduate Center of the City University of New York until age 80. He died in 1988. By the later years of his career his students peopled the French Departments of the United States, maintaining, for their Yale successors, a professional network that Peyre had carefully cultivated.

I remember my first graduate class with Henri Peyre. It was in the fall of 1958, and I had just arrived at Yale. By the end of the class my writing hand was stiff: the two-hour flow of names and book titles and opinions, advice, and judgments was overwhelming. Speaking with few or no notes, from the fund of his years of vast readings and on the basis of his phenomenal memory, Henri Peyre barraged us with contexts, with selected idiocies that had been proffered by other professors (named) at other institutions (also named), with better ways to view the text under discussion and other works to compare it to. Underneath all the fireworks pulsed a great and enthusiastic passion for literature and for the French literary tradition. The reader will see what I mean from the opening paragraphs of "Romantic Poetry and Rhetoric," from *YFS* 13, *Romanticism Revisited* (Spring-Summer 1954).

What Peyre's students learned first was that the literary text was something to be judged always in both a literary and a broader cultural environment. Second, that that context was never solely French. Ranging back through the tradition and across the lands of Western culture, Peyre's vast curiosity, coupled with that extraordinary memory, served him and his students well indeed. Older colleagues from other Yale departments have often spoken to me of a common campus sight of their younger years: Henri Peyre, barely visible behind the foot-high stack of books he was carrying, returning to the library his reading for that day. What I also remember so well from my graduate student days and orals preparation was how many books, in every field imaginable, had their typos corrected in the margins, in Peyre's unmistakable purple ink.

Peyre was a prolific writer and wrote with particular authority on the classical and contemporary periods. His many articles in the 1940s and 1950s in *Yale French Studies* deal not only with these subjects but also with contemporary French painters and sculptors. Peyre's remarkable energy was accompanied by a generosity at least equally remarkable. The hundreds of students, colleagues, and friends he welcomed into his home over the years will remember both the champagne and his excellent collection of contemporary paintings and sculpture. We are all greatly in his debt for the ways in which he encouraged and challenged us, helped us professionally, and showed us how to be passionate lovers of our work and the tradition into which it fit.

Georges May taught in the Yale French Department from 1946–91. He still lives in New Haven, where he is often sought out by colleagues and graduate students, not only because of his vast expertise in many areas of French literature but also because of his accumulated wisdom concerning professional life at Yale (based in part on his eight years of service as Dean of Yale College and two as Provost of the University).

Georges May has often told his younger colleagues about how he came to Yale as a young specialist in the seventeenth century and was soon informed by his chairman, Henri Peyre, that he would teach a course in eighteenth-century literature. May's reputation as a leading scholar of that later period was soon to be solidly buttressed by his series of writings on Diderot (*Quatre visages de Denis Diderot*, 1951; *Diderot et "La religieuse,"* 1954) and other writers (particularly in *Le dilemme du roman au XVIIe siècle*, 1963). Some of his younger friends might not have been aware that those eighteenth-century studies had been preceded by *Tragédie cornélienne, tragédie racinienne* in 1948 and *D'Ovide à Racine* a year later: these two works are mentioned in the "Notes on Contributors" in *YFS* 3 (Spring-Summer 1949) that identifies future Sterling Professor Georges May as an "Assistant Professor at Yale." The piece selected for this anthology, however, is one of three May wrote in the early years of *Yale French Studies* on something else again: Jean Giraudoux. (The other two are "Jean Giraudoux: Diplomacy and Dramaturgy," in *YFS* 5, and "Marriage vs. Love in the World of Giraudoux," in *YFS* 11). Here, it is Giraudoux as literary critic. I don't know the origin of May's interest in Giraudoux, though I suspect that it is one of those many literary interests of his that date back to the enthusiasms and pleasures of his Parisian youth.

"Jean Giraudoux: Academicism and Idiosyncracies" is a fine example of the kind of literary criticism I associate with my graduate school years in the Yale French Department: it is an evaluative reading that arises from both the critic's *esprit de finesse* and his familiarity with the social, intellectual, and cultural, as well as more precisely literary climate out of which the text under study came into being. It is probing, good-humored, and witty. It suggests to the reader the desire to read what is being so agreeably described.

Without a doubt "Those Years: Existentialism 1943–1945" is a very unrepresentative piece from the two numbers of *Yale French Studies* (*YFS* 1, Spring-Summer 1948, and *YFS* 16, Winter, 1955–56) that discuss Existentialism. The majority of the articles in those issues are what one would expect: ideas, literary criticism, philosophical considerations. Yet this one struck me as simply too interesting and too moving not to include in our commemorative issue.

Jacques Guicharnaud's reminiscences of his Parisian late adolescence manage to catch not only his personal experience but also some of the flavor of a notable time and place and the spirit that permeated at least the educated youth of the day. Guicharnaud's Yale students and friends have often commented with amazement on the store of anecdotes he seems to have always at the ready. Those anecdotes are probably so memorable because of his seemingly natural art in telling them; it is this very art that characterizes the following piece. But Guicharnaud, who has frequently taught courses on the classical French "moralists" and on Molière, is also, himself, a wonderfully lucid and objective commentator on the life around him, and such commentary is also an important part of his discussion of France in the mid-1940s

Guicharnaud taught in the Yale French Department from 1950 to 1997. During many of those years he was also very active in the Yale Theater Studies Program. He still lives in New Haven, in the little red house on Bishop Street that so many of his former students have visited.

The author of "On Bonnefoy's Poetry," Mario Maurin, received his Ph.D. from the Yale French Department in 1951, with a dissertation on the thought of André Suarès. After two years in the United States Marines he received a job at Bryn Mawr College, "thanks," he recently wrote me, "to Henri Peyre, who had begun his American career at Bryn Mawr." Mario Maurin is taking retirement in 1999, after his long career at Bryn Mawr, a career that has been characterized by his generosity and kindness to his students. For the past few years he has been collecting Henri Peyre's correspondence, both private and professional: "It will be an interesting document on the activity of a high-powered and, as you know, very influential academic, for whose memory Yale doesn't seem to have done much."

When Mario Maurin wrote the following essay, Yves Bonnefoy had not yet become the major poet and literary critic that he was soon to be. Maurin's article shows the pleasure of making a new discovery and an unusually thoughtful way of trying to understand its relationship to a rich poetic and intellectual tradition.

GEORGES MAY

Jean Giraudoux: Academicism and Idiosyncracies*

When Jean Giraudoux was asked to lecture on La Fontaine in 1936, he entertained his fascinated public with a series of witty, discreetly erudite and masterful lectures. In each he presented what he called one of La Fontaine's "temptations." As he had been requested to deliver five lectures, he discovered, quite naturally, that La Fontaine had undergone precisely five temptations. Two years later these lectures were published in a book entitled *Les Cinq Tentations de La Fontaine*. In 1941 a score or so of articles on literature and drama appeared under the proud and simple title of *Littérature*. These two small volumes, along with some rare uncollected articles and doubtless many unpublished *devoirs*, represent Giraudoux's formal contribution to literary criticism and his right to appear among more commonly accepted critics.

When the book on La Fontaine came out, a professional critic, André Rousseaux, pointed out that Giraudoux's approach was arbitrary and erroneous, since the word "temptation" was hardly applicable to a man like the easy-going La Fontaine. If, as Rousseaux points out, temptation implies resistance, one might feel tempted to apply this method to Giraudoux himself and thus to "Giralducize" him in spite of one's admiration for him. In so enforcing the distributive justice prescribed by the law of retaliation, one would experience a pleasure similar to that of robbing a thief or of burying an undertaker.

Among the many temptations confronting him, the most persistent, and perhaps the most violent, was that of teaching literature. Boy prodigy in the *lycée* of Châteauroux, first in the class of 1913 at the École Normale Supérieure, tutor of the young prince of Saxe-Meinin-

*From *Yale French Studies* 3 (Spring-Summer 1949): *Criticism and Creation*.

YFS 96, *50 Years of Yale French Studies: A Commemorative Anthology*, eds. Porter and Waters, © 1999 by Yale University.

gen, Giraudoux had to put up strong resistance in order to withstand the fascination of teaching to which so many contemporary writers were later to succumb. He settled on being occasionally a critic, as if criticism were the only precarious harmony between his status as a writer and his potential vocation as a professor. And so he chose to write on Racine and La Fontaine, on Choderlos de Laclos and Gérard de Nerval, out of a craving for personal balance. In so compromising he succeeded, as some of his heroes did: Judith, for instance, who managed to be simultaneously pure and impure; Alkmena, who remained faithful to her husband Amphitryon while actually deceiving him; or Siegfried, who for a while combined two of the traditionally most incompatible citizenships.

The personal reasons which thus oriented Giraudoux toward criticism led him to build up his own approach to literature, whereby the conventional and academic methods with which he was so thoroughly familiar were combined with the fanciful and often revealing whims of his most original idiosyncrasies. In spite of the illusion of total liberty which the prestige of his style gives to his readers, Giraudoux often follows the strict discipline of some well-known positivistic critics of the French University, like Taine or Brunetière. These very serious names need not appear more paradoxical than that of Aristotle which Jean-Paul Sartre does not hesitate to bring into his discussion of Giraudoux's last novel, *Choix des élues*. Besides writing about the École Normale which had sheltered Taine some sixty years before it greeted him, Giraudoux himself suggests a possible connection between his elder and himself by entitling his article "L'Esprit normalien"; "Je ne dirai pas que tous ceux qui sortent d'elle [the École Normale] ont de l'esprit, mais ils ont l'esprit." Furthermore, the list of the École Normale alumni is not the only register in which the names of Taine and Giraudoux are to be found—if not side by side, at least one above the other—since they both appear in any good bibliography of La Fontaine.

Taine's *La Fontaine et ses fables*, like his *Essay on Livy* or his *History of English Literature*, is an illustration of his own memorable motto: *race, milieu, moment*. The book endeavors to explain the *Fables* by emphasizing the sociological data of the France of 1670 and the fact that La Fontaine was born in the province of Champagne, an explanation not so far removed from that offered by *Les Cinq Tentations de La Fontaine:* for isn't it true that a careful observation of these temptations—of bourgeois life, of women, of high society, of literary life, of skepticism and religion—allows us readily to pigeonhole them in the three more dogmatic categories of Taine?

In the same manner, the first few pages of Giraudoux's essay on Racine reveal a careful step-by-step Tainian analysis of Racine's background: social environment, family, childhood, adolescence, education. If it were not for the spell of Giraudoux's brilliant metaphorical style, one might think of a study of Lanson or Saintsbury. Again, with the intention in mind of specifying the exact *moment* of Laclos' *Dangerous Acquaintances*, Giraudoux wrote the following lines, which sound like the erudite statement of a Sorbonne professor giving a public lecture:

> Accustomed as we are by our textbooks of literature to link Laclos' name with those of Marivaux or *Crébillon fils*, we still should not forget that his novel was published fifty years after theirs, six years after the first translations of *Werther* and *Ossian*, thirteen years after the French adaptations of *Hamlet;* we should not forget that it is contemporary with Senancour, Bernardin de Saint-Pierre and Chénier, and that it was amid all this sensibility and sentimentality that barrenness had its moment of genius.

Perhaps it would still not be quite safe to consider Giraudoux a disciple of Taine and to bring in the dangerous notion of influence, but the author of *Littérature*—consciously it seems—borrowed from his predecessor an approach to works of literature which is commonly called either academic or scholarly, two adjectives which have the privilege of implying, according to the background of those who use them, praise or censure.

Brunetière had lectured to the students of the École Normale a few years before Giraudoux became one of them. Still he would proudly have recognized his own pet theory of the evolution of literary genres if he could but have read this one page of Giraudoux's essay on Laclos, where the author tries to explain, through the evolution of the tragedy into the novel, the dependence of Laclos on Racine or that of Richardson on Shakespeare:

> Laclos can no longer rely on tragedy—a dead form—, but he is crafty enough to select a genre in which drama subsists: the novel in letter form. A letter, plain and meagre though it may be, preserves its origin which is that of confession, of extemporaneousness and of trust, *i.e.* that of lyricism and poetry. Using the first person singular, limiting the field of human experience, relegating to the background and the backdrop all

the characteristic features of a given period or group of human beings who become that much easier to appreciate, utilizing the very forms which adorn a letter with literary and conventional festoons, all this bestows upon any correspondence the ornate, revealing and inevitable appearance of the tragic epic . . .

Biographical, historical, even comparative—these are the methods to be found in Giraudoux's essays. Even when his criticism becomes more thoroughly fanciful, we can feel that his poetic pen underwent the strict discipline of the Sorbonne. Some dim remembrances of academic criticism are apparent even in such heroic deeds as the unexpected episode in *Églantine,* telling of the deaths of Socrates and Jesus Christ in Chicago, or as the digression where the characters of the *Brothers Karamazov*—including some imaginary sisters Karamazov!—suddenly invade the already unpredictable actions of *Combat avec l'ange.* Also many an essay collected in *Littérature* could have been written for a formal examination: the duel Racine-Bossuet on the drama, for instance, or the lecture delivered for the centenary of *Hernani.*

One more token of Giraudoux's scholarly tradition may be found in the titles of his first books which claim their place in the protective shadows of some famous works, in the same manner that Corneille and Racine deliberately gave their first tragedies titles recalling those of Seneca and Euripides. In spite of discrepancies in subject matter, Giraudoux's *Provinciales* (1909) and *L'Ecole des indifférents* (1911) fall within the outward tradition of Pascal and Molière. The latter was to supply Giraudoux with other titles, such as *L'Impromptu de Paris* (1937) and especially *Amphitryon 38* (1929), for which Molière must share the honor with thirty-six other playwrights. The *Supplément au voyage de Cook* (1937) reminds one of Diderot and the *Cantique des Cantiques* (1938) of the Old Testament; not to mention those subjects which Giraudoux chose to take up again: *Tessa* (1934), after the English original of Margaret Kennedy and Basil Dean; *Ondine* (1939), after the German original of La Motte Fouqué; *Elpénor* (1919), after the Greek original of the *Odyssey;* and even *Le Film de la duchesse de Langeais* (1942), after the French original of Balzac's *Comédie humaine.*

Notwithstanding unmistakable signs of a scholarly tradition in Giraudoux's criticism and several instances of an academic approach, his literary essays remain as genuinely different from those of Faguet or Lemaître as his *Électre* or his *Amphitryon* are unlike those of Sophocles or Plautus. It is however easier to detect the fingerprints of Taine or Brunetière than to recognize those of Giraudoux himself. Only a few of them can actually be observed and shown, as, for instance, his fondness for excessive generalizations, his refusal to approach any subject directly, or his whimsical fancy for those writers in whom he could rightly or wrongly recognize his own most peculiar idiosyncrasies.

The first of these peculiarities is noticeable in Giraudoux's creative work as well as in his criticism and has been pointed out by Claude-Edmonde Magny and by Jean-Paul Sartre: most of his judgments are absolute; he goes directly to the superlative and seeks the unique. This is what we may read in the first page of his "Racine":

> No childhood was further removed than his from the laws and adventures of childhood. . . . Study and the joy of studying supplant in his case all contact with life. . . . There is not a sentiment in Racine which is not a literary sentiment. . . .

In the same manner the first of the five lectures on La Fontaine points out the following singularities:

> There is not one trap which has not been set for our poet to catch him red-handed in the act of civilization with his contemporaries. . . . All the mirages which you can see in the Dutch and Flemish paintings, and which St. Anthony may have dimly seen with the bad eyesight of a hermit, La Fontaine saw their approach. . . . In no single instance did the incredible freedom, which this free man could afford to have, permit itself to be led astray.

As for his friend Charles-Louis Philippe:

> Below the level of the author, Philippe remains above all a unique character and monster in our literary nomenclature.

A niggling critic unafraid of being ridiculous obviously could take up all these judgments anew and demonstrate their inaccuracy. Only the fear of being guilty of the most absolute sort of dogmatism would prevent us from stating that all absolute judgments are wrong. Other childhoods than Racine's may have been as little childish as his: Pascal's for instance; it is not altogether impossible that French society of the 17th century spared La Fontaine the danger of some of its traps: that of military glamour for instance; and the uniqueness of Charles-Louis Philippe may appear less absolute if one thinks of Alain-Fournier or of Charles Péguy for instance. Were Giraudoux in a position to hear this sort of objection, he would undoubtedly answer it as he answered

Fabre's when the latter censured La Fontaine for having his grasshopper crave grain and worms, whereas a normal grasshopper has only a suctorial organ whereby he may suck the sap from the trees:

> This reminds me of my Gazier edition of La Fontaine, where M. Gazier, arriving at the line:
>> *Cependant que mon front au Caucase pareil*
> commented: "Obvious exaggeration. Mount Elbruz in the Caucasus is 18,605 feet high."

To take Giraudoux's pronouncements literally would not only be unjust, but also stupid. His hyperboles are but rhetorical devices deceitfully designed to mean what they don't say and not to mean what they do say. Playing with his authors as he does with the characters of his novels, Giraudoux transforms them into what Jean-Paul Sartre calls "archetypes." This operation implies a critical judgment which we are free to reject on the plea that it informs us about the critic rather than about the object of his criticism. Giraudoux's lectures on La Fontaine shed but little light on the miracle of the *Fables,* but permit a better understanding of the author of *Les Cinq Tentations.* Thus the harsh words directed by Rousseau and Lamartine at the immorality of La Fontaine are of interest primarily to the Rousseauist and the Lamartinian.

Giraudoux's apparent repulsion for a direct critical approach is linked to his phobia of any triteness of expression. In this respect his criticism is governed by the same principles as his creative works. The same inclination leads him to the most traditional subjects—*Judith* or *La Guerre de Troie n'aura pas lieu*—and to the best known poets—Racine or La Fontaine. It is only because they are so worn out that they may be treated with originality and that it is so challenging to avoid banality and repetition. Giraudoux entitled his last novel *Choix des élues,* and, likewise, chose and celebrated writers who had been singled out by posterity and thus "elected" much more effectively than ever were the heroes of the novel: Edmée, Claudie, or the pickle. Giraudoux deliberately found for the legend of Alkmena and Jupiter an interpretation different from those offered by his thirty-seven predecessors, and wrote *Amphitryon 38;* in the same manner, he could not condescend to tell us about Racine as Francisque Sarcey or Jules Lemaître did, or again in the manner of François Mauriac or Thierry Maulnier. His essay could be entitled "Racine 1000." He admits in the preface of *Littérature:*

The make-up with which criticism and habit have smeared our writers is so perfect that one has either to enter our literature by sheer luck,
or to break into it like a burglar.

The paper dedicated by Giraudoux to Valery Larbaud for the special
issue devoted to him in 1922 by the magazine *Intentions* exemplifies
this "back door" approach:

> The point is to honor you. I keep my distance. I unbind myself from
> you.
>
> I did not hear your name for the first time from the lips of Charles-
> Louis Philippe, one evening on the Quai d'Anjou. I did not see your
> mother before I knew you, one morning on the rue Larbaud in Vichy. I
> did not receive you for the first time at night on the fourteenth of July
> on the boulevard de l'Hôtel de Ville in Cusset. . . .
>
> There! Now we are detached from each other and we no longer know
> each other. As if I had rid you of your clothes and not of my remem-
> brances, I see you as a statue, nude. Greetings, Valery Larbaud, un-
> known to me, dear to me, for me ever glorious.

The same apparently flighty method leads Giraudoux to portray La
Fontaine through the temptations which confronted him, and which,
according to Giraudoux, he resisted; in other words, he portrays La
Fontaine by accentuating, in a process of elimination, precisely those
features which he lacked. When seriously applied, this indirect method
is likely to unearth some hidden truths: this is for instance the origin
which Giraudoux finds for Laclos' vocation as a moralist:

> This vocation is neither serene nor is it unbiased. Its origin is not an
> interest in the passions, it is not even a hatred of evil; it is rather a re-
> sentment upon finding out that human beings are bold enough to in-
> dulge in it. His inventiveness, his inspiration as a moralist are not born
> of a kind of optimism, of sympathy for humanity, of hope in its recov-
> ery, but of a jealousy of the wicked on account of their wickedness.

And here are the well-known exordial lines of Giraudoux's
"Racine":

> It is satisfying to think that the foremost writer in the literature of
> France is not a moralist or a scholar or a general or even a king, but a
> man of letters.

For Giraudoux's negative statements always eventuate in affirma-
tions. Like certain acrobats who for a while pretend to be clumsy in order, when they succeed, to get more applause, Giraudoux first thrusts

his scalpels all around his patient, and then stabs him right in the heart, nails him to the operating table, and proceeds with his dazzling "Giralducian" dissections.

Between the moment when Giraudoux tacks toward his goal and the moment when he abandons it with a hyperbole, is a privileged instant when his criticism reaches its point of equilibrium and unearths a metaphor or a single word which is intended to be the key to the aesthetic mystery. This keyword is "man of letters" for Racine, "absentminded" for La Fontaine, "free" for Gérard de Nerval. This again reminds one of Taine's criticism with its "caractère dominant." But, no matter how intelligent and clear-sighted the critic, the method has obvious limitations; there is no pass key in literature. Pretending to elucidate all of Livy with the single word "eloquence," is just as venturesome an undertaking as it is allegedly to explain all of Charles-Louis Philippe by the mere word "innocence."

It is again in the preface of *Littérature* that Giraudoux unfolds the third and most peculiar of his critical idiosyncrasies, as he relates this delightful story of his adolescence, when he spontaneously appropriated the most beautiful and best known pieces of French literature:

> At a wedding party, in the country, I recited *Mignonne, allons voir si la rose*, giving people to believe, without actually saying so, that it was my own. I was congratulated; it was nice, though a little finical, later I would learn vigor. No one suspected any faking, and there wasn't any. It was all my own.

As a matter of fact, Giraudoux never completely overcame this old habit. In later years, though he finally realized that he had written neither "The Ant and the Grasshopper," nor the confession of Phaedra, he still persisted in gazing like Narcissus at his own reflection in the mirrors offered him by the faces of Racine and La Fontaine. There he would recognize and admire his own features because he had been looking for them, and, evoking these poets, like God he recreated them in his own image.

In the very first lecture on La Fontaine, Giraudoux toys with history and supposes that during the trip which La Fontaine took in 1663 in his own native Limousin, the poet conceivably found the time and the opportunity to become his ancestor. He notices further that they both bear the same first name, a distinguishing feature which becomes perhaps less commonplace as we remember that Racine, too, was a Jean. And shouldn't we add to these coincidences that some of the temptations which Giraudoux so lightheartedly attributes to La Fontaine, often without explicit proof, would perchance better fit Giraudoux himself, especially the temptation of women, that of high society and that of the literary life? Shouldn't we also remember, as we read the curious and revealing paper collected in *Littérature* with the title of "The Beast and the Writer," that Giraudoux is, after La Fontaine, one of our most delicate poets of animal life? Some of his animals may be imaginary like the invisible dog which the madwoman of Passy has on leash when she calls on her colleague of Chaillot. Others, more real ones, escaped the volume of *Fables* to caress the tender heart of Jean Giraudoux: the hedgehog of the beggar in *Électre*, the trout of Ondine, the horse of Hans von Wittenstein zu Wittenstein, the eagle of Aegisthus and all the unknown birds which break the solitude of Suzanne's Pacific island.

So, as we leaf through the pages which Giraudoux devoted to his favorite writers, analogies spring forth linking them with him. These sometimes are created only by the will of Giraudoux who, for instance, as he wanted to be more Racinian than he was, had to model new "Giralducian" features on the mask of the poet of *Athalie*. His retouching is not always quite legitimate: we hear at the beginning of the essay that Racine never suffered from the metaphysical anguish which is sometimes attributed to him:

> Of all the great questions which the movement of thought or which circumstances or simply fashion raises during his time, and which leave their mark even in the letters of Mme de Sévigné—not only is Racine never inspired, he has not allowed one of these things to penetrate his inner life.

At this point Giraudoux's profile is so intimately mingled with that of Racine that we have some difficulty in isolating each portrait, in spite of Racine's wig and Giraudoux's glasses, which are known to be the most easily detachable of distinguishing features, precisely those which we don when we want to go out in disguise.

The deliberate confusion between Racine and himself also leads Giraudoux implicitly to disclose, as he mentions Racine's Biblical plays, the motivation of his own *Judith* and *Sodome et Gomorrhe:*

> Passion in Racine is vital and incoercible. Hence the joy with which he wrote *Esther* and *Athalie:* he has at last found a fatality more pitiless than the fatality of the ancients, the virulence of which was tempered by the unbelief of the Greeks and the general poetical outlook. He has found his own people. With the Jews he can barter his Greek Destiny

for a Jehovah who, beyond the native cruelty of Zeus, has precise designs on mankind. He finds beings who, beside their personal fate, bear in addition a general fatality.

Even some of the idiosyncrasies which Giraudoux too generously ascribes to Gérard de Nerval seem to be of an original "Giralducian" nature:

> Remembrance, forgetfulness, gentleness, knowledge of German, love of feminine names not borne by saints, complete lack of vanity: that is the very essence of Nerval.

For wasn't Giraudoux a German scholar at the École Normale? And is there a calendar where one can find the names of Bella and Églantine, of Claudie and Ondine?

As Giraudoux emphasizes more the alleged likenesses which bind him to his favorite authors, as he stresses more those qualities which he would like to share with them, as he seeks more astutely, and perhaps more artificially, affinities which would identify him with them, his criticism becomes more and more a confession. And, since his prose often displays those characteristics which are commonly ascribed to poetry, such as undertones and connotations, unexpected metaphors, brilliant images, subtle rhythms, his critical essays are more and more distant from criticism, and that much closer to lyricism. Hence their stylistic qualities become all-important.

In spite of this priority granted to form, many writers of the past are often quoted as critics, whose pronouncements are scantier and shallower than those of Giraudoux—La Bruyère, for instance, or even Fénelon; whereas their more obscure contemporaries, who perchance may have been genuine critics, like Rapin or the Abbé Du Bos, are no longer consulted except by a few specialists. A man must be a critic of the first magnitude to attain immortality through the value of his criticism alone: even writers like Sainte-Beuve or Taine had other literary talents to ensure the survival of their names. On the other hand a first-rate poet or novelist need not be a gifted critic, for the recognition granted to his creative work will endow his criticism with sufficient prestige. Many writers of our time would substantiate this remark, Proust or Valéry, for instance, not to mention the living.

One may therefore predict a prosperous future for Giraudoux's criticism. The scholarly leaves in his essays will be the first to wither and fall away. The more personal ones, on the contrary, will flourish. And since these too have fed on a fertile classical soil, their polish and their grace are not mere camouflage, but a legitimate aesthetic way of setting off the originality of Giraudoux's intuitive findings. These precious discoveries of his intellect are often misleading and sometimes untruthful, but, though some may deplore it, it is Beauty rather than Truth which is assumed by poets to have the privilege of eternity.

BIBLIOGRAPHICAL NOTE

The quotations from Giraudoux's "Racine" are borrowed from the English translation by P. Mansell Jones (Cambridge: Gordon Fraser, 1938).

The original text of the essay may be found in *Littérature* (Paris: Grasset, 1941), pp. 29–63. It had been previously published in *Tableau de la littérature française (XVIIe et XVIIIe siècles)* (Paris: Gallimard, 1939), pp. 153–169.

Littérature also contains the original texts of Giraudoux's essays on Laclos (pp. 65–88), on Nerval (pp. 89–101) and on Ch.-L. Philippe (pp. 103–121).

The original text of *Les Cinq Tentations de la Fontaine*, before appearing in book form (Paris: Grasset, 1938), was published in the magazine *Conferencia* (April 15, May 15, June 15, July 15 and August 15, 1936).

Jean-Paul Sartre's article "M. Jean Giraudoux et la philosophie d'Aristote. A propos de *Choix des élues*" was first published in the March 1940 issue of *La Nouvelle Revue Française*; it has been reprinted in *Situations I* (Paris: Gallimard, 1947), pp. 82–98.

HENRI PEYRE

Romantic Poetry and Rhetoric*

For approximately half a century in France, and for a slightly shorter
time in Great Britain and America, Romanticism has been the target of
the critics' onslaught. Romanticism *in se*, as a view of life and especially as a vindication of the rights of imagination and of emotional values, fared rather well under the repeated blows which it was dealt. We
recently contended, in the *Modern Language Quarterly* of the Spring
of 1954, that it could well be called "le mort vivant" and that a resurgence of Romantic moods was conspicuous in the recent literature of
France and of England. Romanticism considered historically, in its European manifestations of the early nineteenth century, has suffered the
fate of all that is but one phase in a long evolution: its novelty has worn
off and the beginning of the modern age has been pushed later in time,
around 1860–70 in literature, or earlier, around 1680–1715 in the history of ideas.

Yet the obloquy heaped upon Romanticism by its theological, philosophical and political foes has on the whole redounded to the glory of
that movement. The German Romantics, perhaps the truest of all
(Hölderlin, Novalis, Kleist, even the philosopher Schelling) have never
counted a larger band of enthusiastic zealots than they do today. English Romanticism suffered more from the recent organized attempt to
encompass poetry within a set of criteria evolved from Dryden and
Pope, or from Donne and Marvell, or even from Herbert and Crashaw.
Yet neither Coleridge nor Keats nor even Wordsworth suffered in the
process. Shelley bore the brunt of the attack, and he has weathered it
victoriously. Teachers trained in irony, paradox, structure and ambiguity remark that they do not have to put up an apologetic plea when

*From *Yale French Studies* 13 (Spring-Summer 1954): *Romanticism Revisited.*

YFS 96, *50 Years of Yale French Studies: A Commemorative Anthology,* eds.
Porter and Waters, © 1999 by Yale University.

asking their students to read *Adonaïs*, "Hymn to Intellectual Beauty," nor even "I arise from dreams of thee." Byron himself has won again, if he ever had lost it, his fascination for readers of his biography, of his letters, of *Don Juan* and even of his earlier poems.

But the Romantic movement of Latin countries proved more vulnerable. The Spaniards have never been over-sensitive as to the place ultimately to be assigned to Espronceda, Zorilla or Larra, and to an era of their literature which was not especially conspicuous for its "hispanidad." The Italians are forced to answer "Manzoni, alas!" when questioned as to who is their greatest novelist, but they know that their truest glory lies elsewhere. They have remained justly proud of Leopardi, but they still debate whether he was Romantic or classical. Many of them would not too regretfully proclaim, as one of their critics did in 1908 in entitling a little book thus, that *Il Romanticismo italiano non esiste* (by Gina Martegiani). On the whole, the Risorgimento, not Romanticism, holds the chief place in the cultural history of their early nineteenth century.

Things went otherwise in France, where, between 1875 and 1910, academic criticism had established Romanticism as a great national movement from which fiction, criticism, history had sprung. French anthologies of modern poetry ritually opened with the big four (Lamartine, Vigny, Hugo, Musset) galloping as the fiery French *quadriga*. The novelists of the Romantic era were the last to be acknowledged as "classics." They have fared best with posterity (if one excepts George Sand). The 1949–50 celebration of the double anniversary of Balzac's birth and death was a true apotheosis. Stendhal is even dearer to the youth of France, and he may well some day be hailed as their truest Romantic: for he is cherished for his worship of passion and for his sentiment, for his melancholy and his shyness, for his poetical conception of his characters and for the poetical vibration of his style, he who was strangely insensitive to poetry.

Michelet, the arch-Romantic among the French, is admired by many Frenchmen today as their greatest prose writer, which he may well be (Sartre *dixit*, in *What is literature?* p. 119). Two other names might be added to his as embodying all that was most genuinely Romantic in France between 1820 and 1850: those of Berlioz and of Delacroix. Never had Berlioz captured such a share of our musical programs as he has lately. As for Delacroix, he (not any more than Géricault and even Chassériau) had never suffered from the anti-Romantic reaction. The impressionists, Cézanne, the Fauves all paid him their tribute, and no fresco has yet rivalled the admiration which goes to his ceilings at Saint-Sulpice or at the National Assembly.

Only the attacks against Romantic poetry had struck home in France. We are not taking seriously the naïve teachers who absorbed, without any grain of salt, the pompous and stilted pages, à la Brunetière, of Thierry-Maulnier's *Introduction à la poésie française.* It was an entertaining "canular" to cut the Romantics into shreds and to erect as the giants among French poets Garnier and D'Aubigné (in whom rhetoric reigned supreme) and (a disturbing index to the compiler's poetical taste) Charles Maurras! But even genuine and judicious scholars have, since 1920 or thereabouts, aligned themselves with the foreign critics of French Romantic poetry.[1] They have scored its lack of purity, to which moderns have been made peculiarly sensitive by the prolific priest who, fretting and vaticinating on his academician's tripod like a new swooning abbé Trissotin, set up Valéry's verse, Racine's "La Fille de Minos et de Pasiphaé" and even Musset's "La Blanche Oloossone à la blanche Camyre" as the archetypes of purity. They echoed Mallarmé's claim (regularly misinterpreted, as Aimé Patri showed in *La Revue Musicale* of January 1952) that poetry should "reprendre à la musique son bien" and should neither name objects nor formulate statements, but suggest. French Romantic poetry was also charged with being deficient in mystery, reluctant to submit to the pantheistic ecstasy or to the semi-mystical experience which Rousseau had revealed to Wordsworth and Shelley, which Rimbaud was later to recapture. The hint that they are logical rationalists even in religion, poetry, gastronomy and politics always irks the French. Lately they have cast envious eyes upon the divine, or subhuman, madness which engulfed Hölderlin, Lenau, Nietzsche, and they have gloried in Antonin Artaud among the moderns, and in Nerval who, because he had written six, at the most seven, beautiful and mysterious sonnets, has been disproportionately magnified into a major poet. Both were, at any rate, authentic madmen and a third was

---

1. Paul Hazard, in a polished but not over-profound essay, "Les Caractères nationaux du lyrisme romantique français," in *Quatre Etudes* (New York, Oxford Press, 1940); Louis Cazamian, in "Le Romantisme en France et en Angleterre," *Essais en deux langues* (Didier, 1938) and "Retour d'un infidèle à la poésie française," *ibid.;* the author of the present article, who does not lay any claim to being judicious, pointed out the deficiencies of French Romantic poetry as compared to English in *Shelley et la France: Lyrisme anglais et lyrisme français au XIXe siècle* (Cairo, 1935), p. 155–170. Margaret Gilman has a very penetrating article on the subject in *Yale French Studies* (No. 5, *France and World Literature*, 1950), p. 14–26.

added when Cocteau coined his epigram on Hugo: "a madman who believed he was Victor Hugo."

Our purpose is not to reopen a momentous debate in a brief article. Our conviction is that the delirious enthusiasm for Baudelaire at first, then for Rimbaud and Mallarmé as the only authentic poets of modern France, has run its course. These poets are immensely great, especially for those who, like the quinquagenarian author of these lines, first discovered them before thesis upon thesis, textual analysis piled up upon over-subtle deciphering of their enigmas had converted them into pillars of academic criticism, overgrown with adhesive learned gloss. But they do not epitomize the whole of French poetry, and no example is perhaps more perilous than theirs for poets of the future. Indeed the posterity of Baudelaire has hardly been a prolific one in twentieth-century France: Reverdy has occasional Baudelairean accents and he stands as an isolated exception. The surrealists have proved strikingly cool to Rimbaud; Claudel, with all his admiration for the poet who had served as the angel of the Annunciation to the future convert, is very remote from Rimbaud's *Illuminations*—mainly because he is an eloquent *vates* rather than an illuminated visionary. Valéry sedulously denied that Mallarmé had ever influenced him much, or that Mallarmé could ever have exercised any influence through his poetry. There is far more of Hugo than there is of the trio Baudelaire-Rimbaud-Mallarmé in the best poetry of France at mid-century: in Claudel and St. John Perse, in Michaux and Emmanuel, in P. J. Jouve and Claude Vigée, in Audiberti and Pichette. There is even a little of Sully-Prudhomme in Supervielle and not a little Musset (wedded to Anna de Noailles) in Aragon. Eloquence is a hydra and it would have taken many Verlaines to wring its ever-renascent necks. Besides, wringing its neck successfully would obviously have meant, for poetry itself, decapitation. French poetry has not yet lost its head.

What was lacking in the Romantic poetry of France in the first half of the nineteenth century? Many answers have been proposed, none of which is wholly satisfactory. Music primarily, might we say, and that affinity with folk poetry, with the simplicity of ballads which we cherish in Coleridge occasionally, in Goethe's ballads, even in Heine, or in Lenau's "Postillon" or "Drei Zigeuner." But it is most doubtful whether the music of Swinburne, even that of *Christabel*, and that of all but a few German ballads by Schiller and Goethe constitutes an authentic claim to superiority over the French for the poetry of England and Germany.

Other critics have laid the blame on the French passion for the general, which detracted from the directness of their lyrical poems in Lamartine, Hugo and Vigny and tended to turn spontaneous lyrical effusions into ample and well ordered developments dubbed meditations, contemplations or philosophical poems. Much, it is true, was thus lost. Lamartine's Elvire in "Le Lac," Vigny's Eva have no individual personality. But is Emilia Viviani or Jane Williams more sharply characterized by Shelley, or Ulrike, the girl who inspired seventy-four-year-old Goethe with his most pathetic love and to whom we owe the Marienbad elegy? A case could easily be made for meditative as against narrowly personal poetry and the old-fashioned identification of lyrical as personal, short and musical is no longer accepted by most of us. T. S. Eliot made the latest attempt to explode such a narrow conception of lyricism in his 1953 National Book League Lecture on "the three voices of poetry." Romantic poetry strove for the general and the universal far more than the poetry of Donne and Herrick, or of Théophile, Maynard and other seventeenth-century French poets, had ever done. Indeed, one of the most arresting definitions of Romanticism is the following one: "The truest essence of Romanticism is to make the individual moment or the individual situation absolute, to universalize and to classify it." As the style may lead one to suspect, that definition was not proposed by a Frenchman, but by a German Romantic, Novalis. It reads as No. 970 of his *Fragments* (Minor edition, Jena, III, 363).

Margaret Gilman, in the interesting article mentioned above, offered an ingenious explanation for the inferiority of French Romantic poetry. That poetry did not strike roots in a national tradition, for it was, unhappily, a revolution rather than a revival, and it did not rest on a body of thought around imagination: hence it lacked a content, and relied upon feeling rather than upon vision. The first point seems to us a stronger one than the second. We doubt very much that the achievement of English lyricism from Blake to Coleridge and Keats was due to their rhapsodic but highly confused statements on behalf of imagination. The English painters of the Romantic era, who also raved about imagination, produced very mediocre paintings. We have similar and even stronger doubts where Baudelaire is concerned and his unconvincing tribute to the "reine des facultés." We are still sorely in need, however, of a history of the concept of imagination in France through Dubos, Diderot, Marmontel, Delille (who, like Akenside, wrote a poem on imagination), to Vigny, Baudelaire and Surrealism. Margaret Gilman will soon provide this and she has already treated some aspects of it. But the conclusions to be drawn as to the baneful effects on poetry of the lack of an adequate theory of imagination must doubtless remain highly problematic.

The villain of the piece, who has incurred most of the blame for the deterioration of the French Romantic poets in the estimation of lovers of poetry, is eloquence. The French are, so Caesar declared of the Gauls, a nation of expert talkers. They are, or were until lately, trained in writing Latin or French discourses, broken into the rhetorical devices taught by Isocrates, Cicero and Quintilian. They are also somewhat histrionic, and flourish most conspicuously when they have a public, in wit, in comic observation, and in oratory. Rhetoric was instilled or dinned into their ears from a tender age, at least until the era of Symbolism. Therefore their poets were rhetoricians.

There are many flaws in such a line of reasoning. Rhetoric taught as a separate discipline disappeared from French syllabi in 1885 (see E. Chaignet, *La Rhétorique et son histoire*, 1888). Mallarmé, Laforgue, Verlaine, Rimbaud had been instructed in it no less, indeed far more, than Lamartine and Vigny, who had been indolent schoolboys. So had all English and German poets of most of the nineteenth century. But is there in truth much less rhetoric in the English or German Romantics than among the French? We doubt it. The very first sentence of the first of Novalis' *Hymns to Night* is a most rhetorical question. The sixth and last of those Hymns, "Sehnsucht nach dem Tode," teems with exclamations, rhetorical interrogations and even amplifications. Hölderlin's "Der Archipelagus," which Gundolf shrewdly interpreted, his "Brot und Wein," which has more elegiac tenderness, and indeed all of the poet's prophetic hymns, such as "Der Rhein" or "Patmos," are as rhetorical as Pindar once was, or as anything in Hugo. Schiller, who acted to Hölderlin as a rather stilted mentor, did not fail to advise him, in a letter from Jena on November 24, 1796, to be on his guard against "a hereditary fault of German poets, the prolixity which often crushes a very felicitous thought under an endless development and a deluge of strophes." He held up to his young admirer an ideal of parsimony, clarity and simplicity.

The rhetoric of each of the great English Romantics would deserve a study. It is present in Keats, not only in his long poems, but in his most perfect stanzas:

> Who are these coming to the sacrifice? . . .
> What little town by river or sea-shore? . . .

and in the second stanza of the "Ode to Psyche," invested with sensuous appeal; or in

Where are the songs of Spring? Ay, where are they?

Shelley is far from being the worst culprit (if guilt there be) among the Romantics. Coleridge's "Ode to the departing year," "France—an Ode," even the splendid "Dejection. An Ode" make skillful use of all the traditional devices of rhetoric. Wordsworth did likewise. And few Frenchmen, not even Corneille, certainly not Hugo, have ever established a poem or a tirade on a framework as impeccably logical, as obviously solid and bulging with "if," "therefore," "and so," "nor less, I trust," "once again," "thrice repeated," "not for this I," "nor perchance if I were not thus taught," "nor perchance if I should be," etc., as has Wordsworth in that magnificent description of an ecstasy, "Lines written above Tintern Abbey."

An anthology of the most eloquent passages in French poetry might include "Le Lac," "Ischia," "Paroles sur la dune" (and, if it were an anthology of bad poetry, a sorely needed one, "Le Dernier Chant de Childe Harold," "Rolla" and the "Lettre à Lamartine," even some of the most atrocious poems of Hugo such as "Regard jeté dans une mansarde" in *Les Rayons et les ombres*). But it should also comprise "Bateau Ivre," Mallarmé's "Toast funèbre" and even "Prose pour des Esseintes," samples from Claudel's odes and hymns so numerous that selection would prove embarrassing, reams of verse from La Tour du Pin, Emmanuel, Milosz and others, even one third of Paul Valéry. The peril for the anthologist would be to decide what to exclude from Lautréamont and, indeed, from St. John Perse. André Breton remarked in his recent and very rich volume, *La Clé des champs* (Sagittaire, 1953) that the cast of Apollinaire's thought is revealed by his favorite leitmotif, "Il y a," just as Perse's key-formula is "Celui qui," which opens the flood-gates of his sumptuous census of men's multifarious and non-utilitarian activities. "Celui qui," introducing a balanced series of enumerations, is a device straight from Bossuet, to which Lamartine (in the passionate and musical eloquence which concludes "Ischia") and other Romantics resorted, as they did to "Puisque, puisque," cumulatively proving that "il faut aimer sans cesse après avoir aimé" or to the "maintenant que" of "A Villequier" and "Paroles sur la dune."

The loss or, to use the untranslatable French word, the *déchet* in Symbolist poets (when, like Verlaine, Henri de Régnier, Verhaeren, Vielé-Griffin, they were imprudent enough to write more than one vol-

ume) is frightening, as the *déchet* in Claudel, in Jouve, nay, even in
Valéry is likely to be. It is probably more considerable than the similar
waste in the so called great Romantics. And we are led to wonder
whether the most original and durable achievement of French Romanticism was not, in verse, its eloquence. De Quincey, who wrote a long
essay "On Rhetoric" in 1829, quoted Bacon's definition of the duty and
office of rhetoric as "to apply reason to imagination for the better moving of the will." He himself, unashamedly borrowing Wordsworth's
definition of great poetry, saw in eloquence "the overflow of powerful
feelings upon occasions fitted to excite them."

Poetic eloquence at its best is characterized by an abundance of feelings or of ideas emotionally experienced, by that saturation which is often found in the powerful creators; then by an intoxication with one's
powers, that Romantic imperialism denounced tirelessly by Seillière,
which leads one to impart some of that overflow to others. Persuasion
was a noble art among the ancients, and eloquence was, in Aristotle's
word, its handmaid. Eloquence requires the mastery of a number of rules
and devices which rhetoric taught. I. A. Richards, Kenneth Burke and
Jean Paulhan have rehabilitated the word rhetoric among us, and transformed its content. But they have not as yet trained a generation of college students—or of philosophers, social scientists and politicians—to
ponder sufficiently over the warning uttered by Pericles to his country-
men, as reported by Thucydides: "The man who thinks but who does not
know how to express what he thinks is on a par with him who has no
idea at all." Dialectics, which for the Greeks was the counterpart or the
complement of rhetoric, has sprung into fashion again since Hegel and
Marx. Rhetoric may not have too long to wait for the rehabilitation
which is due to it. It had been associated with sophistry. In actual fact
the stoics viewed it as a virtue and as a branch of ethics, which taught
how to discriminate between good and evil, as Jean Cousin recalled in
his voluminous study of Quintilian (Boivin, 1935, I, 780).

The poetics which stressed images above all else was for a time
beneficent. It ended, however, by belittling poetry and by leaving it
with a dwindling audience of over-subtle aesthetes. Many a younger
poet today would gladly echo the concise remark of one of them: "Images seem to me means, not ends" (Randall Jarrell). The isolation of poetry from the main stream of life and its divorce from reality have been
concealed from some of us by the fervor of a few for Hopkins, Mallarmé
or the later Yeats. Professors still succeed in inflaming their students,
who are at the receptive and romantic age, with the love of esoteric po-

etry. But such love hardly ever survives their graduation from college. Adults are irretrievably divorced from poetry as they are not from music or painting: the niggardly place granted to verse (most of which hardly deserves the name of poetry) in our magazines today bears witness to the failure of poets and interpreters of poetry to enlarge their scant band of readers, in spite of a marked growth in population and in the size of the literate and of the college-graduated public. It is our fond belief that the radio programs grossly underestimate their public when they grant, in America at least, such a miserable place (when it is not a glaring absence) to the reading of poetry. Those of us who do not totally despair of the future of literature in this age of mass media hope that the poetry which has a content, because it embodies a passionate understanding of human emotions ("Wer das Tiefste gedacht, liebt das Lebendigste," proclaimed Hölderlin), and which has wind or breath ("le souffle" which Jean Prévost has searchingly analyzed in his *Baudelaire*) may survive the curse cast upon it by the tenants of purity and of form or pattern divorced from content.[2]

Space is lacking for a detailed analysis of the original eloquence, "the good one," which is occasionally found, among much dross and much immature declamation, in each of the leading Romantic poets of France. One example alone may be given here. The *Harmonies* is probably the least successful volume of Lamartine's youth (excluding the later *Recueillements*): "Your 'gloria Patri' diluted in two tomes," wrote to the poet one of his detractors. Yet three or four poems in it scale heights to which French lyricism had never soared before, and they are the eloquent ones—among them this fragment from "Novissima Verba" in which the poet, casting a backward glance at his life in a supreme farewell (he survived that crisis of melancholy of 1830 to die only in 1869), pays the following tribute to love and woman, by whom alone living was justified.

---

2. Marcel Arland, a refined and perspicacious critic who has usually been more devoted to Marivaux or Constant than to the Romantics, has, as had Claudel before him, lamented the distrust of eloquence in recent poetry. "Many poems today lack that broad flow, that deep murmur in which, sparkling as they may be, images and lovely details can both be fused and seek their exact value. Without them, a poem may be a succession of pleasing fragments, but not the living thing which a beautiful work must be. 'Prends l'éloquence et tords-lui son cou.' For the last sixty years, we have been doing precisely that; but we overlooked the fact that there is a certain kind of eloquence which no great work can do without. Distrust of eloquence has brought about distrust of poetry itself. Luckily, eloquence can survive many deaths" (M. Arland, in *Essais et nouveaux essais critiques*, Gallimard, 1952, p. 130).

Amour, être de l'être, amour, âme de l'âme,
Nul homme plus que moi ne vécut de ta flamme!
Nul, brûlant de ta soif sans jamais l'épuiser,
N'eût sacrifié plus pour t'immortaliser!
Nul ne désira plus dans l'autre âme qu'il aime
De concentrer sa vie en se perdant soi-même,
Et, dans un monde à part de toi seul habité,
De se faire à lui seul sa propre éternité!
Femmes, anges mortels, création divine,
Seul rayon dont la nuit un moment s'illumine,
Je le dis à cette heure, heure de vérité,
Comme je l'aurais dit quand devant la beauté
Mon cœur épanoui, qui se sentait éclore,
Fondait comme une neige aux rayons de l'aurore,
Je ne regrette rien de ce monde que vous!
Ce que la vie humaine a d'amer et de doux,
Ce qui la fait brûler, ce qui trahit en elle
Je ne sais quel parfum de la vie immortelle,
C'est vous seules! Par vous toute joie est amour,
Ombre des biens parfaits du céleste séjour,
Vous êtes ici-bas la goutte sans mélange
Que Dieu laissa tomber de la coupe de l'ange,
L'étoile qui brillant dans une vaste nuit
Dit seule à nos regards qu'un autre monde luit,
Le seul garant enfin que le bonheur suprême,
Ce bonheur que l'amour puise dans l'amour même,
N'est pas un songe vain créé pour nous tenter,
Qu'il existe, ou plutôt qu'il pourrait exister,
Si, brûlant à jamais du feu qui nous dévore,
Vous et l'être adoré dont l'âme vous adore,
L'innocence, l'amour, le désir, la beauté,
Pouvaient ravir aux dieux leur immortalité!

These thirty lines, the magnificent long ode on "Les Révolutions" composed in 1831, and, in spite of several flaws which the poet carelessly left in it, his powerful poem on his daughter's death, "Gethsémani" (1834), rank in our eyes among the truly great achievements of French lyricism. They all belong to the eloquent type of poetry which Lamartine, around and after 1830, recognized as the one best suited to him. On September 22, 1835, after delivering a speech at Mâcon, he wrote: "I now see the effective truth of what I had always felt: that eloquence was in me more than poetry, the latter being only one of its forms." He similarly noted later, of one of his favorite Girondins, Vergniaud, that

"his imagination first overflowed in poetry before it burst out into eloquence."

Such a dynamic kind of poetry may appear verbose, too sumptu-
ously ample, too prone to approximate and to skirt the inevitable image or the strikingly concise and enigmatic line. It is entitled to its right-
ful place in France, however, alongside the more fashionable finds of
Valéry, less eloquent but in no way less rhetorical (indeed far more
"arty" and tricky) than Lamartine's rolling periods.

> Qui pleure là, sinon le vent simple à cette heure? . . .
> N'entends-tu pas frémir ces noms aériens,
> O Sourde!

and the exquisite but most rhetorical and artificial questions addressed
in the presence of "La Dormeuse":

> Quels secrets dans son coeur brûle ma jeune amie? . . .
> De quels vains aliments sa naïve chaleur
> Fait ce rayonnement d'une femme endormie?

We refrain from mentioning Valéry's more obvious failures, such as "La
Pythie," and the bad stanzas (there are several such) of "Le Cimetière
marin." Static poetry occasionally creates delightful miniatures and
delights in serpentine folds and volutes. It appeals to the feminine half
of ourselves which confesses, with Mme Emilie Teste: "A good part of
the soul can enjoy without understanding; it is a large part in me." But
the invasion and the conquest of our whole being by a surge of poetical
eloquence carried by an "élan vital" are not to be easily banished from
the kingdom of poetry. When all is said, if French Romanticism had
been more similar to the best of German and English Romanticism, we
should deplore it today. For it would probably have spent all its force
between 1820 and 1840, and have dried up or crushed the rest of French
poetry, as came to be the case in Germany from Heine to George, in England from Tennyson and Browning to Yeats (Hopkins being for all practical purposes absent until 1918).

Instead, just as the French Renaissance, blossoming long after the
Italian Renaissance, timid, awkward at first, borrowing lavishly and
slavishly from the ancients and from beyond the Alps, turned out to be
the slow dawn of a perdurable and original classicism which outlived
the earlier attempt of Italy, French Romanticism in 1820–40 was only
one phase by which literary history, taken in as it often is by manifestoes and debates, has been hypnotized. The so-called Romantic

movement of 1820–1840 was in fact only one wave (and probably the most timid, the most classical or pseudo-classical one) in the long history of French Romanticism. The first now conveniently termed pre-Romanticism (1760–75) was far bolder and more authentic in everything but poetry. The second was the timid ripple of *Atala,* Mme de Staël's novels and criticism, *Obermann,* in 1800–1810. The third one began, in the pattern which Malraux has proposed as the law for all artists, by imitating pseudo-classical models before it became aware of its own originality.[3] Only on and through the stage could the liberation of French literature occur, after 1827–30. Parnassianism, Baudelaireanism, Bovarysm, were, in our view, chiefly a new and fourth Romantic onslaught, carried on by a liberated generation which no longer had to vituperate against classicism to conceal how close it was to it. Symbolism was, especially in its precursors, the most revolutionary of those successive Romantic waves, and psychologically the most profound.

Yet too many of the Symbolists appear to us today as failures: they were satisfied with a languid and nerveless poetry, poor in intellectual content, distrustful of motion as well as of eloquence, fearful to commit itself to the great issues of the age. They paraded the word mystery, and attempted to put mystery by force everywhere; but they seldom yielded to the marvelous and failed to follow up that "renascence of wonder" which an English writer glorified as the achievement of Romanticism. Such at any rate is the charge of André Breton, in an essay on "Le merveilleux contre le mystère," in which he praises the best of the Romantic accomplishment against an overrated Symbolism.

Romantic rhetoric is not to be equated with the sense of wonder or with poetry, to be sure. But we believe that, after half a century of vituperation against eloquence, many lovers of poetry and many poets have become aware of the perils of a poetics evolved from an indiscriminate repudiation of French Romanticism. Valéry's poetics, which his poetry often contradicts, has led several younger poets, unable to read the professor at the Collège de France with the required irony and to see through the finery of an aged coquette, to an impoverishment of their gifts. Claudel, that inveterate Romantic in revolt against Romanticism, may well have been wiser when he tirelessly called mod-

---

3. One of the very best works on Romanticism which made this point (of Romantic poetry being a supreme neo-classical achievement) is the old study by Emmanuel Barat, *Le Style poétique et la révolution romantique* (Hachette, 1904).

ern poetry to the task of attempting the slow, progressive commotion of the whole man, alone worthy of a truly Catholic poet. Curiously enough, he thus met with another literary potentate, the pontiff of Surrealism, whose poetical achievement, from the cascade of amplifications of "L'Union libre" to the rhetorical invocations of the "Ode à Charles Fourier," has not been averse to eloquence. Eloquence is after all one of the ways in which literature, and poetry in particular, can escape the perpetual nightmare of art: immobility which is death, and capture that prerogative of life: motion. One of the shrewdest critics of modern French poetry, Gabriel Bounoure, rightly said: "Tout poème est un itinéraire pour l'âme. Il n'y pas de poème immobile."

JACQUES GUICHARNAUD

Those Years: Existentialism 1943–1945 *

> "The names we give past events just don't matter; what matters is the future."
>
> —Anne, in *Les Mandarins*, by Simone de Beauvoir

New Haven, September 1955. Some local station is endlessly grinding out its "rock-'n'-roll." I can write only against a background of music, and the worse it is the better: no temptation to stop and listen.

In 1943, our "gods" were Louis Armstrong, Fats Waller and Jelly Roll Morton. They were *verboten* in Paris (at least their records were) and instead we had the jazz of the new, Nazified Europe—whose sane Teutonic ideals inspired Peter Kreuder's "piano medleys." On the cinema screens *Jew Süss* had replaced *The Awful Truth*. In the book stores, translations of Hemingway and Faulkner fetched black-market prices; in our classrooms Heine (but our teachers whispered his name to us) had become an "unbekannter Dichter"; on town hall and police station walls, red or yellow notices every day listed those who had just been shot. All were accused of "Communism." (A man could not be disposed of by simply branding him anti-Nazi, anti-Vichy or anti-New-Order, it was all too negative. And to accuse him of patriotism would have been equivocal, for who deserved that label apart from Marshal Pétain and his followers? No, some positive charge was needed, and one that would please the mediocrities of the Reaction. But, thank God, the genius of Propaganda and historical circumstance conspired together, after the rupture of the Russo-German Pact, to provide the sin of *lèse-trahison* with a new, positive, bloodcurdling name: Communism.)

The foregoing deals with what is no more. But eleven years have now elapsed since France was "liberated," and so these recollections are no longer truly personal, containing as they do the most meaning-

*From *Yale French Studies* 16 (Winter 1955–56): *Foray through Existentialism*.

YFS 96, *50 Years of Yale French Studies: A Commemorative Anthology*, eds. Porter and Waters, © 1999 by Yale University.

ful details of a sunken period of History. But the aim of these pages is to give individual testimony and the author, consequently, must strive to be both a witness and himself too. He must commit no one but himself, while claiming to be the pattern of an age and of a universe.

Thus I alone am committed by what follows. Other contributors who would advance objective scholarship have every right to question this individual perspective—and especially those mentioned, personages both public and private, will have the right and the duty to reject this nasty, naive or biased deformation of the truth. Of their "truth." In a word, I am trying in all sincerity to recall a past that is theirs no less than mine. (Sincerity, of course, is the crossroads where entire good faith has a splendid chance of colliding with error. In this case any error would be particularly regrettable, since many of the names to be evoked belong to men who besides their other undertakings sought to make sincerity and truth coincide.)

Yet I have been asked to be subjective, on the grounds that in 1944 I was in my twentieth year, that I frequented the Café de Flore and, for various reasons, was often in contact with Sartre and the Existentialist "group." Often I shall say "we": "We were sitting outside the Flore . . . Sartre told us . . ." This "we" obviously needs definition. In the first place it means myself, or what I remember about myself, revised by the intervening ten years of sometimes tangential development; and it means some of my friends, what I remember about them or imagined I knew. It is an abstract "we." It is historical; and a handy category for imposing a significance that transcends personal experience on these souvenirs of a time that, by a rather considerable margin, transcended me.

WHEN HUMANISM WOVE ITS SPELLS

At this present moment Sartre is in Peking. Although most of the critics lashed into it, his satirical comedy *Nekrassov*, which pokes fun at the anti-Communist press, continues to pack the Théâtre Antoine. Twelve years ago Sartre was in Paris, teaching philosophy at the Lycée Condorcet, and Charles Dullin was directing *The Flies*. At that moment the flies of the uneasy conscience were buzzing like the very devil in the murky atmosphere of occupied France.

But they did not buzz in everyone's ears. The Pétainist numskull, along with the collaborationist puffed up with neo-feudal notions, enjoyed complete tranquillity of soul or even exaltation, as each went his opportunistic way or savored the consequences of his placing order before justice.

Nor did the flies torment those who had plunged at once into direct action, nor those who were stopped from thinking by their routine occupations or the speed of events. But a hesitant mass, whose very conditions of existence barred any protest, sensed them in the air and, for reasons still to be given, appeared ready to be their passive victim. Found in it were young men of the upper and lower bourgeoisie, yet of an age when in our democratic lands every bourgeois is an intellectual.

We were between fourteen and eighteen years old when war descended upon us. The clearest indication of the effectiveness of French secondary schooling is the irresistible fascination it exerts on so many of the young. How hard it is to abandon Homer, Plato and Racine just as one begins, at the time of the *baccalauréat*, to understand them a little. Literature and philosophy, presented as an eclectic, smiling and somewhat irresponsible humanism, are the two wings of a golden door. Centuries of culture labored over it lovingly, in order that the stripling bourgeoisie, future guardian of Values, might be enticed into the garden of Epicure. Or even into the garden of tortures, the delicious tortures of the Intellect.

It is rather less harsh to have to put up with regimented under-nourishment, with the roping off of certain streets, with police raids, curfew and other minor miseries of the occupation or of fascism, when at the heart of one's existence is the obligation to translate elegantly a page of Cicero or to interpret the *Réponses aux objections*. This is not to inculpate our educational system or the teachers who man it. This teaching is the very *summa* of our culture, and not one of us would wish to repudiate it. Organized almost entirely under the Third Republic it has, for the most part, courageously chosen to set Truth above any civic propaganda. But its interpretation of culture is wise and moderate: Culture is universal and thus, though offering the citizen the joys of knowledge in peace time, it may be pursued, untainted, during war. This may be the sign of its eternal worth, but with "the Nation in danger" History leaves this harmonious institution dangerously in the rear. I know at first hand that the partisans read Montaigne in their forests; that maquis members in the Vercors organized at least one mountain school where, between one tough exploit and the next, they taught La Fontaine's fables and the secrets of Latin composition to the Jewish and other children they were trying to save. These men, who were hastily disarmed at war's end for fear they might force their purity on the new peace when compromise again offered the easy way out, had actually fought to save culture and the education that maintained it.

But after all it was they who had personally taken the decisive step. The humanism in whose name they killed and were killed had not, in so many words, demanded that they take up arms and become apprentice murderers—perhaps because those who organized and represented it could not conceive that in an era of universal Democracy men would seek to enslave men, as Nazi Germany had set about doing. These representatives—I am being unfair, for many of our teachers were active Resistance members. Some disappeared, either executed or burnt in the crematoriums. In their classes they had often appeared the least "committed" of any. Was this personal prudence? Why risk arrest for some daring remark that would have won the barren applause of anti-Nazi pupils? Or rather was it not that, fully aware of the frightful dangers of direct action, they would not use their facile prestige as teachers to lead adolescents into torture and the dirty work of terrorism? Besides, it is not easy to look on men as tools when the aim of the struggle is to restore their dignity and personal freedom. See, in this connection, Sartre's lecture (called *Existentialism* in the English translation) where he relates how a young man came to ask his advice. The dilemma was: "If I join the Resistance I will be responsible for my mother's death, for she will die of fright. If I do not enlist, I will be a scum who has betrayed France and the cause of Freedom." I quote from memory and may be textually inaccurate, but I remember that it was not hard to discern Sartre's own problem behind the young man's.

"We are fighting," Giraudoux had rather foolishly declared during the phony war, "so that French schoolchildren may still toil over the problem of the faucets and not over others that speak of cannon."[1] The metaphor is undeniably silly. But beneath it the hopes of men were at stake. I said that some Resistants died for the sake of Montaigne who, himself, had fled the plague at Bordeaux. The faucets are the merest piddle-poetry, Montaigne may have been a coward (a debatable point), yet it was the faucet problem and the reading of Montaigne that helped form the concrete entity, if so it may be called, of the French consciousness. Despite all defeats and aberrations, a civilization that aims at the happiness of mankind no less than others do is far from negligible. Certainly no less, and maybe more! There were many reasons for taking up arms, and since 1945 their irreconcilability has become evident. But some did it for Montaigne and the faucets.

1. He alluded to a problem found in all French arithmetic manuals: A barrel of such and such a volume is filled from a faucet at such and such a rate; it is being emptied via another faucet that has another rate of flow; how long will it take to fill the barrel?

A serious spirit directed at every manifestation of the spirit, a lively indignation at every debasement, a keen recollection of that not-so-remote time when poets were *assassinated* for demanding poetry's rights, and when one of their greatest survivors, René Char, with his own hands executed the traitors in his Resistance group (men of this caliber became heroes in spite of themselves, so that Malraux could call a newspaper article "Those who wage war without liking it"), finally, confidence in Man. (For the second time I use this cliché, and I shall not refrain from using it again.) These are some of the areas where the intellectual Resistant was concerned and active. His greatness, his ambiguity, the reasons for his political failure in the post-Liberation years, can now be understood: without always realizing it, he transcended the concepts of France, Europe, Western World.

Never in the history of the world, it seems to me, no, not even in the sixteenth century, when the armed struggle turned on factional ideologies, or in the eighteenth, whose revolutions took place on behalf of white, adult, civilized men who, into the bargain, were bourgeois through and through, with a notion of man fostered, in each period, which was limited by the state of actual knowledge, not even then, I believe, were men willing to die and to kill for an idea of Man so pure, so universal, so "unconditional" and so fecund as that forged by a part of the European Resistance between 1942 and 1945. The expression "part of the Resistance," I hasten to add, offers no slight, essentially at least, to the rest of the movement, whether of Right or Left: I was merely seeking to define this part.

Well then, what actual experiences are reflected in the systematization and "historicization" I have just practiced? I could easily compile a whole list of pertinent memories. My classmate Levy, who wore the yellow star and in order not to embarrass me, when we were walking together, used to throw his raincoat over his shoulder, told me one day that he belonged to a Resistance group. Some of our teachers were suddenly demoted for having disobeyed the Marshal. Months passed. Levy vanished (less unlucky than others, he was sent to a prison in Italy and at least emerged alive, after the Liberation). Some teachers also disappeared, into the silence of a smoothly functioning administrative machine. When one is very young, when there are no personal reasons to worry and the family's main problems concern the food supply, while individual preoccupations revolve around the possible reactions of one's girl friend (who waits every day outside the *lycée*, with her short skirt, hair piled up in a topknot, shoulder-strap bag and sandals with triple wooden soles)—in a word, when one is a non-political *petit bourgeois*—an occupying power and a native fascism eager to keep up appearances employ all the velvet needed to establish the mailed fist as a part of the daily routine. The *petit bourgeois,* with his longing for tranquillity (which he confuses with happiness), has no desire to compromise himself: smile at him a little, and the trick works. "Yes, times are hard; yes, it's a wicked world, it's outrageous and absurd, but what's to be done? That's the way things are." All this is without any reference to those who swallowed the teachings of Vichy and of a section of the clergy, mouthpieces for the demoralizing Nazi propaganda: "France has erred; she is paying the penalty. She must accept the fact and resign herself."

The occupation was the normal landscape, so to speak, of our adolescent years. To explain our lack of concern, mention should be made of the discretion shown in supervising the Sorbonne and the whole educational set-up in Paris. Nothing occurred here to match, for instance, the bloody and spectacular surgery the Nazis performed on the Charles University in Prague. As a consequence, a young French novelist teaching in an American college could reassure the audience at his public lecture that "France was not occupied." I almost protested, but he was speaking for himself, for me, for a whole group of young bourgeois intellectuals who had not *really* suffered. I said nothing. Fortunately there were some European refugees in the room who made it their duty to refute him.

No immediately apparent relationship existed between the technique of the *explication de texte* and the disappearance of my friend Levy. Then, too, we had bouts of rebelliousness that took little account of the real situation. During our "rural public service" at a wood-cutting site, the rumor or the news of an allied landing served as a pretext for us to seize our axes and choppers and go off to storm an airfield used by the Germans. The venture was not carried through, in part because one of us expressed his skepticism about the likely results. Later we were to learn that he was the only one among us who had participated actively in the Resistance. Isn't that so, Pedro? Thoughtlessness and muddleheadedness (playing tennis with a German soldier as a preliminary to distributing Gaullist tracts in the stadium dressing room, and with no clear realization of the contradiction involved), also a sense of impotence, but which was largely accepted—this was not a final resignation, but to some imagined miracle was left the responsibility for changing the absurd order that beset the world—this about characterizes quite a few of us at the time.

One of our teachers, with a quaver in his voice, read us a paragraph from Pascal: "Imagine a number of men in chains and all condemned to death, some of them slaughtered every day in sight of the others, while those who remain see their own lot in that of their fellows and, looking at each other in grief and without hope, await their turn. That is the image of man's lot." This saddened us, no doubt, but it had little effect. Yet this was the right tone in which to speak to us.

THE APPRENTICE EXISTENTIALIST (1943 – 44)

Our earliest existentialist "apprenticeship" was spent, in the main, in reading Kafka, Sartre's *Nausea* and *The Stranger* by Albert Camus. In these works we found (more readily than in Pascal, for we were infidels) the great metaphors that rendered intelligible for us our own lot, made up of solitude and of a complex of slavery and freedom. This coming to consciousness can be achieved only through anguish—and although this may not have been experienced for the first time, now we could give it a name and understand it better.

One cannot begin one's philosophical education at the end, and even less can wisdom be forced on one from the outside. Each man on his own account has to relive the philosopher's progress. At a particular moment in history, for young people of a particular station, the first step, the becoming aware of the actual state of things, must be despair. Anguish and despair were certainly better than thoughtlessness. We were overly happy (if I may put it thus) at having found the writings and the men able to express us, so that our attitude perhaps was not free of a certain pose, of a little snobbery. At all events, it had nothing in common with the spectacular manifestations of romantic despair. Sartre and Simone de Beauvoir, whom we were beginning to frequent, and later Albert Camus, with their seriousness and their rejection of all scandal and frivolity, scarcely invited us to take that path.

They invited us, indeed, to very little. They were not "masters" on the prowl for disciples. We sought them out. Refusing to betray their own time by a flight or refuge into inoffensive literature, they knew that we like others were the representatives of the time; they were less anxious to guide us than to express us, and were convinced that by expressing us and exhorting us (for we all more or less prided ourselves on writing) to express ourselves, they would assist in the burgeoning of our freedom.

The tone of the meetings and conversations whose meaning I have tried to make plain could not exactly be characterized as tender. The violence of the era, and what was at stake in these discussions, namely our lives or, at least, our consciences, hardly encouraged that. Nevertheless, from more than ten years' distance, I cannot help feeling a sort of tenderness as I recall the immediate setting and the savor of this turning-point in our lives. For example, the smoky warmth of the Café de Flore on certain winter afternoons. Sartre and Simone de Beauvoir usually sat at the back, toward the right. With their pipe, cigarettes, glass of tea or spirits, paper and pen, they wrote on (*Being and Nothingness, She Came to Stay*). They were undisturbed there, and warm. One of us would enter, shake hands, chat with them for a moment and then settle down at another table, usually to write also. In the late afternoon Camus, coming from his work at Gallimard's, put in an appearance. Or, perhaps, one of us showed up with a manuscript under his arm: short stories, the first pages of a novel. The thing was read during the next few days by Sartre and Simone de Beauvoir, and duly criticized. If it deserved it, it was passed on to Camus. Throughout these years I can't recollect any of the three having refused substantial criticism and abundant literary counsel to any young author of good faith who asked for their opinion.

Of course, all this had rather the air of a "conventicle." But unlike some other conventicles, this one did not resemble a house of ill-repute, and even less an ivory tower. Above all, the journalists and other outsiders who have satirized the group failed to record, either from ignorance or in deliberate misrepresentation, the cordiality that prevailed. "Despair" does not necessarily imply bitterness and a "difficult character." At times despair and hatred are necessities, or at least realities, there is no sense in closing one's eyes to them; there is no sense, either, in yielding to them: one lives *with* them. Sartre, in any case, with his entire lucidity and his violence, and in the sincerity of his personal drama, has always seemed to me a "good-humored" man. The real Sartre bears no resemblance to the atrabilious and sordid character which certain papers have seen fit to depict. In this connection, here is an anecdote. One evening as with Jean Genet I walked along the banks of the Seine, still quite dazzled by the NRF crowd I was getting to know, I was called to order by Genet, who found my naivete irritating. After hurling vehement diatribes at some of the establishment's great names, he summed up: "Fundamentally, among all French writers there are only two I really respect: Cocteau because he is intelligent, and Sartre because he is kind."

Some of the thoughtless laugh to hear speak of Sartre's seductiveness. Perhaps that is not the right word. Let us say that he attached us to him by his patent kindness, by the clarity of his articulation, by his refusal of any polite compromise in argument, by the call that went out from him to what we really were, to what our solid education as civilized young intellectuals forced us to hide. After my first meeting with Sartre (it was in a little café behind the Lycée Condorcet—a friend, a former pupil of Sartre's, had taken me along) I was bursting with problems. Everything had become important, lighting a cigarette, stirring a cup of coffee, using certain words and intonations. The world had become an immense trap for catching crimes. I had discovered the uneasy conscience in connection with little things. Sartre had talked on, in the little café, quite unaware of all this; it was my friend who had sized me up shrewdly and judged his shot well. Right, J.B.? I like to think that this individual experience is typical. To employ a term that Sartre himself would detest, he played for some of us the part of an "awakener." "The world is yours," he seemed to say. This did not mean that we should undertake to ensure its continued existence on the lines laid down by our elders, in the hypocrisy of the clear conscience and of the exploitation of Man, camouflaged as fidelity to the traditions of bourgeois humanism. We understood, on the contrary, that the only way to achieve this kind of continual creation of the world was to change it. The majority thought such a procedure ridiculous: those, that is, who lived in accord with a philosophy determined in advance. There were two sections: the bourgeoisie, whether collaborationist or resistant, which (and this quite sufficiently demonstrates the abstractness of its attitude) had chosen one side or the other *for the selfsame reasons;* and the Marxist proletariat, supplemented by some intellectuals who long before had been enfeoffed and enrolled in a universe where these trivial questions could be solved by the utterance of slogans.

By word of mouth, before the Liberation, and subsequently in the newspapers, the Marxist Left indulged in a vigorous criticism of the Existentialists, even in the days of "unity of action against the Nazi invader." That distressed us, at the time: for like these people we too placed our hopes in a better earth. The indignation voiced by the Right, which after its war-time divisions was once more united in reaction, always delighted us. To be dragged through the mud by certain papers is, if not a mark of distinction, at least the indication that one is on the track of a few truths. Pious souls took pleasure—as indeed they still do—in dissecting the incoherence, the flaws and certain sleights-of-hand to be found in the Sartrian "system." Apart from the fact that no system can withstand, from beginning to end, a relentless criticism of detail, the dishonesty of these criticisms becomes patent when one considers that (1) they are made by people who, quite frequently, were moved to ecstasy by the "system" of Maurras and his acolytes, either fully realizing (and then they were contemptible) or unaware (and then they were dupes) that Maurras' views were based on an astonishing misreading of history; (2) at the very moment that Europe was undergoing the most gigantic attempt at enslavement, it was criminally frivolous to blame a philosophy that put the concept of liberty in the forefront for confusing Cartesian liberty and political freedom and for giving too little weight to heredity, and to blame its begetter because too often, in his literary works, he used such words as "merde" and "con."

For liberty is the root of the matter. As a general notion it was perhaps hard to grasp, even for intellectuals: we began to take excessive liberties with it in our philosophy papers, at the Sorbonne or in *Première Supérieure*. Some of our teachers condemned the excessive use we were making of it. It's true: on paper we juggled too freely with such words as "anguish," "Dasein," "nothingness," "liberty," "commitment." But it's no fluke, after all, that they could so readily enter our speech: they aroused in us the consciousness of what we were and of what we might be. And reduced to an over-simple definition, but accurate enough for young bourgeois of eighteen or twenty, Sartre's "Soyez libres" resounded with a note quite different from the "Fais ce que veulx" of Rabelais' Abbey of Theleme.

This makes sufficiently clear how Sartre had brought philosophy down to earth for us. I envy those of us who were his pupils at the Lycée Condorcet or elsewhere. Many indeed have claimed to "have brought philosophy down to earth." They succeeded but ill: they touch earth but they abandon philosophy, and all ends in a pseudo-positivism, an imbecile drooling that exalts the illusions of the convenient to the rank of a value. Sartre, I mean to say, and Merleau-Ponty, and Simone de Beauvoir, both in their purely literary works and in their "phenomenological" essays or studies have made our world intelligible to us, and the circumstances of our lives.

I repeat: we became horribly entangled in the subtleties of phenomenology,[2] we said plenty of silly things, we reveled in argument—

2. It has not been my intention here to explain existentialist ontology, the priority of existence over essence, the distinction between in-self and for-self, the phenomenological method, etc.—but only to evoke our attitude and conduct vis-a-vis the world.

in school, in the cafés, during our "surprise parties." We could refer our disputes to Sartre, who never refused to explain (after all, he was a teacher), and to whom we perhaps rendered a service by compelling him to clarify for himself certain notions and crucial points in his argumentation. These "supplementary classes" did not destroy but rounded out the teaching we received elsewhere, at the Sorbonne or in the preparatory classes for the "Grandes Ecoles." Some of our teachers had adopted a certain mark of dignity: I remember one of them who closed the classroom door himself and then turned to us. "Once this door is shut," he said, "we are free. Truth is a prisoner along *with* us." And then he went on to execute, in all its perfection, the death leap of an *explication de texte* on Théophile Gautier's "Symphonie en blanc majeur," for example. One can too easily forget that, with his preliminary remark, he risked Fresnes and the concentration camp. But when all is said and done it was Sartre who, by his private conversation, enabled us to see in the proper perspective this sort of courage—and Gautier also. More generally, the world ceased to be absurd because we knew it was absurd, and in what way. Food shortages, the disappearance of our Jewish friends and of those in the Resistance, the broadcasts of Radio Paris and the BBC, our own behavior, our surprise parties under the menace of aerial bombardment, they all acquired a meaning: tears and sentimental outpourings are an acceptance of the absurd, whereas the intellectual identification of the absurd leads to rebellion.

Gide and Cocteau are excellent masters in subversiveness. But only for peace time. In time of war, whether international, internecine or ideological, they are of little help. Gide's Nathanael is, possibly, a hero; only by the sheerest fluke could he be a hero of the Resistance: it is just as easy to become "the most irreplaceable of beings" in the anti-Bolshevik Legion as in the underground. We esteemed and still esteem Gide and Cocteau, for they belong to the race of writers who mold men. The French tradition is behind them, also Montaigne and Rousseau. Beside them, opposed to them, is Montherlant.[3] (There is a way of personally endowing oneself with a kind of greatness, through the very contempt one bestows on Man. We desired and still desire greatness, but not at the expense of Man.)

What we discovered in the course of those years is this, that the

---

3. He imagines he is Corneille, without for a moment suspecting that in actual fact he is the anti-Corneille.

words greatness, patriotism, citizen, Man, humanism (and with them, of course, Work, Famine, Fatherland) are terribly equivocal, and that a man is not justified by the "names" of the characteristics recognized as his, for the name is the height of abstraction. Naive it certainly was, but when we were about eighteen years old part of our apprenticeship was to learn this: that the concept of crime is reversible, depending on its historical context. A man kills, a judge condemns him to death. There are moments in History when it is the judge who is the criminal. An American mob hangs a negro who is believed to have tried to rape a white woman: that's a lynching. A European village rebels against established authority and shoots the head of the local *Kommandantur:* it's . . . that's a lynching too, but the word has changed its meaning, for the relation of oppressed to oppressor has been inverted.

There can be no doubt that to refer thus to the concrete content, to examine closely the actual consequences of some gesture, to strive for "historical realism," to resolve to attribute to every act its true meaning, tend to destroy immediate efficacy. At a time when some choice must be made at once, total knowledge is an impossible luxury. For this requires time, and there are periods when the "rhythm" of History is violently stepped up. The Trotskyites turned their backs on Terrorism with the justification that "a dead German is merely a corpse. A living German, if we set about it properly, is potentially on our side." As others saw it, "one German dead means one less henchman of Nazism." Whatever judgment History may pronounce concerning these points of view, this was the sort of answer that had to be given, and fast, to the choice that faced us.

I have spoken in terms of Terrorism and civil war (after all, German and collaborationist amounted to the same thing), in terms, that is, of a phenomenon with which the American reader has been unfamiliar for almost one hundred years. Scattered instances, limited to mass psychoses, imprisonment, the electric chair or banishment, and reserved for the favored few, give only a faint idea of what national psychology may become, when the same phenomena find expression (with the aid of a foreign occupying army) in systematic assassination, the Terror practised by the resisters having its counterpart in that put into force by reigning authority.

But "those years" have been holding my attention for too long. Let it not be forgotten, however, that at stake was the life of each individual, that the death of a member of the underground or of a helpless victim of Nazism did not mean the same thing as the death of a volunteer in the anti-Bolshevik legion. That is to say that we restored the concrete significance of the term "hero," that heroism was not appraised according to its military importance, but placed in the historical situation. If this is not done, communication by means of language remains abstract and illusory. The same was true for such expressions as martyr, patriot, etc. And with the end of hostilities the terms Communist, fascist, etc., were to require the same treatment.

We knew well the meaning of "virtus" in Latin; yet, without admitting it to ourselves, we had no idea what "Man" signified. By taking us as we were, and going beyond both classical humanism and anthropology, Existentialism became for some of us the only possible bridge between our thoughtlessness, which our milieu had assiduously fostered, and our entering the world. Thanks to this "philosophy," and to those who had founded it in France or had adopted it, we became conscious of the position we occupied and of its possibilities. Whether we availed ourselves of them or not, on each one of us rested the responsibility. Yet nonetheless, and quite apart from the question of our individual deeds, for many of us those particular years were a time of purity. No doubt we had bumped into the problems of retarded adolescence that mark the young bourgeois intellectual. But our fresh attacks of puberty and the minor setbacks of our love life were readily disposed of, to the extent that we succeeded in realizing that the world we lived in and were a part of had other worries, and could not allow itself the luxury of yearning over an adolescent's blackheads.

On June 6, 1944, I was to meet Sartre on the terrace of the Brasserie Lipp, at Saint-Germain-des-Prés. He didn't show up that morning: the Allies had just disembarked in Normandy.

Each of us lived through that following summer as his convictions, possibilities, vocation and destiny permitted.

THE GALA (1944 – 45)

In the months that followed the Liberation, the "group" came together once more, impoverished, enriched, and a stage farther on. We lived under the sign of happiness, or at least of that which betokened an extraordinary thirst for happiness. The final victory of the democracies was in sight, we were dazzled by the prospects of freedom suddenly presented us, the world was ours. The intellectual world celebrated the triumph of the writers of the Resistance. Thanks to Sartre, every door opened before us: those of the publishing houses, of Radio, of the Cinema. This had nothing in common with any "Restoration," it was a renewal, and we believed in Revolution. I neither aspire, nor in the framework of these recollections have I the right, to allot the shares of individual blame for the collapse of our hopes. But in all sincerity I declare that, during those months, France missed its chance for a new 1789. Was it Communist intransigence, or the Gaullists', the timorousness of other leftist groups, the presence of American troops and the associated fear of a repression, or the myth of the unity of the Resistance and an associated spirit of procrastination? In any event, the Revolution did not take place. Must I say that we did not know how to set about it? For lack of anything better the country fell back on a Christian Democratic regime (the M.R.P.), the inadequacy of which has become all too painfully apparent.

In any case—to get back to our little "Existentialist" world—the immediate post-war period was a regular gala. To begin with, we could utter truths which until then one dared only to whisper. Newspapers and periodicals were founded on every side, or emerged from clandestinity. Camus, as director of *Combat,* awakened in us the conviction that an end had been made of journalism "à l'américaine," greedy for sensation and enslaved to private interests, of "political" journalism, enslaved to a party or faction, and of the "official" press, with its subjection to the financial bourgeoisie so tightly ensconced in power. Sartre, Merleau-Ponty and their friends were getting ready *Les Temps Modernes:* this was to be a new *Nouvelle Revue Française* that would have absorbed the lesson of History. Everything could be said, no one was afraid of anybody. A journey, a conversation, an incident of the war years, anything was a possible theme. For everything had become meaningful for us, in terms of oppression and liberty. Many of us had suffered enough to have a keen insight into the suffering of others and to write about it with a concern for justice and not out of maudlin sentimentality. Here was none of the exoticism of the preceding post-war era. Our journalistic work did not aim at soothing our readers or plunging them in a reverie beside their hearths. "I am a camera," yes, but with the whole cruelty and "totalitarianism" of the photograph. In this respect, "Existentialist" reporting takes its place in the movement later called, and quite wrongly, "neo-realism," made illustrious by Italian Cinema (in the days of *Open City* and *Paisan*). Simone de Beauvoir, Jacques Laurent Bost, Scipion, as independent travelers or war correspondents, with varying success recreated French reporting. Confronted by the opposition of greatness and ignominy, of beauty and debasing poverty, the reader is no longer summoned to coo at the dexterity of the writer or the picturesqueness of the scene, but to be revolted by it. The beggar on the steps of the magnificent baroque church is no longer "a part of the scenery," he refutes the church. In the terminology of the "Existentialist" reporter, "land of contrast" ceases to be a slogan to attract tourists and becomes a reason for indignation. This reassessment of travel and the reporting of it, although the "Existentialists" did not invent it (just reread Dos Passos), fits in well with their outlook. The "appeal" of a piece of writing is not directed at the reader's tear ducts, but toward his liberty. The world's miseries are conjured up, not to induce the reader to rejoice in his own good fortune, but on the contrary to spoil his enjoyment of it, when faced by a wretchedness to which previously he had thought himself immune.

Nevertheless, in our own persons, we had just escaped hunger, oppression and fear. We accorded ourselves, as did the whole of France, a few months of "permission to stand at ease." Not that everything was ideal: in those months provisioning was at its worst. And then, too, between the freeing of Paris and the war's end blood continued to flow, some of us were at the front, and we began to receive official news of the fate of our vanished comrades. Yet the "victory" was near, War lay in its death agony, and though it still engulfed thousands of men in its last convulsions our thoughts turned above all to the "singing tomorrows." With no premonition of Hiroshima or the Berlin blockade, we danced once again.

In our eyes, Saint-Germain-des-Prés had become the world's navel. Perhaps my memory telescopes the dates, but it seems to me that almost simultaneously with the restoration of freedom, with the appearance of new papers and new reviews and the cleaning up of Radio and Cinema, life in our Quarter took on the proportions of a national and even international phenomenon. The Café de Flore remained the "Existentialists' " bastion. André Breton and the surrealists showed up once more at the Deux Magots. A group of young Communist writers and intellectuals used to meet at the Montana Bar. There were countless uniforms, both French and American—as if they sought a justification, and wanted to be reassured about the future consequences of their acts.[4] This was the time when the Latin Quarter was a positive

---

4. These "uniforms," to speak only of the Americans, have now become "names," in *The New Yorker, Partisan Review* and documentary films.

international cocktail shaker for ideas. Since then? It's still international, but the tourist trade has evicted the ideas. Such must be the lot of every Paris street crossing, it would seem, of Saint-Germain-des-Prés no less than of Montmartre and Montparnasse.

What was a Saint-Germain-des-Prés evening like, at this time? The group of friends or associates was at one, in any event, in its relief at enjoying freedom once again. Some wore uniforms, as correspondents or soldiers on leave. The civilians were students (with the examinations of May 1944 to worry about, as these had been put off until December 1944 or January 1945), young actors or technicians, Jews or Resistance members (suddenly confronted by their first big part, their "first production"). Both sexes were included in these categories, the second sex represented in the main by girls of the kind we liked: not much make-up, hair worn very long, in any case easy on the eyes and able to take part in conversation.[5] The setting for these reunions was the Cave des Lorientais in the Rue des Carmes, and later the Club Saint Germain and the Rose Rouge. Cognac teamed up with jazz. This period saw the beginnings of Claude Luter, perfervid devotee of the New Orleans style. "The catacombs of the early Christians," murmured Raymond Queneau as he entered the Cave des Lorientais, fascinated by externals first of all but then by the "community of tastes" that appeared to reign. All that once was forbidden in the name of a so-called "moral order" could now spring up again: Judeo-Negro-American music, dancing in public, the drinking of spirits, the right to speak one's mind and to go to bed at four in the morning. Don't overlook the fact that we were *petits bourgeois* for whom such privileges have great importance. Whole pages would not suffice to inventory all the aspects of those gala days. Perhaps one disagreed with American policy, which had already begun to exercise a perceptible pressure, but how could one fail to be won over by the charm of a young American soldier initiating one of the girls into the mysteries of jitterbugging, who passed on to us the latest news of Hollywood and Broadway, testified to the effects of penicillin and related deeds of violence that seemed to come straight from the pages of Hemingway or Faulkner? In our experience the boundaries of the world moved farther away, and we gulped down indiscriminately all that so suddenly was thrust upon us, postponing choosiness until a later occasion. In our endless conversations we rebuilt the world, a world in-

---

5. Among us were Juliette Greco and Mouloudji, whose later fame as major stars of the French *chanson* no one could have predicted. He wrote poetic and "miserabilist" short stories of the utmost violence. She was satisfied to be there and to be beautiful.

finitely richer, more just and more sincere, where the right to pursue happiness would no longer be a vague constitutional guarantee but a living reality. Conversations did not make up the whole of our carnival, I need scarcely say, but each of us has the right to an ungossiped-about life of his own.

Beyond a doubt, it was easy during those months to confuse Existentialism and the life of pleasure. Ordering the girl friend to let her hair grow, give up lipstick and wear polo sweaters, believing one will cut a figure in History after executing a particularly difficult jitterbug movement—it's true, we didn't always put the right price-tag on things. This somewhat bewildered the outsiders: they looked on Saint-Germain-des-Prés night life as merely a particularly explosive continuation of "zazouism." Putting aside the question of outrageous garb, it must be admitted that many of our "Existentialists" would have been astounded to learn that, since Existentialism is a philosophy of human freedom, it involves anti-colonialism, anti-militarism and the proclamation of the rights of racial minorities. But for all Sartre's declarations, over the radio, that he did not buy his clothes from "Freddy, the Existentialist tailor," and that his philosophy had no more to do with the raging fashion than Voltaire with the armchair of the same name, the appellation had entered the public domain.[6] Praise, invective . . . it was served up in every imaginable sauce. And what proves that these eccentricities had their value, is the indignation they provoked among the reactionaries. Alongside the Communists who accused us of mistaking childish naughtinesses for the Revolution, the Right depicted us as sunk in perversion, Negro rhythms and lechery, and seeking to drown our despair in some potently alcoholic cocktail. It was Sartre, of course, who had corrupted us, and he was unmasked as Satan.[7] A colossal blunder! Never had we felt so joyous, or so confident in the future of Man.

Our sleepless nights did not stop us working. We had our exams and our jobs to think of. But our real labor was consecrated to that novel, to the collection of short stories, to the piece of reporting or book review. The French book trade had never been so flourishing: young authors with something to say trod on each other's heels, readers were both numerous and insatiable, and a new world awaited its mirroring in liter-

6. The more cautious Italians preferred to call their latter-day zazous "Sangermanisti."

7. This motif is highly favored on the right. Gide, the surrealists, and then Sartre. Who's the next Socrates on their list?

ature. The new wine needed new bottles: every form was renewed, in novel, short story, radio and films. If the results sometimes disappointed, at least they were stimulating.

Our literary models were no longer Stendhal or Gide, but (in translation) Dos Passos, Faulkner, Hemingway and Steinbeck, and of course Sartre and Camus themselves. Their techniques did not always suit our themes, and Camus, rather embarrassed by the pastiches of his *Stranger* that inundated him, discreetly reminded us that in an earlier age there had been French writers, a Stendhal, a Proust . . . Nevertheless, our unintentional pastiches, our blunders, exaggerations and leg-pulls (Boris Vian had a best-seller with his "translation" of an alleged American novel *I'll Spit on Your Tombs*) established the American technique in the French novel. These ways of "telling a story" had no doubt existed for a long time, but they were not really absorbed and put to profit by French writers until after 1945.

But by this time Sartre, Camus and a few of their friends were faced by other problems. Now the "men of the day," they had come to occupy the first rank in French literature and philosophy beside their greatest elders. In addition, they were the sport of fashion, and the papers and magazines continually referred to them. Everything concerning them was made public, to be adulated or dragged in the mud: the possible prolongation of their intellectual path, their projects, their private lives. Thus they suffered the fate of cinema stars and of first-magnitude intellectuals at the same time. The publicity was scandalous, their responsibilities were most real. With the war definitely over, political tensions both internal and international cast a shadow on the delights of the newly won peace. Camus and the Existentialists had become historical characters, willy-nilly. They had spoken to excess of *commitment:* now they were committed. More than ever before, French political tendencies sought an outlet for expression through certain writers: the notion of the literary man, of the uncommitted writer, had disappeared from the French intellectual landscape. What Mauriac was doing for Christian Democracy and Aragon for the Communists, the non-Marxist Left expected Sartre and Camus to do, especially after Malraux had become the spokesman of the Gaullist Rassemblement. With the Liberation, the helmeted poet of the Resistance had yielded to the "politically responsible writer." Sartre himself had put this notion in circulation, and since his personal success now turned on him the full glare of public curiosity, he could not refuse to play the leading role. And this he set out to do, with considerable uneasiness but without hesitation.

At Saint-Germain-des-Prés, the gala went on. And, be it added, became increasingly commercial. The epithet "Existentialist" served for everything, from Boris Vian's trumpet playing to the fantastic clowning of the Frères Jacques, Orson Welles' visits to the Tabou, the revelation of be-bop, homosexuality and common or garden Bohemianism.

CONCLUSION

We were twenty years old or more. Marriages, the first stages of a career, the choice of a profession and the normal conditions of existence were beginning to separate us. On the other hand, the political scene was becoming more and more animated. In *Les Temps Modernes*, under the title "Born in 1925," a young intellectual began by declaring that "God and the Communist Party have been the two great disappointments of my life." This did not stop other members of the group from throwing themselves into the Party's welcoming arms. But the Right seemed too close to the pre-war or collaborationist model. All the same, some of us approached it flirtatiously. As for the non-Communist Left, it became more and more divided and undecided. Sartre and his friends did indeed essay a "Rassemblement Démocratique Révolutionnaire," but the experiment turned out badly, and the mass meetings in the Salle Wagram were too much like a slightly expanded Saint-Germain-des-Prés. The Rassemblement came to an end. Disagreements arose concerning the concrete steps to be taken with regard to the concentration camps in the U.S.S.R., the attitude to adopt vis-a-vis the proposed Atlantic Pact and NATO. The ranks held firm, however, for the Indo-Chinese War, and on the issues of racial minorities and the meaning of literature.

A divergency of view between Sartre and Camus led to a rupture, whose details can be studied in *Les Temps Modernes*. Although this gave no cause for rejoicing, it certainly characterized these two men, who respected each other but who preferred the open clash so that they could continue their search for truths that may save the world from catastrophe, rather than sacrifice their integrity in an amicable compromise.

I—we—find it difficult to string together any valid souvenirs for these more recent years, we are too widely scattered.[8] Teachers in the

---

8. Simone de Beauvoir's novel *Les Mandarins* deals at length with the atmosphere of this period and with the development of some writers and journalists belonging to the group.

French provinces or abroad or launched on the most varied careers, radio, cinema, medicine, our political evolution has also borne us in different directions. Yet I do not believe that any one of us has repudiated his apprenticeship of 1943–1945. In spite of our scattering and our political differences, we have preserved a common vision of the world and a common language.

A certain attitude toward others and toward life, distinguished by its confidence in Man's labors and a keen awareness of any affronts, individual or collective, offered this one value that really counts, leads the Existentialist to a precarious optimism, for, if Man stumbles, all values collapse along with him. Only men can dominate the flies, and this they can do only with the help of their purity and with a ready shouldering of responsibility: no eye of God will keep the tally of one's good intentions. This gives rise to plenty of indecisiveness, since not everyone has the force of an Orestes. The ends are clear, the means are disturbing: what should one pay for freedom, or for justice? There is something of Orestes in the Existentialist, there is also something of Musset's Lorenzaccio and even of Hamlet.[9] Bourgeois morality and Communist morality, each in its own way and with different aims, have solved the problem and had a familiar outcome: lies and the perversion of justice, when they are deemed necessary, are pronounced holy in the name of pompous abstractions. "Sacrifice men to save Man," or vice versa, "the lesser of two evils," and many another time-hallowed formula, together with the actions they claim to justify, may be both true and necessary. But it is permissible to accept them without the least joy, and in this connection the Existentialists have often been accused of idealism. They at least have the merit of not being taken in by the hoaxes that have deceived others.

In today's world, that summons to a clear consciousness, which Sartre and his philosophy voiced in 1943, is still valid. Let it not be said that he has hit on nothing new for, even were this true, he would still have been the only one to give it utterance at that time, and to express it in terms we could understand.[10] Today, the evolution of his thinking, of his activity and of his group continues to hold the forefront of our interest. It is more important and more vital to know and grasp why

---

9. The young Communist novelist Pierre Courtade in his "Elseneur," a Marxist interpretation of the Hamlet myth, could not refrain from making his hero a disciple of Heidegger's.

10. This "we" still refers to a section of the young intellectual bourgeoisie.

Sartre adopts one course or another than to mull over the fancies of Mlle Sagan or the latest metamorphosis of Jules Romains. Those pious souls whose essential mission it seems to be to unload their feelings of guilt upon others will accuse us of dwelling in the allegiance of our adolescent years. To which it is easy to rejoin that so far we have seen no reason to change allegiance, and that quite objectively it can only be said that the world, in the last decade, has set nothing before us that would make such a change possible.

—Translated by Kevin Neilson

MARIO MAURIN

On Bonnefoy's Poetry*

Yves Bonnefoy's arresting title, *Du mouvement et de l'immobilité de Douve,* may at first glance have puzzled critics, accustomed to more laconic labels; it did not deter them from expressing their enthusiasm. In the field of contemporary poetry, where landmarks were few and already weather-beaten, no work had arisen in recent years that was more immediately rewarding and seemed better prepared to wear the patina of time. To be able at least to praise unconditionally was delightful, and critics were pleased with themselves as much as with the poet. To be sure, there were a few reluctant voices, Jean Grosjean's for example, but what could one expect from a possibly disgruntled competitor? One line which he adduced as evidence of Bonnefoy's attempt at "nobility" of style was singled out for praise in the *Mercure de France.* Where one objected to the heaviness of words, the other admired the weightiness of language. Grosjean's reservations were drowned in a roar of acclaim. He seemed condemned to the part he had assumed in his poetry: that of an anchorite crying out and grumbling in the wilderness.

Yet in denouncing the neo-classic character of Bonnefoy's poetry, he had put his finger on one of the reasons which had most contributed to its reception. It was a welcome relief, as it had been in 1917 with Valéry's *La Jeune Parque,* to find in 1953 a poet whose work effortlessly inserted itself in the body of French poetry and secured the backing of tradition without the least evidence of retrogression. The comparison is neither forced nor fortuitous. Just as one was led to think of Racine and Mallarmé without disparaging Valéry's dazzling creation, *Douve* gravely recapitulated, as it moved on its dark journey, the achievement of the past. If a characteristic adjective such as "infuse" confirmed the

*From *Yale French Studies* 21 (Spring-Summer 1958): *Poetry since the Liberation.*

YFS 96, *50 Years of Yale French Studies: A Commemorative Anthology,* eds. Porter and Waters, © 1999 by Yale University.

Scèvian resonance of this poetry, in its compact and emblematic secrecy, hints of flowing majestic litanies pointed to St. John Perse's use of language ("Il s'agissait d'un vent plus fort que nos mémoires"), only to harden immediately into Char's rock-crystal, Surrealist imagery or Michaux's ferocious matter-of-factness ("A présent se disloquent les menuiseries faciales. A présent l'on procède a l'arrachement de la vue"). Were not lines like

> Etre défait que l'être invincible rassemble,
> Présence ressaisie dans la torche du froid

> *A being undone which invincible being assembles,/ Presence seized anew in the torch of the cold*

torn from some unpublished draft of *Le Cimetière Marin!* Even Péguy's obstinate plodding shuffles for a moment at the threshold of the volume's concluding segment. Most of these reminiscences occur, however, in the first part titled *Théâtre.* This fact leads us to wonder whether, besides other areas of meaning later to be discussed, this review of poetic signatures in the glow of the footlights, as it were, is not intended to strike the balance of the process in its historical unfolding, to pay homage to its outstanding realizations by consciously appropriating them, but in so doing to destroy and transcend them.[1] That this is the very motion of the work under consideration, these remarks, however spotty and inadequate, will endeavor to make plain.

The familiarity of the poems is delusive, therefore, but nonetheless operates on the reader. He feels on safer ground than usual. If respect means looking back, he is confronted with an essentially respectful poet. Bonnefoy's backward glance, however, is also Orpheus' glance: inspired by impatience and love, it destroys what it brings to the light. What appears to be the gravitational pull of traditional prosody may be interpreted as a centrifugal force. To use the author's own image—in a recent book review of Jouve's *Mélodrame*—a wound is reopened in classic meters, less blandly than by Baudelaire, more blatantly than by Mallarmé.

The main asset of *Du mouvement et de l'immobilité de Douve,* however, is its unity. This is no agglomeration of disconnected poems, but a tightly-knit sequence that relates or, more accurately, un-

---

1. A side-view of the care which Bonnefoy brings to his work is supplied by a comparison of the text found in the volume and as published in the *Mercure de France,* May 1, 1953. Several unimportant but noticeable changes have been made.

dergoes an experience which we are called upon to share. This experience takes the mythical form of the journey, of the metamorphosis. Before attempting to assess its implications, a few superficial observations on *Douve's* structure may be in order. The volume is divided into five parts: *Théâtre, Derniers Gestes, Douve parle, L'Orangerie, Vrai lieu.* The first part, a series of nineteen untitled poems, is the longest. The last one, on the other hand, is the shortest and with seven poems is roughly three times briefer than *Théâtre.* The central panels form a triptych of fourteen poems each: whether by sheer coincidence, I cannot say, though I am inclined to doubt it. Some will probably lament that the first part was not made up of 21 poems, as may well have been the author's original intention. This would have clinched the position of 7 as the key to the whole structure.[2] As it is, the work avoids mathematical rigidity while adhering to firmly organized patterns, and the final movement, *Vrai lieu,* appears more intense and compressed than any of the preceding parts. This configuration is, on the whole, repeated within the movement itself by the growing predominance of short lines over the initial alexandrines. The last poem of the book is a mere quatrain that hurls its question into silence. And just as *Théâtre* formally looked back on the past to carry on its own forward movement, throughout *Douve* recurrent secondary motifs act as echoes of the poems that preceded and confirm the coherence of the whole, already insured by the dominant themes. Each poem is grounded on its own past, no material is left dangling. However doubtful the sense may remain in each particular case, reiteration establishes significance. Such is the typical mode of operation of an important range of "symbolist" literature, where it is possible to discover meanings if one is willing to apply specific coordinates, but where what is actually being communicated is a certain structure of experience. Beckett's *Waiting for Godot* may be considered an admirable example of this type of work.

The central experience of *Douve,* as the complete title implies, is dialectical. It is a passage from life to death, from day to night and light to darkness, from Summer's warmth to cold, from motion to immobility, from white to black, from high to low; but a passage without end, for these polarizations exist only in function of each other. Who is Douve? What is Douve? The most frequent meaning of the word, in

2. Bonnefoy is obviously, though perhaps not very thoroughly, acquainted with hermetic and alchemical literature.

French, is that of "moat" or "trench filled with water." Bonnefoy acknowledges it at least once, when he addresses Douve as "Eau basse irréductible où l'effort se perdra." But at other times Douve is a flowing river, a forest, a stretch of low land, a woman. In all these impersonations, one common character is shared: the pull of gravity, a tendency to lie low or recline, a downward movement, a descent which is cosmically mirrored by the waning of Summer and the setting of the sun. I shall quote examples of this general motion from one part alone, *l'Orangerie*, in order to emphasize its predominance: "Le ciel trop bas pour toi," "Le soleil était déjà très bas sur toute terre," "Regard puisé plus bas que tout regard épris," "Mais toi, mais le désert! étends plus bas . . . ," "Je la coucherai dans le froid," "Tu coucheras ton cœur," "Le soleil tournera, de sa vive agonie."

This last example conveniently underscores the traditional connection between the imagery of descent and the theme of death. Indeed, the whole first part is occupied by Douve's acceptance of and submission to death. Her body is picked clean by insects, she merges with the landscape in a series of poems reminiscent of Lautréamont on the one hand, on the other of Arcimboldo's and Dali's visual puns or double images. Is not this merging the return to substance which Bonnefoy, in an intricate article on the painter Balthus (*Mercure de France*, March 1, 1957), indicated as the goal of the artist's quest? Her funeral journey willingly, ecstatically undertaken, Douve disappears like water absorbed by sand. But this disappearance is the necessary condition of her resurrection, and she is greeted by the names that cannot fail to suggest the ambiguity of her experience: salamander and phoenix.[3] Both these emblematic animals survive the ordeal of the flame, they thrive in it, and an odd image like "les basses flammes de la mer" makes it plain that in Bonnefoy's order the waters of death and the fire of the spirit are but two aspects of a single inextricable element. We reach here the core of the poet's attempt, the key to the series of gestures "mimed" by the poems and gathered into what Bonnefoy proudly calls ". . . plus grand cri qu'être ait jamais tenté."

Douve is the Word, her death is the life of the spirit. One wonders whether the author has not been attracted by the linguistic and the-

3. The stag, one of the symbols of Christ in Christian iconography, also appears. One could glean interesting materials for comparison in Scève's *Délie*, where phoenix, stag, salamander, lamp and many other of Bonnefoy's emblems recur (cf., for instance, *dizains* 158, 199, 274). Could the connection between the *sand* and *phoenix* motifs be ensured by the Hebrew *chul*, which happens to mean both "sand" and "phoenix"?

matic proximity of the emblem of the Holy Ghost, the Dove. The suggestion, I think, is not entirely preposterous, since Bonnefoy knows English well enough to have translated Shakespeare's *Julius Caesar*. Douve is white as well as coal-black, she is winged as well as irreducible and low. Be that as it may, from the very start the reader is given an indication as to the significance of the journey he is about to undertake, for a quotation from Hegel ushers him into the poet's syncretic Hades: "Now the life of the spirit does not cringe in front of death nor keep itself pure from its ravage. It supports death and maintains itself in it." No references are given, but the passage is taken from the Preface to the *Phenomenology of the Spirit*.[4] Alexandre Kojève, in his *Introduction à la lecture de Hegel*, describes it as capital for the understanding of the philosopher's thought and comments upon it at length. "For the Understanding, by its colloquy," he writes, "reveals the real and reveals itself. And since it is born of finiteness, it is only by thinking death and by speaking of it that it is truly what it is: a colloquy conscious of itself and of its origin." (p. 546) Compare this statement, which aptly summarizes Hegel's involved exposition, with one of Bonnefoy's purest lyrics:

Que saisir sinon qui s'échappe,
Que voir sinon qui s'obscurcit,
Que désirer sinon qui meurt,
Sinon qui parle et se déchire?

Parole proche de moi
Que chercher sinon ton silence,
Quelle lueur sinon profonde
Ta conscience ensevelie,

Parole jetée matérielle
Sur l'origine et la nuit?

What shall I seize except what eludes me, / What shall I see except what grows dark, / What shall I desire except what dies, / Except what speaks and tears itself?

Word close to me / What shall I seek except your silence, / What gleam except the deep gleam / Of your sunken consciousness,

Word material jetty / Over origin and night?

---

4. It may be worth noting that Bonnefoy has used neither Hyppolite's nor Kojève's versions.

The Spirit, for Hegel, is Being revealed through the word. Consciousness is for itself its own concept, the negation of its limited forms and of its own death, which is nevertheless a necessary moment of the life of the spirit, through which consciousness survives itself and rises to a new form. If spirit is to retain its power, it must, says Hegel, sojourn with the Negative and look at it in the face. "This sojourn is the magic power which converts the negative into being."[5] When Bonnefoy writes: "Et je t'ai vue te rompre et jouir d'être morte" or again: "Mourir est un pays que tu aimais," he merely concretizes or personalizes the Hegelian concept that man's death is an immanent or autonomous end, that is to say, a conscious and voluntary end, and emphasizes that willingness to die which is the only possible way of life for consciousness. Awareness of this self-activating process makes it easier to understand how, in *L'Orangerie,* after a continuous thread of downward motion, the last line of the final poem can become: "Que faire d'une lampe, il pleut, le jour se lève," just as the last line of the preceding part was: "Quand la lumière enfin s'est faite vent et nuit." The dialectical conversion has taken place, the lamp of consciousness destroys itself but, in so doing, like the phoenix, insures its own rebirth.[6] The same reversal is pointed at by another terminal poem, "Art Poétique." It also occurs in the experience of love, which is an essential facet of Douve's itinerary: the moment of "death" is that which gives life, and there is no need to insist on the traditional connection between the act of love and *knowing,* here explicitly stated: "Ayant vécu l'instant ou la chair la plus proche se mue en connaissance." *Douve* temporaralizes an experience which is of course instantaneous and timeless, and so it ends by a victory which, hollowed out and denied by Becoming, already begins to doubt itself:

> Le jour franchit le soir, il gagnera
> Sur la nuit quotidienne.
> O notre force et notre gloire, pourrez-vous
> Trouer la muraille des morts?

> *The day strides over the evening, it will win/ Against quotidian night./ Oh, our strength and our luster, will you be able/ To pierce the rampart of the dead?*

5. In addition to Kojève's work, one should consult Jean Hyppolite, *Genèse et structure de la Phénoménologie de l'esprit de Hegel.* I have used both.

6. At various points, lamp and stone are associated: "Lampe de pierre," "pierre . . . lampe secrète," "cette lampe rocailleuse." The rocky lamp may well be the moon, an old and obvious symbol of reflection.

The journey is forever to be started all over again, the new beginning is but a continuation, the interrogation is raised in anxiety, the plural "the rampart of the dead" denounces this unending descent into Hell which is the life of the spirit and which opposes the perspective of its massive unalterability to our joy, and yet exerts this very joy by allowing it to be born and to die. The *Théâtre* of the first part has become the *Vrai Lieu* of the last.

The aridity of Bonnefoy's poetry is its wealth and its plenitude. As he would phrase it, it lives in opulence on the very scene of disaster. Through absence, presence is regained, and presence is salvation. If this be the authentic theme of our time, little wonder that critics found in *Douve* a work whose spell could not be shaken. What is amazing—and this final digression may be of help to more exhaustive commentators—is *one* critic's abstention: one critic, for whom *Douve* seemed made to order, indeed who might well have inspired it. That writer is Maurice Blanchot. To look at his essays is to discover, inexorably sought out, the central problem and sometimes the very wording of Bonnefoy's poetry. "La Littérature et le droit à la mort," in particular, is nothing but a long and searching comment on that sentence of Hegel's which we found pointing in *Douve* like an initial signpost—a dark exploration of the ambiguity of literature, of language as life-in-death. "But this ceaseless reiteration of words devoid of content," he writes, "this persistence of speech throughout an immense holocaust of words, this itself is the profound nature of silence which speaks even in total muteness, which is speech emptied of words, an ever speaking echo in the midst of silence." (*La Part du Feu*, p. 335) Bonnefoy echoes this:

Je ne suis que parole intentée à l'absence,
L'absence détruira tout mon ressassement.[7]

I am but speech instituted against absence,/ Absence will destroy all my reiteration.

7. One of Bonnefoy's most striking images, "Et ta robe tachée du venin des lampes," may have its origin in the following passage of Blanchot: "We understand . . . only by infecting what we understand with the nothingness of death."—if we bear in mind the suggested equation: lamp, consciousness. Or again when Bonnefoy writes the already quoted line, "Ou plus grand cri qu'être ait jamais tenté," he may merely have been thinking of Blanchot's statement on the writer's work in general: "His work is a prodigious deed, the greatest and most important that can be." (p. 319)

Why did Blanchot remain silent? The first time a man sees himself in a mirror, does he refuse to recognize his image? Or did he have nothing to say, because he had already said everything, already written the commentary required by *Douve?* One thing is certain, although what Bonnefoy has achieved stands on its own merits, to what he has attempted Blanchot alone holds the master key.

II. 1960–1969

FRANÇOISE JAOUËN

Introduction: Answering to the Authorities

What is at stake, then, if not desire and power?
—Michel Foucault

The three essays that follow in many ways do not represent their time, nor do they make any claim of the sort, no more than *Yale French Studies* ever did. They are not "symptomatic" of the sixties, they are not historical bubbles rising to the surface memories of a bygone era. They have been selected in their own right, and as such, if they represent anything, it is my own idiosyncratic, biased approach to the question of anthology. They are a reflection of the mostly overlooked "irrationality" of criticism, that is, the degree of personal involvement in the selection, endorsement, and use of authors and texts. It is overlooked because it has no real legitimacy, no clearly defined boundaries, no existence even, except in the most fleeting, anecdotal, of fashions. And yet . . . Essentially, the three essays "agree" with me. It is the fundamental rationale for their inclusion in this issue. Which is not to say that I learned nothing from them, that they have no insight or originality, that they could be mine. Far from it. I am simply stating a fact of reading. Matching comes before discovering, my own self precedes the text, I agree and disagree before I know why. Pascal said it best: "Everything I see in Montaigne comes from me." Which most emphatically does not mean that he learned nothing from Montaigne. Reading for knowledge is a paradoxical fallacy that applies to literature and criticism alike. Texts teach me something I already know. The lesson has been repeated throughout history on a grand scale, from Socrates to Freud: we learn nothing that is not "always already there." This, of course, does not mean that knowledge is the exclusive realm of science, that there is madness in the method, and that literary criticism is hopeless, self-serving, or fraudulent. Its worth lies in its practice, in the constant reassessment of dominant values, in the reevaluation of distance, in the search for a new "method." Too much has been made of the transat-

YFS 96, *50 Years of Yale French Studies: A Commemorative Anthology,* eds. Porter and Waters, © 1999 by Yale University.

lantic controversy surrounding the publication of *Impostures intellectuelles* by Alan Sokal and Jean Bricmont (Paris: Odile Jacob, 1997). At best insignificant, at worst laughable, it has none of the redeeming features of the great historical clashes focusing on the role of books and critics. No Erasmus, no Swift in sight, no minions of institutional terrorism, no head-on collision between French intellectualism and American pragmatism, not even a good old ideological feud. A let down compared to Barthes's achievement in the early sixties. His inaugural *Sur Racine* (Paris: Seuil, 1963) was a rocket launch that put him in stable and durable orbit; twenty-five years later, René Pommier, in a book published with a grant from the Centre National de la Recherche Scientifique, still felt compelled to call him a fraud. From the sixties also originates what appears to be turning into the new hot French intellectual potato: Bourdieu. His seminal article on "champ littéraire" appeared in 1966 in *Les temps modernes*. Its effect was felt, however, only a decade or so later, and does not have the grandiose dimensions of *Nouvelle Critique*. Furthermore, he has become a controversial figure mostly for his attacks on the media, not for his approach to literature. Still, he is worth mentioning because he is both the shadow of, and the antidote to, Barthes. Both are pure products of educational elitism, both criticize it, and the two of them sit at the opposite ends of the inescapable quagmire that lies between text and context, between production and significance, between origin and interpretation, sixties style.

They also embody the great paradox of intellectual subversion: the threat comes from inside the fortress, the institution fosters its own disruption. Therein lies the value of criticism (and the value of institutions). It is always the same struggle in different garb. Eventually, subversion becomes mainstream, is absorbed and loses its uniqueness. Barthes is now a classic and his own brand of structuralism is, undifferentiated, part of our daily fare. Deconstruction is probably not worth a fight any longer, for much the same reason. But the struggle had merit and value, and did affect the world outside, if only because critics are also teachers. The three essays selected, then, perhaps refresh my memory of a time that was never mine. They are traces of my fake nostalgia, my inefficient relics of the sixties: insurrection and laughter (Swinburne and Sade), a vigorous sense of the absurd (Lewis Carroll and the modern) and the flat, yet hopeful acknowledgment that the sentiment of the tragic has left us, to be replaced with a weakened and diffuse sense of guilt with no redemption in sight (Nietzsche and tragedy).

What is the significance and value of the critical sixties nowadays? It is what I make of it, it is what the institution makes of it. Reading and interpretation are a sly appropriation of something that does not belong to anyone. And, once in a while, there is also the uncanny feeling that the text has somehow found me, that it was intended for me alone. The appropriation then becomes a response. *Sur Racine* is still a great book, biased, provocative, and quite wrong in many places. But it also shows a rare self-awareness and deft handling of objective narcissism. The last word, perhaps, from its preface:

> Let us try on Racine, by reason of his own silence, all the languages our time has invented; our response will be short-lived, and can therefore be exclusive; dogmatic, yet responsible, we do not need the caution of "truth" applied to Racine, a truth that our time would alone presume to uncover; our response to Racine will find its justification in engaging fully, far beyond ourselves, with the language through which our world speaks to itself and which is part and parcel of its self-given history.

I like that.

JEREMY MITCHELL

Swinburne—
The Disappointed Protagonist*

Swinburne was Sade's enthusiastic champion before he had opened a page of his books. Sir William Hardman, after meeting the twenty-four-year-old Swinburne in 1861, described him as "strongly sensual; although almost a boy, he upholds the Marquis de Sade as the acme and apostle of perfection, without (as he says) having read a word of his works."

Swinburne knew of Sade's work from his new acquaintance, Richard Monckton Milnes. Part of Monckton Milnes' vast library at his country house in Yorkshire consisted of a varied and comprehensive collection of erotica, including Sade's work. Monckton Milnes has been portrayed by Mario Praz, among others, as a sinister *guru* who corrupted the much younger Swinburne and released his latent preoccupation with flagellation by introducing him to Sade's writing. But as James Pope Hennessy, the biographer of Monckton Milnes, has pointed out, what happened was neither so simple nor so sinister as has often been assumed. Although Monckton Milnes was, as Pope Hennessy describes him "the first serious English amateur of the writings of Sade," there is evidence that he held back from lending *Justine* or *Juliette* to Swinburne for fear of the effect they might have on him. In October 1861 Swinburne wrote to Monckton Milnes: "Reserving always your corresponding promise, which I do not forget, that I am yet to live and look upon the mystic pages of the martyred marquis de Sade; ever since which, the vision of that illustrious and ill-requited benefactor of humanity has hovered by night before my eyes, and I have run great risk of going as mad as Janin's friend,[1] but with curiosity alone."

*From *Yale French Studies* 35 (December 1965): *Sade.*
1. Jules Janin had at one time been counted among the more morbid romantics—his necrophilic novel, *L'Ane mort et la femme guillotinée,* was published in 1829. But his

YFS 96, *50 Years of Yale French Studies: A Commemorative Anthology,* eds. Porter and Waters, © 1999 by Yale University.

Just under a fortnight after writing this letter, and still without having read any Sade, Swinburne wrote a long poem in French, "Charenton
en 1810." This extraordinary work remained unpublished until 1951
when it was printed in the second part of Pope Hennessy's biography of
Monckton Milnes. It takes the form of a pagan hymn to Sade, seeing in
his physical features the quintessence of all that can be known or felt
about life and death, good and evil. Pope Hennessy points out how closely
the poem's meter and style are modelled on Victor Hugo's "La Judée":

> En ce temps-là c'était un vieillard calme et fort:
> Il avait le front grave et l'oeil serein: la Mort
> Avait peur à l'aspect du satyre sublime;
> Et la Douleur qui ronge et mord comme une lime
> Se tordait sous son pied comme un chien écrasé.[2]

Here, as in so much of Swinburne's work, there is a strong autobio-
graphical element as Swinburne anticipates the moment when he will
have the chance to read Sade:

> Or, un soir, un jeune homme âgé de vingt-quatre ans
> Vit ce front blême et fier chargé de cheveux blancs,
> Ces yeux noirs, cette bouche impérieuse et fine;
> Il frissonna.
>   L'enfant lisait ce jour *Justine*;
> Il levait ces regards, comme on fait en priant,
> De la page proscrite au vieillard souriant.

The poem ends with the old man's revelation of his identity:

> —Enfant, dit le vieillard, je m'appelle de Sade.[3]

----

views seem to have changed considerably, and he became the John Gordon of his day. In
1834, he attacked Sade in the *Revue de Paris*, justifying his article by asking his readers
to accept it "comme on accepte en histoire naturelle, la monographie du scorpion ou du
crapaud." A lengthy set-piece in the article describes, in prim, eyeball-rolling tones, how
a boyhood friend became an incurable epileptic after chancing on a copy of Sade in the
curé's library. Five years later, Janin assaulted Petrus Borel's *Madame Putiphar* in the
Journal des Débats, comparing Borel to Sade.

2. At that time he was a calm and determined old man. His forehead was sturdy and
his eye calm: Death was frightened by his resemblance to a sublime satyr. And the sorrow
which pecked away and bore into him like a file twisted under his foot like a crushed dog.

3. Now one evening a young man of twenty-four saw that pale and proud brow, covered with white hair, those black eyes, that fine and commanding mouth. He shuddered.
The child that day was reading *Justine*. He raised his eyes, as one does in prayer, from the
forbidden page to the smiling old man. "Child," the old man said, "my name is Sade."

Swinburne's anticipatory enthusiasm for Sade did not survive a reading of *Justine*. In August 1862 he wrote to Monckton Milnes:

> You retain my Charenton and desire me to clear my head of the subject. I am in a very fair way to do so; for I have just read *Justine ou les Malheurs de la vertu* . . .

> At first, I quite expected to add another to the gifted author's list of victims; I really thought I must have died or split open or choked with laughing. I never laughed so much in my life: I couldn't have stopped to save the said life. I went from the text to illustrations and back again, till I literally doubled up and fell down with laughter—I regret to add that all the friends to whom I have lent or shown the book were affected in just the same way. One scene between M. de Verneuil and Mme d'Esterval I never thought to survive. Then Rossetti read out the dissection of the interesting Rosalie and her infant, and the rest of that refreshing episode: and I wonder to this minute that we did not raise the whole house by our screams of laughter.

If this description of Swinburne's first reactions to Sade has all the unfuniness of a comedy film trailer—"You'll split your sides laughing at Cary Grant and . . ."—the criticisms that follow it are serious enough. They are especially valuable and bear quotation at length because Swinburne was neither overwhelmed by Sade's liberation from conventional moral values, nor outraged by the subject matter of his works. He condemned the book as a literary failure, because it did not achieve what its author set out to do:

> Of course the book must be taken on its own grounds; well, assuming every postulate imaginable, I lament to say it appears to me a most outrageous *fiasco*. I looked for some sharp and subtle analysis of lust— some keen dissection of pain and pleasure—*quelques taillades dans les chairs vives de la sensation:* at least such an exquisite relish of the things anatomized as without explanation would suffice for a stimulant and be comprehensible at once even if unfit for sympathy. But in *Justine* there seems to me throughout to be one radical mistake rotting and undermining the whole structure of the book. De Sade is like a Hindoo mythologist; he takes *bulk* and *number* for greatness. As if a crime of great extent was necessarily a great crime; as if a number of pleasures piled one on another made up the value of a single great and perfect sensation of pleasure. You tear out wombs, smash in heads, and discharge into the orifice. *Après?* You scourge and abuse your mother and make dogs tear off her breasts, etc. *Après?* Suppose you take your grandmother next time and try wild cats by a way of change? . . . Shew me the point,

the pleasure of all this, as a man of genius ought to do in a few touches; *that* will be worth something as a study. Dumas says of you, my poor friend, "Le marquis de Sade, voluptueux étrange, poursuit l'idéal de l'esprit infini dans la torture de la matière bornée." A splendid character, which might do for Nero, perhaps for Gilles de Retz; but for you? Take the simplest little example of your way of work. You have, say, a flogging to describe. You go in for *quantity* in a way quite regardless of expense. You lay on some hundreds of cuts, behind and before; you assert that they drew blood; probably they did; that the recipient wept and writhed; which is not unlikely; that the inflictor enjoyed himself and was much excited in his *physique;* which is most probable of all. Well? You have asserted a great deal; prove it now, bring it face to face with us; let the sense of it bite and tickle and sting your reader. Assertion is easy work. Shew us how and why these things are as they are. I on my part assert that you never do this once. "Tu radotes, tu rabâches, tu baisses, tes coups ratent; tu n'es qu'un ganache; c'était bien la peine de se faire enfoncer à Charenton!" . . . Why, there is more and better sensual physiology in that *Manon-la-Foutteuse* than in all your great lumbering Justine. *There* one finds some relish of the style, and catches it of the writer.

After criticizing *Justine* as a piece of literature, Swinburne turns to Sade's philosophical attitude:

You take yourself for a great pagan physiologist and philosopher—you are a Christian ascetic bent on earning the salvation of the soul through the mortification of the flesh. You are one of the family of St. Simeon Stylites. You are a hermit of the Thebaid turned inside out. You, a Roman of the later empire? Nero knows nothing of you; Heliogabalus turns his back on you . . . Paganism washes its hands of you. You belong to Christian Egypt; you smell of Nitria; you have walked straight out of some Nile monastery; you are twin brother to St. Maccarius; you are St. Anthony and his pig rolled into one . . . Your one knack is to take common things, usual affections, natural pleasures and make them walk on their heads; by the simple process of *reversing,* any one may write as good a Justine as yours . . . We took you for a sort of burlesque Prometheus; you are only a very serious Simeon Stylites—in an inverted posture. You worship the phallus as those first ascetics worshipped the cross; you seek your heaven by the very same road as they sought theirs. That is all.

The one good thing that Swinburne finds to say about Sade is, unexpectedly to praise him as a lyric poet. He describes the song in the eighth part of "Aline et Valcour" as "about the most exquisite piece of simple finished language and musical effect in all eighteenth-century French literature."

In an apparently final dismissal of Sade, Swinburne writes: "I drop my apostrophe to M. de Sade, having relieved my mind for good and all of its final judgment on a matter of some curiosity and interest to me."

This was, however, far from being the end of Sade's influence on Swinburne. Swinburne's subsequent letters bubble with open and veiled allusions to Sade. He addresses Monckton Milnes as "Cher M. Rodin" and "Mon cher Rodin," the name of a character in *Justine*. He parodies Sade in a joke reply to a *Punch* advertisement, purporting to come from Zulma de Cordoville. He tells C. A. Howells that he has added ten verses to "Dolores" that are, he wrote in French, ". . . très infâmes et très bien tournés. 'Oh! Monsieur—peut-on prendre du plaisir à telles horreurs?' 'Tu le vois, Justine, je bande—oh! putain, que tu vas souffrir.'"

Sade's influence went much further and deeper than these allusive references. It acted as a catalyst to Swinburne's obsession with flagellation. It would be unfair to say that Sade's writings were entirely responsible for this preoccupation. When he was 12, Swinburne went to school at Eton, where birching was a frequent punishment. Ritual beatings were his first perisexual experiences, and they are vividly and enthusiastically remembered and described in his letters. This preoccupation is evident even in his early writing, certainly before he had read, and probably before he had heard of, Sade. Lafourcade points out the references to it in *Laugh and Lie Down*, an "Elizabethan pastiche" Swinburne wrote when he was at Oxford in 1858–59, and says that Sade's novels "confirmed Swinburne in his instincts. He learnt from them not to be afraid and ashamed at the tendencies of his own nature . . . Thanks to Sade Swinburne reached a full conscience of his personality, and was no longer disconcerted at his own feelings."

There is no need here to explore the repercussions this sense of liberation had on Swinburne's personal life—these are described in an essay by Edmund Gosse, deliberately withheld from Gosse's *Life of Swinburne*, and first published as an Appendix to Lang's collection of *The Swinburne Letters*.

From a literary viewpoint, should Swinburne's preoccupation with pain be treated merely as an unfortunate fact of his private life, which spilled over into his writing in the form of the flagellation passages in *Lesbia Brandon*? Gosse, who knew Swinburne, thought so: "Extravagant, even vicious, as might be some sides of Swinburne's conduct, they were not essential, but accidental: that is to say, they might have been entirely absent without the nature of his genius being affected by that absence." A more recent critic, Bonamy Dobrée, agrees: "Most men and women have in them vestiges of such destructive impulses, which normal human beings turn into more beneficent channels, or suppress, but which Swinburne had no wish to hide. Such things need not concern the reader who seeks in poetry for imaginative release, for support in the more directive energies, for relations he can contemplate and ramify; they belong, rather, to the realm of psychiatry . . ."

It is necessary to look at Swinburne's own work more closely to see that pain, far from being an accidental and occasional disturbance to the balance of his writing, is absolutely central to his genius. The conjunction of pleasure and pain, their fusion to form two aspects of a single sensation, is a theme which occurs again and again in Swinburne's poems and novels, often presented in the context of love or death, or of both together. In "Rococo," for example:

> We have trod the wine-vat's treasure,
> Whence, ripe to steam and stain,
> Foams round the feet of pleasure
> The blood-red must of pain
>
> The snake that hides and hisses
> In heaven we twain have known;
> The grief of cruel kisses,
> The joy whose mouth makes moan;
> The pulse's pause and measure,
> Where in one furtive vein
> Throbs through the heart of pleasure
> The purpler blood of pain.

Here, even the imagery of red and purple, blood and throbbing, has the most obvious associations, and can be compared with the specific instructions Swinburne wrote to Monckton Milnes on how to compose flagellation poems: "Make fair weals . . . tingling ridges of throbbing purple and darkening crimson."

This theme of the mingling of pain and pleasure is especially evident throughout the First Series of *Poems and Ballads* which was published in 1866. These poems also make clear that Swinburne's attitude was essentially masochistic rather than sadistic, confirming Randolph Hughes' analysis of Swinburne's character in his magnificently vituperative commentary on the posthumously published novel, *Lesbia Brandon*. Swinburne's masochism takes its most extreme form in desire to be killed by a lover. In *Lesbia Brandon*, there is an intensely pas-

sionate love scene between young Herbert Seyton (a confessedly auto-
biographical character) and his elder sister, in which this theme recurs:
"Oh, I should like you to tread me to death! darling!"—"I wish you
would kill me some day; it would be jolly to feel you killing me." A further clue is given in the anticlimactically school-boyish remark: "I
should like being swished even, I think, if you were to complain of me
or if I knew you liked."

Death as the final fulfilment of love is also the theme of "Anactoria:"

> . . . and pain made perfect in thy lips
> For my sake when I hurt thee; O that I
> Durst crush thee out of life with love, and die,
> Die of thy pain and my delight, and be
> Mixed with thy blood and molten into thee!
> Would I not plague thee dying overmuch!
> Would I not hurt thee perfectly? not touch
> Thy pores of sense with torture, and make bright
> Thine eyes with bloodlike tears and grievous light?

Sometimes, Sade's influence goes beyond acting as a trigger to Swinburne's self-awareness and is more directly evident—as in the passage
from "Anactoria" quoted above and more especially in "Dolores,"
which rephrases, in poetic terms, one of Swinburne's criticisms of *Justine:*

> There are sins it may be to discover,
>   There are deeds it may be to delight.
> What new work wilt thou find for thy lover,
>   What new passions for daytime or night?
> What spells that they know not a word of
>   Where lives are as leaves overblown?
> What tortures undreamt of, unheard of,
>   Unwritten, unknown? . . .
>
> Hast thou told all thy secrets the last time,
>   And bared all thy beauties to one?
> Ah, where shall we go then for pastime,
>   If the worst that can be has been done?

The sea is another obsession which pervaded Swinburne's life and writing. Although he was far from being an athlete, he was a good and foolishly heroic swimmer (". . . I was swept out to sea for over two miles
and picked up at the last gasp by a French fishing boat," he wrote to his

cousin, Mary Gordon Leith). The sea provides images for his poems, descriptive passages for his novels. In the novel, *Love's Cross-Currents,* the slow tumescence of two adulterous love affairs, which threaten to tear down the tightly-woven social fabric of an aristocratic English family, comes to a sudden stop when one of the characters is accidentally drowned. This drowning, although it takes place off-novel, as it were, is the only event in the book. After the sea has acted, love dies, and the matriarchal Lady Midhurst maintains her ironic social imperative: "Married ladies, in modern English society, *cannot* fail in their duties to the conjugal relation . . . The other hypothesis is *impossible* to take into account."

Swinburne's absorption with the sea is directly linked with his masochism. Flagellation and sexual images are often an integral part of the descriptive passages: in *Lesbia Brandon,* the wind plays upon the sea "wilfully, lashing it with soft strokes, kissing it with rapid kisses." Sometimes sea, love, ecstasy, and masochism become entwined when Swinburne succeeds in doing what he accused Sade of failing to do— "proving it"—:

> Herbert wanted no teaching to make him face a heavy sea; he panted and shouted with pleasure among breakers where he could not stand for two minutes; the blow of a roller that beat him off his feet made him laugh and cry out in ecstasy: he rioted in the water like a young sea-beast, sprang at the throat of the waves that threw him flat, pressed up against their soft fierce bosoms and fought for their sharp embraces; grappled with them as lover with lover, flung himself upon their limbs that laboured and yielded deliciously, till the scourging of the surf made him red from the shoulders to the knees, and sent him on shore whipped by the sea into a single blush of the whole skin, breathless and untried . . . he was insatiable and would have revelled by the hour among waves that lashed and caressed him with all their might and all their foam.

In a letter written in French to Monckton Milnes, there is an instant of self-awareness when Swinburne directly links his own engrossed interest in the sea with Sade:

> Il est dommage que ce cher et digne marquis n'ait pas imaginé des supplices de mer. J'ai vu la semaine passée un effet admirable de bourrasque sur les grèves de la côte du nord. En contemplant les grandes lames blanches et roussâtres de cette mer houleuse, et les rochers crénelés qui soufflaient l'écume par mille bouches et mille narines de pierre, j'ai trouvé des supplices à faire bander un cadavre.

In most of Swinburne's writing, the influence of Sade is less direct than this. It is there, none the less, transmuted into the twin dualities of pleasure and pain, and life and death, which permeate so much of his best work. If final proof is needed of the importance of these two ideas, Swinburne himself provides it in a letter he wrote to Howell in 1865. He quotes a couplet from "Dolores:"

> Pain melted in tears, and was pleasure;
>   Death tingled with blood, and was life.

Then he comments, in French: "Voilà, mes amis, une vérité que ne comprendront jamais les sots idolateurs de la vertu."

With this issue, the Editors find themselves obliged to augment the price of *Yale French Studies* for the first time in fifteen years. We make this move regretfully, but higher production costs render it indispensable. We wish to express our gratitude to our subscribers for their loyalty in the past, and our hope that they will remain with us for what we believe will be a highly interesting future.

The new rates are as follows:

Single issues: $1.50.

Subscription for one year (2 issues): $3.00.

Subscription for two years (4 issues): $5.00.

All requests for subscriptions or single issues should be addressed to the Business Manager, Yale French Studies, 323 W. L. Harkness Hall, New Haven, Conn. 06520.

From *Yale French Studies* 38 (May 1967).

KURT WEINBERG

Nietzsche's Paradox of Tragedy*

> Only as esthetic phenomena are existence and the universe forever
> justified.
>
> —Nietzsche**

For Nietzsche, convention "is the condition of art, not its hindrance"
(III 754), and tragedy, in particular, is predicated upon the most basic of
human conventions: upon language, both as verbal expression and gesture. Not in a confused *laisser aller* does the classical dramatist attain
his ends but rather by rigidly controlling "invention"—in the traditional sense: the "finding" of, the "coming upon" striking images,
rhythms, sound and rhyme patterns within the narrow confines of traditional plots, metric forms, and genres. His freedom resides in *con-
traintes*, in his ability to "dance in fetters," to vanquish self-made
difficulties while covering them up with "the deception of facility"
(I 932 [§140]). In so doing, he conforms in his own way to the same rules
of artistic artificality which govern the acting of the dummy-like hero
of Greek tragedy (or the stylized protagonist of French classical
drama). All art is serious play and as such is stylization: in the strict-
est meaning *play-acting*, per-*form*ing, representing; in short, *histri-
onics* or *hypocrisy* (literally, the "playing of a part," Greek *hypo-
crisis*).

Hypocrisy, mimicry, an unconscious but infinitely artful cunning
is the very law by which organic life seduces, for the sake of its own re-

*From *Yale French Studies* 38 (May 1967): *The Classical Line: Essays in Honor of
Henri Peyre*.

**Quotations, if not otherwise indicated, refer to the three volume edition of
Nietzsche's *Werke*, edited by Karl Schlechta, Carl Hanser Verlag, Munich (1954–1956)
which, although not complete, offers the advantage of not having been bowdlerized by
Frau Elisabeth Förster-Nietzsche. Number of volume is shown in Roman numerals, followed by page number in Arabic numerals, and also in Arabic numerals, preceded by §
sign and inserted in [ ] the number of aphorism, section, or chapter.—Other editions
used: *Historisch-kritische Gesamt-ausgabe*, C. H. Beck, Munich 1933 ff., abbrev.:
HKGA; and *Gesammelte Werke*, Musarion-Verlag, Munich 1922–1929, abbrev.: *Musarion-Ausgabe*.—The translations are mine. The epigraph is from (I 40 [85]; I 131 [§24]).

YFS 96, *50 Years of Yale French Studies: A Commemorative Anthology*, eds.
Porter and Waters, © 1999 by Yale University.

production, the improvement and the evolutionary outstripping of the species. In this sense, the psychology of Nietzsche's Dionysian ideal of the actor—the polar opposite of the nineteenth-century artist who, in his schizophrenia, vicariously acts out his own fantasies in the characters of his novels and plays (*"Madame Bovary, c'est moi!"*)—provides an insight into the physiology of deception, the *sprezzatura*, one might say, by which all organisms seem to plot the triumph of the strongest individuals over the mediocrity of their race.

The paradox of art as a sexual device of Nature, the procreative and fertilizing stimulus provoked by enticing colors, perfumes, sounds, and rhythmic movement as organic functions of plant and animal life demonstrate to what an extent beauty as dissimulation, as play-acting, as hypocrisy, reaches far beyond man and human consciousness: *"Dissimulation* increases, according to the ascending hierarchy of living things. . . . It seems to be absent from anorganic Nature: [there] power [is pitched] against power, quite crudely so—*ruse* begins with the world of organic beings; already plants are masters of ruse. . . . Cunning multiplied a thousand times belongs to the *essence* of man's rise . . . problem of the actor, my Dionysos-ideal . . ." (III 578). One and the same type of energy or "will to power," a physiological and psychological drive for intoxication, blindly animates and metamorphoses all living things. It attains its goals by devious means, by sham and deception. From plant to animal and man, all sexual activity takes place through a triumph of art. Not Nature but productive and sexual fantasies, set in motion by the illusion of beauty, lead to procreation as well as to the creation of works of art. In man's unique case, "it is one and the same energy that is spent in the conception of art and in the sex act" (III 924). For the very existence of art, "one physiological preliminary is indispensable: *intoxication,*" and "above all the intoxication of sexual excitement, great cupidity, strong emotions." Idealization is no more than "a rape of things, a manner of forcing the dominant features into the open by way of that intoxication which is a feeling of increased energy and exuberance" (II 995 [§8]). The artist's creative instinct is closely related to "the distribution of *semen* in his blood" (III 870). An inquiry into his psychology would involve a critique of his play instinct as "a pouring out of energy, the enjoyment of change" and of willful transformation, a curious pleasure taken in "impressing one's own soul upon foreign matter," the artist's boundless selfishness, the kind of "instincts he sublimates" (III 867). Intoxication as a phallic experience constitutes the heightened feeling of power which brings about artistic creation: it is that inner need which drives the artist, "to make of things reflexes of his own perfection" (II 995 [§9]).

Against the esthetics of "disinterested contemplation, by means of which the emasculation of art tries today . . . to give itself a clean conscience" (II 598 [§33]), against Kant's and Schopenhauer's assertion that the contemplation of art neutralizes sexual desires, Nietzsche suggests that Stendhal comes closer to the truth with his contention that art is "a promise of happiness." All theorists of art, from Aristotle to Schopenhauer, have failed to see the essential aspects of the esthetic experience, because, rather than envisaging art from the creative artist's viewpoint, they have always looked at it from the spectator's perspective. Nietzsche, turning to the psychology of the artist, points bluntly to the myth of Pygmalion (II 845 ff. [§6]) as a key to the understanding of the motives behind artistic creation: Far from being disinterested, the creative instinct takes its impetus from a heightening of sensual appetites and a state of intoxication. With "the divine Plato," Nietzsche upholds that "all beauty excites the procreative powers: this precisely is its property, from the most sensual to the most intellectual and spiritual" things on the ladder of being (II 1003 [§22]). The desire for art and beauty "is an indirect longing for sexual thrills which the procreative instinct communicates to the *cerebrum*" (III 870). Just as situations which are transfigured and enhanced by our sexual and emotional fantasies will reflect our own vitality, so, inversely, if we come into contact with objects which rank high on our personal scale of sensual values and which, accordingly, show "this sort of transfiguration and enhancement, then our animal existence responds with an excitement of those spheres where such states of pleasure are imbedded—and a mixture of these very delicate dispositions for animal enjoyments and desires is the *esthetic condition*" (III 535; cf. II 995 [§8]; III 755). It can only be found in persons who are endowed with an excess of "procreative vigor" in which "always inheres the *primum mobile*" (*ibid.*). In short, as Freud himself acknowledges it, the Freudian concept of "sublimation" preexists in Nietzsche's psychology of the esthetic experience, and so does the word itself: It originates in *Human, All Too Human* (1879), with Nietzsche's realization that "there is no unselfish action, nor is there such a thing as disinterested contemplation: both are but sublimations . . ." (I 447 [§1]). The creative act overpowers the artist, turning him into its mere tool: The *paternal, patterning* "Apollonian," and the *maternal, matter*-providing "Dionysian" (cf. Aristotle, *On the generation of animals*) take possession and dispose of him with the violence of natural *forces majeures*, "whether he is willing or not: compelling him, on one hand, to become a visionary, on the other, to orgy. Both conditions are present in normal life too, only more weakly; as dream and intoxication" (III 788). These latter, too, "unleash in us artistic powers which are at variance: dream releasing the power to see, to connect things in logical sequence, to create poetry; intoxication endowing us with the gift of *mimicry*, passion, song, dance" (*ibid.*). Rimbaud in 1871, and Nietzsche in 1872, independent from one another, enounce the same truth about the lyrical poet as a quasi passive instrument, a voice and mime ("Je *est un autre*") in the hands, as it were, of a creative power that works through him (Rimbaud to P. Demeny, May 15, 1871, and *The Birth of Tragedy* I 38, I 40 [§5]).

"All perfect *doing*, to be exact, takes place unconsciously and is not willed" (III 746). For Nietzsche, the will to power is "not a being, not a becoming, but a *pathos*—the most elemental fact to begin with, from which as a consequence 'becoming' and 'producing' result" (III 778). Since *pathos, passion*, implies passivity, a suffering, in a way a *maternal* state, the difference between "committing" one's actions and "enduring" them as they arise spontaneously from the blind "will to power" is, to say the least, negligible. In Nietzsche's world, where consciousness falsifies all values by rationalizing them, and where the individual never senses the true role he plays within the overall plans of the species, one does not "do": one is *"being done*, at every instant! Mankind has at all times confused the active and the passive: that happens to be its eternal grammatical blunder" (I 1096 [§121]). Wherever our ignorance begins and our vision is blocked, we "place a word, *e.g.* the word 'I,' the word 'do,' the word 'suffer': those, perhaps, are the horizons of our knowledge, but they are no 'truths' " (III 863). In the very separation of the concept of "action" from that of "suffering," Nietzsche sees a misunderstanding which is rooted in language itself, and hence in consciousness: Language and thought, in their stumbling manner, can only proceed by way of "distinctions," and only distinguish or categorize by positing "pairs of opposites" where, in truth, seeming opposites occur organically intermingled as a complex and, as it were, hermaphroditic unity. "Acting" and "suffering" are simultaneously present in artistic creation, in the Apollonian-Dionysian polarity and duplicity of *poiein*—for Nietzsche (the classical philologist) not merely a "making," but as in Hesiod a "bringing into existence" (*Works and Days* 110; *Theogony* 161, 579 etc.), in Andocides a "begetting" (1.124; 4.22), and in Plato literally a "conceiving" of children

(*Symposium* 203b). Artistic creation wholly depends on a sexual stimulation which, in the final analysis, is identified by Nietzsche as an excess of procreative strength, an overflowing and sublimation of the will to power: "Without a certain overheating of the sexual system, a Raffael is unthinkable," and "music making, too, is a way of making children" (III 756).

Nietzsche's erotic concept of poetry (in the broadest sense, as a "making of works") affords remarkable insights into the psychology and physiology of the artist as "the maternal type of man" (II 251 [§376]), who is "constantly pregnant" (II 243 [§369]), and far beyond that, on the cosmic level, into the self-creating nature of "the universe as a work of art giving birth to itself" (III 495). The problem which, from the outset, intrigues Nietzsche, in retrospect is formulated by him in these terms: "How far does art reach into the innermost recesses of the world? And do there exist, apart from the 'artist,' other artistic powers?" To the second question, he unhesitatingly answers "yes." As to the first, he elaborates: "The world is nothing else but art!" And once more he passionately affirms the superiority of art over philosophy: "There is something contrary to nature in *wisdom* that is revealed by its hostility to art: to ask for *knowledge* where *illusion* alone gives deliverance, salvation—this indeed is perversion, the instinct for nothingness!" (*Musarion-Ausgabe* XIV 324): words which echo the major thesis of *The Birth of Tragedy* and "The Pathos of Truth," one of five prefaces for unwritten books presented in 1872 as Christmas gifts to Cosima Wagner: "Art is mightier than cognition, for it *wills* life, and cognition attains as its ultimate goal—destruction" (III 271).

Aisthesis, sense perception, establishes the link between art and science; it facilitates the understanding of the artful workings of the organic and the anorganic world. Like artistic production and receptivity for art, all worthwhile knowledge is fully dependent on the subtlety, vigor, and alertness of the senses: "Today our science reaches exactly as far as our determination to accept the testimony of our senses" (II 958 [§3]). To be meaningful at all, the "realm of concepts" cannot be absolutely severed from "the world of the senses"; nor can the identity of "being" and "thinking" be abolished (III 394 [§13]). In the final analysis, all true cognition—in its anthropomorphic relativity—amounts to no more (and no less) than an *esthetic* experience: It cannot transcend the organic prison walls of the human senses. To the mind of the Ancients, the esthetic experience rated above all other forms of knowledge. The sense of taste in particular, as the most subtle tool of *touch* and *testing*, for them was so closely related to the idea of "wisdom" that "the Greek word which designates the *sage* etymologically belongs to *sapio* I taste, *sapiens* the one who is tasting, *sisyphos* the man with the keenest taste; an acute feeling out through tasting, a significant aptitude for *distinguo* by the palate: this was the specific art of the philosopher, such as popular consciousness saw it" (III 363f. [§3]). Where taste, sensuality, wisdom, and knowledge are said to be interrelated, esthetics has clearly conquered the epistemological scene, and the object of its inquiry, no matter *what* the domain, will be art, that very force which, for Nietzsche, in all organisms stimulates life and excites its reproduction: "Art and nothing else but art! Art is that great power which alone makes life possible, the great seducer of life, the great stimulus for life" (III 692 [§2]). Wherever art, i.e. the will to power, commands, it works through "agents" that only "act out" whatever *it* wills while they are under the impression that they are acting of their own accord, at their own discretion. Psychologically seen, "the concept of *cause* is the sensation of power we experience in the exercise of our so-called [free] 'will';—our notion *effect*, the superstition that this *feeling* of power is the power itself which moves . . ." (III 775). When, as in Nietzsche's thought, the entire universe determines like an organism the functions of even the smallest of its parts by the animating and destructive force of a blind will to power, haphazardly, and without the benefit of a guiding Hegelian *Weltgeist* (that obligingly would become conscious of itself in the cataclysms of "world"—i.e. "human"—history) then there can be no such things as "moral" or "immoral" acts; then "free" and "spontaneous intentions" and the concept of "action" itself must needs be relegated to the world of imagination and fiction (III 612). In such a scheme, nothing would remain of the mystery of the universe but the dual and pulsating lust and rhythm of a permanent self-creation and self-destruction in great things and small, a constant metamorphosis of the "actor," the mask, while the play and the role would essentially stay the same in the eternal return of the life cycle. On the largest scale, the universe itself would perform in eternal repetitions (and rehearsals) the parts of Nietzsche's Dionysian actor: "Dionysian universe of eternal self-creation, eternal self-destruction . . . This world is the will to power and nothing else! And you are yourselves that will to power—and nothing else!" (III 917).

Life, in all its manifestations, would then be *one* infinite and eternal *pathos*—a suffering, a fate, a *moira*—personifying itself in countless "actors" on all ranks of its hierarchy. The theatre, as a dark mirror to life, would then show the tragic hero as a *sufferer* at the hands of a power that wills and acts through him, and over which he exercises practically no control whatsoever. A determinist view of this magnitude, organic rather than mechanistic, would also lead to an idea of the "drama" and to a "poetics" in some ways different from Aristotle's. It is then not surprising that Nietzsche should deplore what he considers to be one among a number of errors in Aristotle's rather insensitive interpretation of the nature of "drama" in general, and of the tragic hero in particular. A casual footnote in *The Wagner Case* (II 921 [§9]), in fact, calls into question the Aristotelian views on tragedy, pointing out that the Doric word *drama* by no means designated "action"; instead, it meant a hieratic *event*, a sacred "story": The oldest drama enacted the holy legend on which the local religious cult was founded. Substance is lent to Nietzsche's hypothesis by more recent commentaries on the extended Attic form of "drama," *dramosyne* "sacred service" (cf. Frisk I 416), "ceremony" (*Inscriptiones Graecae* II² 1358 ii 34, 40: IVth century B.C.). Aristotle himself explains that Doric *dran*, the root of "drama," meant the same as Attic *prattein* (i.e., "to go through," only later "to achieve," "to accomplish," "to effect," etc.) (*Poetics* 3.6). Nietzsche suggests that by mistranslating *dran* as a *doing*, the German classical philologists—who, ever since Wilamowitz-Möllendorff's violent attacks on *The Birth of Tragedy* ("*Zukunftsphilologie!*") have observed a hostile silence—are guilty of spreading misconceptions on the character of tragedy. What Nietzsche seems to imply is that *dran* and *prattein* alike express a "bringing about," an "effecting" which is its own end and has no moral connotations: It turns the subject through whom it works into a *sufferer*, not into a "free" agent. Instead of *spontaneously acting*, the tragic hero in the end recognizes that he is and has been no more than a plaything in the hands of a *fate* to which he consents (*amor fati*), and which coincides with those uncontrollable forces that through his immolation, his consciously accepted sacrifice, fulfill themselves. Here again, Nietzsche's contention seems to be borne out by the derivatives of *prattein: praxis*, the mythological *event* (and *not action*) which according to Aristotle (*Poetics* 6.8), rather than the hero's character, is to be acted out through the hero's *persona; pragma* (pl. *pragmata*)—misleadingly translated as *actus*, "act(s)"—in the language of the theatre: the principal divisions of the play (in Latin, originally, the role of the actor), means primarily "events," "circumstances," i.e. *happenings* rather than actions (cf. Herodotos 1.207; Thucydides 1.89; 3.82); while in Euripides' *Helena* (286), *pragmasin* "by circumstances" is expressly contrasted with *ērgoisi* "by acts." Whatever the merits of Nietzsche's reinterpretation of the concept of "drama," he makes short shrift of the meaning which, since the Renaissance, classical scholars have read into the Aristotelian idea of *mimesis* as the purported "imitation of an *action*," for he sees in it the representation of *suffering, passion, pathos* (pl. *pathé*), which befall the hero by a fatality that he cannot escape, and against his *conscious* will. Thus Nietzsche resolves in an ironic and tragic *coincidentia oppositorum* the age-honoured antinomies of *praxis* "action," *pathos* "incident," "accident," "chance," and *pathé* "suffering," "misfortune." He can conclude: "Tragedy had in mind great *pathos scenes*—action, as it were, was precluded from it ([in time] situated *before* the beginning and [in space] *behind* the scene") (II 921 [§9])—words which could stand as a gloss to Boileau's: *Ce qu'on ne doit point voir, qu'un récit nous l'expose* (*Art poétique* 3, 51)—but which ultimately touch upon what Nietzsche considers as the essence of tragedy: Those poignant *pathos scenes* (Aristotle, *Poetics* 14, 9) where the tragic hero, suffering from an excess of tensions which explode into "action," moves toward his doom without consciously becoming a "culprit," a "sinner."

This idea, a major theme, a *leitmotif*, the esthetic foundation underlying Nietzsche's entire work, is expressed as early as 1864 in the student essay *Primum Oedipodis regis carmen choricum:* "The Greeks thought differently from us about the tragic effect; it was brought about by way of the great *pathos scenes* . . . where action meant little but lyricism everything . . ." (*HKGA, Werke* II 375). With the exception of the seventeenth-century French, no modern playwright has understood what Nietzsche elsewhere (and without reference to the French) calls "the awesome Gorgon-head beauty of the Classical" (III 159), which destroys the tragic hero without "adequately" relating his misfortune to any "guilt"—for there is such a thing as "pure, innocent misfortune" (I 1065 [§78]).

Christianity, in particular in its Northern manifestations where it has lost contact with its Mediterranean origins, has falsified all psychological values: it has abolished the innocence of suffering by causally linking it with the concepts of "sin," "justice," "punishment"; it has branded as "sinful," "suspect," and "seductive" all great emotions of overflowing lust and strength, such as haughtiness, pride, voluptuousness, triumph, self-assurance, temerity, self-love; it has sanctified meekness and made it desirable; it has distorted the meaning of love by interpreting it as altruism and, in doing so, demanded unselfishness, the forsaking of the "self," the "ego," its *alter-ation* (the true significance of "altruism"); it has made a punishment of life itself, a temptation of fortune; it has condemned the passions as diabolical, man's trust in himself as godlessness. Christian psychology, as Nietzsche sees it, is a psychology of inhibition, a walling-in against life—out of fear of life's tragic sense (III 519 f.). "The doctrine of [the free] will was, on the whole, invented for the purpose of punishment" (II 976 [§7]; III 822). Against the Christian exorcism of human passions by the frail dogma of the "free will," Nietzsche's depth psychology affords abysmal insights into the blind "will to power" which is impersonal and disposes of the individual, allowing—if one accepts these premises—equally terrifying apprehensions about the obscure forces which drive certain Cornelian and Racinian heroes to their orgies of destruction and self-immolation. For Nietzsche asks questions such as: "whether all conscious willing, all conscious aims, all valuations are not mere means by which something essentially different must be effected than what might appear within consciousness" (III 901). Man is at the same time much more and much less than an individual; it is impossible for him "*not* to be possessed by the qualities and preferences of his parents and ancestors . . . Provided that something is known about the parents, a conclusion is permissible as to the child" (II 738 [§264]). No traits of character, however small, are insignificant. Nor do they occur as a matter of chance. Everything in a "personality" obeys the iron law of an ineluctable determinism which organically extends into the past and into the future of mankind. "On the whole, everything is worth exactly as much as one has paid for it . . . 'Heredity' is an erroneous notion. For *what* someone *is,* his ancestors have paid the price" (III 552). If one applies Nietzsche's views to French classical tragedy, even such monsters of "will power" as Corneille's Horace, Polyeucte, Auguste, and Attila appear to be guided by an instinctive "will to power" prepared by the preceding generations: their generosity, their sense of honor, their *terribilitas,* their religious or political fervour then seem no longer matters of choice but predestined, the unique and only form which their inescapable fate can take. They represent rare culminating points where mankind, after decades or centuries of blind elaboration, produces its healthiest and strongest exemplars in whom it attains perfection: the end toward which in ever returning cycles the human race moves in its tireless and unconscious efforts to overcome itself. And yet, they are nothing more than incarnations of Nietzsche's Dionysian actor who consents to a tragic fate over which he has no control and which is acting through his mask, his *persona*, his person.

There is no escape for the individual from the fatal chain of mankind; "every human being is himself a piece of fate" (I 905 [§61]). Inexorably, Nietzsche demonstrates the utter vanity of everyone else's and his own attempts to break through the prison walls of fate and to seek his personal salvation: "You are yourself that invincible *moira*; in you the entire future of the human world is predestined; little does it avail you if you shrink from yourself in horror" (*ibid.*). From the lowest cell to the universe itself, all existence *suffers* the will to power, in the final analysis, a permanence of tensions and of constant changes. On the cosmic scale: "The world subsists, without becoming, without perishing. Or rather: it is becoming, it is perishing, but without ever having begun to become or ended perishing—it persists in both conditions . . . It feeds on itself: its excrements are its nourishment" (III 703). On the human scale: the same cycle; in the strongest exemplars, in the type of the tragic hero, a frail balance: a tension of power quanta, each striving for greater intensity, for usurpation; all competing with each other, and producing in the subject a rapid change, a pendulum movement of violent passions, an imperious desire for the total possession or (if this should prove impossible) for the total destruction of the coveted object; in other terms, an insatiable appetite for an absolute ascendency which, feeding on itself, corresponds to a maximum of pleasure or a maximum of repugnance, but which is *not* identical to a platitudinous, plebeian, Darwinian "instinct of self-preservation," nor to a sense of "order" or to a devotion to "lawfulness."

Racine's Pyrrhus, Hermione, Néron, Agrippine, Roxane, Athalie (among others) do not pursue "happiness" but absolute power over the objects of their persecution, in a spirit of total and passionate commitment, at the risk of their own immolation, and as prisoners tied to the pendulum swing of their alternating emotions. In so doing, they blindly obey their chameleon-like instincts, "they *change*, but they do not *evolve*" (to use Nietzsche's terms which, however, do not specifically refer to Racine's characters) (III 725). "Every instinct is a type of despotism" and establishes its "own perspective" (III 903; cf. II 571 [§6]), and since "all instincts are unintelligent," no instinct proceeds from a utilitarian viewpoint (III 909). The life of the instincts is explained by Nietzsche as "a structure and a branching out" of that basic and thoroughly subconscious form of will, the will to power, whose commands are promptly rationalized by consciousness: "To the strongest of our instincts, to the tyrant in us, submits not only our reasoning but also our conscience" (II 638 [§158]).

When all is said, the conscious exercise of our will amounts to a delusion, a rationalization of dark instinctive forces which dispose of us on all levels of our being. Whatever we may take for our "activity" is at heart only something that comes to *pass* by way of our existence, and that we are fated to do. It is no more than a *passing*, a *passion* that we undergo; both literally, a *happening*, and etymologically (German: *Geschehen* "event," *Geschick* "fate," *Geschichte* "history"—all stemming from the same root), an *event* that by *fate* and *historically* is bound to come into being through and by our existence: paradoxically, an "act" of ours that we must *suffer* to be performed by us.

Man is *what* he is by a higher and innate necessity, and to speak of him "as he *ought* to be is as absurd as: a tree as it ought to be" (III 671). In this sense, every human being is a unique and prodigious phenomenon (I 287 [§1]); and yet, he but exists as a necessary link in a sequence, "concretized out of the elements and influences of things past and present . . . He cannot be held responsible: neither for *what* he is, nor for his motives, nor for his actions, nor for their effects" (I 479f. [§39]). The entire history of the human emotions amounts to "the history of an error, the error of responsibility which rests upon the error of the freedom of the will" (*ibid.*). Nietzsche never tires of repeating that man is totally without responsibility for his actions and innocent of their consequences (I 513 [§107]; I 544 [§144]; I 709 [§588]; I 908 [§69]; I 912f. [§81]; etc.). The doctrine of responsibility is founded on the naive assumption that "only the will can be causal, and that a person must *know* that he actually willed in order to be entitled to believe in himself as a cause" (III 745). We are as little responsible for the things we do while we are awake as we are for our dreams (I 1098f. [§128]). If for Fr. Schlegel "the historian is a prophet turned backwards" (*Athenaeums-Fragmente*), for Nietzsche (as for the Ancients), the past is like the voice of the Pythia, darkly but infallibly foreboding the future: "The judgment of the past is always an oracular response" (I 251 [§6]).

In this manner, the fatality incarnate in Racine's Phèdre, as well as her guiltlessness for the persecution she suffers at the hands of Aphrodite (Vénus), are forecast and, as it were, subsumed, right from the very first scene of the play, in Hippolyte's portentous line: *La fille de Minos et de Pasiphaé* (*Phèdre* I.i.36). Similarly, in *La Thébaïde*, the recurrent words *sang* and *nature* (= *naissance, famille, race*) and *dé-*

naturé foreshadow the inescapable doom of the unfortunate children of Oedipus who bear as little responsibility for their existence as does their father for his incestuous marriage with Jocasta or for the death of Laius. "No one is responsible for his deeds, no one for his nature" (I 481 [§39]). In speaking of *morality* where all is a matter of predestination, one would risk making a mockery of the very spirit of tragedy, which Nietzsche defines in these terms: "To understand the world from the viewpoint of *suffering:* that is the tragic essence of tragedy" (*das ist das Tragische an der Tragödie*) (III 338). Would not "moral" actions depend on the triumph of *reason* over excessive passions and desires? Yet, any attempt to distinguish between "reason" and "passion" would amount to a misconstruction of both: For, reason is no more than "a relationship between different passions and desires" (III 648).

All intentions, all actions, as it were, are amoral, since all reasoning about underlying motives and emotions—as we have seen—turns out to be a fabric of rationalizations. In fact, "the healthier, the stronger, . . . the more enterprising a man feels, the greater his amorality" (III 919); any rise in vitality inevitably brings with it "an increase in amorality" (III 583). In what precisely consists the preeminence of any great civilization, e.g. the Renaissance in Italy, over a barbarian state of affairs? "Always in *one* thing: the great quantum of frankly admitted amorality" (III 572). The higher species of man differs from all lower ones not for reasons of greater *moral* distinction but because of a more refined *esthetic* organization which lies beyond "good" and "evil," enabling them to "see and hear infinitely more and to think while they are seeing and hearing" (II 176 [§301]). For Nietzsche as for Baudelaire (whom he depreciates), esthetics and bourgeois morality are diametrically opposed, ideal beauty and greatness incompatible with the meekness of a "virtue" which allows the secret showings of criminal fantasies in the theatre of the mind but with feigned indignation shrinks from the admission of criminal fantasies, out of hypocrisy, cowardice, and the fear of being caught. "All great men were criminals, not in a miserable sense . . . Crime and greatness belong together," proclaims Nietzsche (III 521f.)—always speaking from the viewpoint of esthetics and tragic knowledge, and somewhere in the neighborhood of Baudelaire's ideal beauty (*Ce qu'il faut à ce coeur profond comme un abîme / C'est vous, Lady Macbeth, âme puissante au crime,* etc.).

Seen in the perspective of life and its stimulation, the ascetic values of "virtue" *diminish* man: "One is a thoroughly small type of man if one is only virtuous" (III 603); "a virtuous man: a lower species" (III

604)—in fact, a living lie, a denial of human reality. Modern man in his worm-like, purely economic and social existence is striving for an even smaller meaning of life, for smaller risks, lesser dangers, perfect security. "Has not the self-diminution of man made irresistible strides since Copernicus?" (II 893 [§25]). In order to enjoy "security," men have declared their equality (I 892 [§31]). Greatness in man results from the free reins he gives to his senses, to the free play of his appetites, and from "the still greater power that knows how to employ in its service these monsters" (III 528): the amoral, ancestral, and tragic will to power—for "the only power which exists is equal in kind to [this] will" (III 473). All great works and deeds which were not swept away by the ages—were they not, asks Nietzsche, "in the deepest sense, *amoralities*?" (III 920). Morality itself, when seen from the only valid perspective, from the viewpoint of the tragic heightening of *life,* is not truly a "moral" force but merely one tool among many used in the economy of vitality: in the service of life itself, the apparent opposites of "good" and "evil" do not appear as absolutes, they merely "express *power-degrees of the instincts,* a temporary hierarchy by means of which certain instincts are kept under control" (III 615).

The heroes and heroines of Greek and Racinian tragedy, driven by *hybris* and violent passions to their own immolation, live in a state of tension, pathos, insecurity. They approach with every step they take their imminent fall. Idealizations of the *great criminal* in his utter isolation, they are examples of a hard, cold, and tragic greatness which, for sentimental nineteenth-century man in his quest for material comfort and security, had lost its meaning. For the Greeks, even "theft, as in Prometheus' case, even the massacre of cattle as the expression of a mad envy, as in Ajax' case" could have *dignity:* "In their need to ascribe dignity to crime . . . they invented tragedy" (II 132 [§135]). The ethical background of tragedy is seen, in *The Birth of Tragedy,* in the "*justification* of human evil" (I 59 [§9]). In this sense, the pathos of tragedy is the life-asserting pathos *par excellence* (II 1129 [§1], the very opposite of the will- and life-denying pessimism of Schopenhauer: it accepts and gives meaning to the dual necessity of becoming and of annihilation. "The depth of the tragic artist consists in the ability of his esthetic instinct to see at a glance the farthest consequences, and not myopically to stop at the nearest point: he is capable of accepting the *economy* of the whole *on the largest scale,* which justifies, and not merely justifies, *the fearful nature of evil and all that is questionable*" (III 575).

Life is illogical, hence unjust (I 471 [§32]; cf. I 443 [§6]; I 229 [§3]). To

Aristotle's *catharsis*, Nietzsche opposes the esthetic enhancement of life by an art form which cannot be explained in moral terms (I 131 [§24]). The purpose of tragedy is *not* to move the spectator to fear and pity; it is to awaken in him the "poetic state"—a thought which is echoed by Valéry (*Variété V* 138). To see in tragedy a *purgative* which releases a state of depression is to misunderstand its *tonic* effect, the stimulus it provides for life: the festive spectacle of human suffering "ignites pleasure (i.e. the awareness of strength)" (III 753; III 828f.; cf. I 571 [§212]; etc.).

Nietzsche's Dionysian concept of tragedy as a tonic to life, an intoxication for the senses, in the final analysis is not so far removed from (and considerably more palatable than) that of Tertullian and Thomas Aquinas—who advise the believer to abstain from the sin of visiting theatres on earth, all the more to enjoy in after-life the edifying and eternal spectacle of the damned roasting in hell (II 794 [§15]). Nietzsche's theories on the guiltless and fated misfortune of the sacrificial tragic hero, in the end, replace all Leibnitzian and post-Leibnitzian *Théodicées* by a *Tyrannodicée* which amounts to an esthetic justification of human evil and injustice.

Finally, Nietzsche's perennial exaltation of life over intelligence, his distrust of reason and "virtuous" intentions seems to present an unexpected twist by which his abandoned Lutheran faith takes its revenge for its long inhibition. It turns out to be a variation on a traditional Augustinian theme: the corruption of man's original state of nobility by the knowledge of "good" and "evil." By leaving the noumenal for the phenomenal, ethics and consciousness for esthetics and aisthesis, intellectual knowledge for the intuition of the instincts, in short by substituting what N. O. Brown has so aptly named "polymorphous perversity" for an illusory morality, Nietzsche's road to the recovery of a tragic and Dionysian innocence—as in all apocalyptic schemes of the nineteenth century—leads for modern man "down and out," through nihilism.

MICHAEL HOLQUIST

What is a Boojum?
Nonsense and Modernism*

> The other project was a scheme for entirely abolishing all words whatsoever; and this was urged as a great advantage in point of health as well as brevity. . . . An expedient was therefore offered, that since words are only names for things, it would be more convenient for all men to carry about them such things as were necessary to express the particular business they are to discourse on.
>
> —Swift, *Gulliver's Travels*

> What am I to do, what shall I do, what should I do, in my situation, how proceed? By aporia pure and simple? Or by affirmations and negations invalidated as uttered?
>
> —Samuel Beckett, *The Unnamable*

Because the question "What is a Boojum," may appear strange or whimsical, I would like to begin by giving some reasons for posing it. Like many other readers, I have been intrigued and perplexed by a body of literature often called modern or post-modern, but which is probably most efficiently expressed in a list of authors: Joyce, Kafka, Beckett, Nabokov, Borges, Genet, Robbe-Grillet—the list could be extended, but these names will probably suffice to suggest, if very roughly, the tradition I have in mind. The works of these men are all very dissimilar to each other. However, they seem to have something in common when compared not to themselves as a class, but to past literature. In casting about for specific terms which might define this vaguely felt sense of what was distinctive and yet shared in these works, two things constantly inhibited any progress. The first was one's sense of the ridiculous: aware of other attempts to define the modern, one knew that it was difficult to do so without becoming shrill or unduly chiliastic. There is a group of critics, of whom Ihab Hassan and Nathan Scott might be considered representative, who insist on an absolute cut-off

*From *Yale French Studies* 43 (1969): *The Child's Part*.

YFS 96, *50 Years of Yale French Studies: A Commemorative Anthology*, eds. Porter and Waters, © 1999 by Yale University.

between all of previous history and the modern experience. They have in their characteristically humorless way taken seriously Virginia Woolf's remark that "on or about December, 1910 human nature changed." The work of these critics is easily recognized in the apocalyptic rhetoric which distinguishes their writing, and in the irresponsible application they make of terms derived from modern German philosophy. Some rather thick books on the subject of recent literature could easily be reduced in size through the simple expedient of excising any mention of *Heimweh, Geworfenheit,* and that incantory word, *Angst.* So one thing which made it difficult to get at distinctive features in recent literature was the sense that it was very different from previous literature; and at the same time to recognize that it was not the end of history.

Another stumbling block, much less serious, was the constant recurrence of a phrase, which continually passed through my mind as I would read new works. I would read that Gregor Samsa woke up one morning to discover that he was an *Ungeziefer,* and immediately a ghostly refrain would be heard in my inner ear: "Aha, for the Snark *was* a Boojum, you see!" The same thing would happen when in *Lolita,* one discovered that all those strange men following Humbert were Quilty; or when reading in Gombrowicz that there was nothing to identity but the grimace [gęba]; and so on and on—one kept hearing "The Snark *was* a Boojum, you see." Pausing to reflect on this, the association of Lewis Carroll with modern literature seemed natural enough: his name figures in the first Surrealist manifesto (1924); Louis Aragon and André Breton write essays on Carroll; the former attempts a translation of *The Snark* (1929), the latter includes selections from Carroll in his *Anthologie de l'humour noir* (1939). Henri Parisot publishes a study of Carroll in 1952, in a series called, significantly, *Poètes d'aujourd hui;* Antonin Artaud tried to translate the Jabberwocky song; Joyce's use of portmanteau words, without which there would be no *Finnegans Wake,* is only one index of his high regard for Carroll; Borges admires Carroll, and Nabokov translates all of *Alice in Wonderland* into Russian (*Anja v strane chudes,* 1923). But such obvious associations of Carroll with modern authors were not, it turned out, the reason why the *Boojum* kept raising its head as I read these men.

Finally, I picked up again, after many years, *The Hunting of the Snark,* and it soon became apparent why its final line kept popping up in connection with modern literature: Lewis Carroll's "agony in eight fits" was not only among the first to exemplify what is perhaps the most distinctive feature of modern literature, it did so more openly, more paradigmatically than almost any other text one knew. That is, it best dramatized the attempt of an author to insure through the structure of his work that the work could be perceived only as what it was, and not some other thing; the attempt to create an immaculate fiction, a fiction that resists the attempts of readers, and especially those readers who write criticism, to turn it into an allegory, a system equatable with already existing systems in the non-fictive world. In what follows, I propose to outline this pattern of resistances in some detail as it exists in *The Hunting of the Snark*, and then, in a short conclusion to suggest the significance the pattern may have for readers of experimental modern fiction. But before looking at the poem itself, it might prove helpful to have some background information.

Lewis Carroll is, of course, a pseudonym. Characteristically for its bearer, it is an acrostic, based on an inversion of the re-Latinized forms of his two Christian names, Charles Lutwidge. Charles Lutwidge Dodgson is a fascinating object of study in himself, but in what follows I propose to mention only those aspects of his career which bear directly on the significance of the *Snark* poem.

Dodgson's whole career can best be understood as a quest for order, in some ways not unlike that of the White Knight in *Through the Looking Glass*. He begins his career as a student of mathematics, and was for many years a teacher of the subject in Christ Church College, Oxford. In his later years even the precision of Euclidian geometry failed to satisfy his lust for order, and he turned to symbolic logic. There are many anecdotes which further point up his compulsive orderliness: when he had packages to be wrapped, he drew diagrams so precise that they showed to a fraction of an inch just where the knots should be tied; he kept congeries of thermometers in his apartments and never let the temperature rise above or fall below a specific point. He worked out a system for betting on horses which eliminated disorderly chance. He wrote the director of Covent Garden telling him how to clear up the traffic jams which plagued the theater; to the post office on how to make its regulations more efficient. And after having written all these letters (more than 98,000 before he died), he then made an abstract of each, and entered it into a register with notes and cross references. When he saw the first proofs of *Alice in Wonderland*, he refused to accept them because, as his illustrator Tenniell had pointed out, they were not clear enough, a scruple which, however, did not keep him from selling the 2000 copies of this rejected printing to an American publisher, for whose colonial audience he felt the plates were adequate. When going over the plates for the illustrations to his last books, *Sylvie and Bruno* and *Sylvie and Bruno Concluded*, prepared by the artist Harry Furniss, Dodgson put them under a microscope in order to count the lines in the etchings. And then, in a gesture that is pure Nabokov, he compiled an index for these novels, complete with listings for "crocodiles, logic of" and "frog, young, how to amuse," all arranged from A ("Accelerated velocity, causes of") to W ("wilful waste, etc., lesson to be learnt from"). It should be clear that Dodgson's life, in the large outline of his whole career and in the smallest details of his everyday existence, was dominated by the quest for a more perfect order. I will return to the significance of this point in a moment. But one further aspect of Dodgson/Carroll's existence should first be mentioned. It concerns the necessity of the slash or hyphen which one must use when referring to this author. That is, he is both Charles Lutwidge Dodgson, student (or Fellow) of Christ Church, and Lewis Carroll, author of books of nonsense.

Queen Victoria herself became aware of the split when, having been delighted in 1865 by *Alice in Wonderland*, she asked that a standing order be left for the author's next book; in 1866 she was not amused when she was given Dodgson's formidably technical *Condensation of Determinants*. Another revealing story is told by one of the child friends from Dodgson's later years, Isa Bowman, who grew up to write a book about her benefactor. As a young girl he took her to see one of those static panoramas so beloved by the Victorians. It was a diorama of Niagara Falls, with the figure of a dog in the foreground. Dodgson amused her by spinning a tale in which the dog was really alive, but trained to stand motionless for hours on end. He ". . . added other absurd details about the dog, how, if we waited long enough, we should see an attendant bring him a bone, how he was allowed so many hours off each day when his brother, who unfortunately was rather restless, would take his place, and how this badly behaved animal on one occasion jumped right out of the panorama among the onlookers, attracted by the sight of a little girl's sandwich, and so on. Suddenly he began to stammer and looking round in some alarm, I saw that a dozen grown-ups and children had gathered around and were listening with every appearance of amused interest. And it was not Mr. Carroll but a very confused Mr. Dodgson who took me by the hand and led me quickly from the scene."[1] Much has been made of this dichotomy between Mr. Carroll and Mr. Dodgson, and psychoanalytical studies, such as Phyllis Greenacre's *Swift and Carroll* (New York, 1955), suggest that the man was simply a schizophrenic who found a unique means of adjustment.

A more balanced view has been provided in what are probably the two best studies of Carroll: Elizabeth Sewell's *The Field of Nonsense* (London, 1952) and Alfred Liede's *Dichtung als Spiel* (Berlin, 1963, 2 vols.). These two critics have suggested that the split between Dodgson and Carroll is only an apparent dichotomy, quickly resolved if one sees that there is a common pursuit at the heart of each avatar, a *Drang nach Ordnung* which Dodgson/Carroll sought in mathematics and logic, in the strictly ordered life of an Oxford scholar, in the severely proper existence of a Victorian gentleman—and last but not least, in nonsense. In fact it was in nonsense that Dodgson's compulsion toward order found its most perfect expression, a point that has also been made by a professor of logic at Leeds University, Peter Alexander.[2] I would further add that the most nonsensical nonsense which Carroll created is *The Hunting of the Snark*. There is an ascending progression toward the apex it represents in 1876, from the first Alice book (1865) through the second (1872); and all the work after the *Snark* was a decline, a falling away which is painful in the last books, *Sylvie and Bruno* (1889) and *Sylvie and Bruno Concluded* (1893).

The *Snark* is the most perfect nonsense which Carroll created in that it best exemplifies what all his career and all his books sought to do: achieve pure order. For nonsense, in the writings of Lewis Carroll, at any rate, does not mean gibberish; it is not chaos, but the opposite of chaos. It is a closed field of language in which the meaning of any single unit is dependent on its relationship to the system of the other constituents. Nonsense is "a collection of words of events which in their arrangement do not fit into some recognized system,"[3] but which constitute a new system of their own. As has recently been said, "what we have learned from Saussure is that, taken singly, signs do not signify anything, and that each one of them does not so much express a meaning as mark a divergence of meaning between itself and other signs . . . The prior whole which Saussure is talking about cannot be the explicit

1. Cited in R. L. Green, *Lewis Carroll* (New York, 1962), p. 25.
2. *Logic and the Humor of Lewis Carroll* (Leeds, 1951).
3. Sewell, p. 25.

and articulated whole of a complete language as it is recorded in grammars and dictionaries . . . the unity he is talking about is a unity of coexistence, like that of the sections of an arch which shoulder one another. In a unified whole of this kind, the learned parts of a language have an immediate value as a whole, and progress is made less by addition and juxtaposition than by the internal articulation of a function which in its own way is already complete."[4] My argument here is that *The Hunting of the Snark* constitutes such a whole; it is its own system of signs which gain their meaning by constantly dramatizing their differences from signs in other systems. The poem is, in a small way, its own language. This is difficult to grasp because its elements are bound up so closely with the syntax, morphology, and, fleetingly, the semantics of the English language.

Some illustrations, taken from Carroll, may help us here. In the book which most closely approximates the completeness of the system in the *Snark, Through the Looking Glass,* Humpty Dumpty says in a famous passage: " 'When *I* use a word . . . it means just what I choose it to mean—neither more nor less.' 'The question is,' said Alice, 'whether you *can* make words mean so many different things.' 'The question is' said Humpty Dumpty, 'which is to be master—that's all.' " This last remark is a rebuke to Alice, who has not understood the problem: it is not, as she says, to "make words mean so many *different* things." It is to make a word mean just *one* thing, the thing which its user intends and nothing else. Which is to be master—the system of language which says " 'glory' doesn't mean 'a nice knock-down argument' " or Humpty who says it does mean that, and in his system, only that. Nonsense is a system in which, at its purest, words mean only one thing, and they get that meaning through divergence from the system of the nonsense itself, as well as through divergence from an existing language system. This raises, of course, the question of how one understands nonsense. It is a point to which I will return later; for the moment suffice it to say that if meaning in nonsense is dependent on the field it constructs, then the difference between nonsense and gibberish is that nonsense is a system which can be learned, as languages are learned. Thus the elements of the system can be perceived relationally, and therefore meaningfully, within it. Gibberish, on the other hand, is unsystematic.

4. Maurice Merleau-Ponty, "Indirect Language and the Voices of Silence," *Signs,* tr. Richard C. McCleary (Northwestern U. Press, 1964) pp. 39–40.

What this suggests is that nonsense, among other things, is highly abstract. It is very much like the pure relations which obtain in mathematics, where ten remains ten, whether ten apples, ten horses, ten men, or ten Bandersnarks. This is an important point, and helps to define one relationship of nonsense to modernism. For it suggests a crucial difference between nonsense and the absurd. The absurd points to a discrepancy between purely human values and purely logical values. When a computer announces that the best cure for brain cancer is to amputate the patient's head, it is, according to its system, being logical.[5] But such a conclusion is unsettling to the patient and absurd to less involved observers. The absurd is a contrast between systems of human belief, which may lack all logic, and the extremes of a logic unfettered by human disorder. Thus the absurd is basically play with order and disorder. Nonsense is play with order only. It achieves its effects not from contrasting order and confusion, but rather by contrasting one system of order against another system of order, each of which is logical in itself, but which cannot find a place in the other. This distinction may help to account for the two dominant modes of depersonalization in recent literature. The absurd operates in the theater, where the contrast of human/non-human serves to exploit the presence of living actors on the stage. Nonsense, understood as defined above, dominates in prose fictions, where the book may become its own hermetic world, its own laboratory for systematic play, without the anthropomorphizing presence of actors. Thus the difference bewteen, say, Beckett's *Waiting for Godot,* and the same author's *Comment c'est.*

Lewis Carroll is one of the most important figures in the movement Ortega y Gasset has called the "dehumanization of art." Kafka was not the first to reduce his hero to an integer; his K has an earlier analogue in one of the many essays Dodgson wrote on Oxford university issues. In 1865 the Regius chair in Greek fell vacant, and Dodgson used the occasion as an inspiration for a little paper called *A New Method of Evaluation of* π: "Let U=the university, G=Greek, and P=professor. Then GP=Greek Professor; let this be reduced to its lowest terms and call the result I. Also let W=the work done, T=the times, p=giving payment, π=the payment according to T, and S=the sum required; so that π=S. The problem is to obtain a value for π which shall be commensurate with W . . ."

5. For raising the problems of the relationship between nonsense and the absurd, and for the computer example, I am grateful to my friend Jan Kott.

"Let this be reduced to its lowest terms . . ." What Dodgson has expressed here in satire is a fundamental principle of his nonsense. For to reduce a word to one meaning is surely to reduce language to its lowest terms. The effect is to create a condition of what the Russian critic Viktor Shklovsky has called *ostranenie,* or "making it strange." But, again like so much modern literature, the effect in the *Snark* is not just to estrange a character or an event, but to estrange language itself. The technique is usually employed to render some familiar action unfamiliar by describing it naively, as if perceived for the first time. And this is what nonsense does to language. But it has a purpose for doing so, one which Merleau-Ponty has hinted at in another context: "If we want to understand language as an originating operation, we must pretend never to have spoken, submit language to a reduction without which it would once more escape us by referring us to what it signifies for us, [we must] *look* at [language] as deaf people look at those who are speaking."[6] Or, it should be added, *look* at language as children or Lewis Carroll *look* at language.

In order to understand "language as an originating operation" we must, in other words, see it as a process, as a system in itself. By so doing, one becomes aware of its capacity to present us with something new. But in order to achieve this state of radical linguistic innocence it is necessary to put aside all expectations which arise from the habit of creating meaning through systems other than language. Perception has recently been defined as being "primarily the modification of an anticipation."[7] The unfamiliar is always understood in terms of the familiar.[8] This may seem a bit opaque, but it is really quite simple, and an operation we engage in and see performed every day around us. The most common example of it in literary criticism is found in the work of critics who bring to bear on any given text a procrustean system, the sort of thing T. S. Eliot had in mind when he referred to the "lemon-squeezer school" of criticism. A rigidly Freudian critic will never perceive a dark, wet setting as anything but a womb symbol, or an object which is slender and vertical as anything but a phallic symbol, regardless of the fact that, in the system of the text he is treating, the former is a bower in a forest, say, or the latter a cane or spear. This critic has not seen bowers or spears in the one system because his expectations

6. Merleau-Ponty, *Ibid,* p. 46.

7. J. R. Beloff, "Perception and Extrapolation," *Bulletin of the British Psychological Society,* XXXII (May 1957), 44.

8. See E. H. Gombrich, *Art and Illusion* (Princeton U. Press, 1960), pp. 63–92.

are a function of another system. In order to see a new thing we must be able to recognize it as such, and this is done by the willed inhibition of systems we have learnt before coming upon the novel object, an act performed in the service of learning new systems. If this is not done in literary criticism, all texts become allegories. The *Odyssey* ceases to be an epic system with properties peculiar to it alone, and becomes an Allegory of Quest; *Gulliver's Travels* ceases to be a satiric structure with its own distinctive features, and is turned into an allegory of Swift's psychological development, an orgy of Freudian Anality; Dostoevsky's novels become equally orgiastic allegories of Sin and Redemption.

Critics of Lewis Carroll have possibly developed this allegorical urge to its ultimate limits. Phyllis Greenacre, a practicing psychiatrist, cannot forget that Dodgson loved to photograph little girls in the nude, with results for her interpretation of the Alice books which are as predictable as they are unfortunate.[9] Louis Aragon, in a 1931 article in *Le Surréalisme au service de la révolution* does a Marxian interpretation of the Alice books, notable for such insights as: "in those shameful days of massacre in Ireland . . . human liberty lay wholly in the frail hands of Alice . . ." William Empson has combined Freudian and Marxian techniques in his reading, "The Child as Swain."[10] Alice experiences birth trauma, and her tears become amniotic fluid; commenting on the famous scene at the end of *Through the Looking Glass* where Alice pulls off the tablecloth, sending plates, dishes, and guests hurtling to the floor, Empson remarks, "It is the High Table of Christ Church we must think of here . . ."[11] A. L. Taylor makes the Alice books into that easiest to find of all allegories, the Christian.[12] I have argued that the Alice books are less perfect nonsense than *The Hunting of the Snark*; therefore they are less hermetic, less systematic in their own right, and thus more porous to other systems.

But even the *Snark* has not escaped the allegorist. Alexander Taylor sees it as an anti-vivisectionist tract[13] and Martin Gardner, in his otherwise fine annotated version, suggests a crude existentialist reading, full of *Angst's*, and in which the Boojum somehow becomes the atomic

9. Greenacre, *op. cit.*
10. *Some Versions of Pastoral* (London, 1935).
11. *Ibid.*, p. 294.
12. *The White Knight* (Edinburgh, 1952).
13. Taylor, *op. cit.*

bomb.[14] A former dean of the Harvard Business School has argued that the poem is "a satire on business in general, the Boojum a symbol of a business slump, and the whole thing a tragedy about the business cycle."[15] I will not go into F.C.S. Schiller's theory, which states that the *Snark* is a satire on Hegelian philosophy, because Schiller presents his theory as a send-up. But even W. H. Auden has said that the *Snark* is a "pure example" of the way in which, "if thought of as isolated in the midst of the ocean, a ship can stand for mankind and human society moving through time and struggling with its destiny."[16]

Now there is something remarkably wrong about all this. Dodgson himself would be astounded. We have his word that "I can guarantee that the books have no religious teaching whatever in them—in fact they do not teach anything at all."[17] It may be that, knowing how drearily and relentlessly didactic Victorian children's books were, readers have not been able to accept that the most famous representative of the class is without uplift of one sort or another. However a quick comparison of *Alice* or the *Snark* with Charles Kingsley's *The Water Babies* (1863) should be enough to convince any unprejudiced reader of the fact. Kingsley's book, it will be remembered, ends with Tom, the erstwhile fairy, "now a great man of science [who] can plan railroads and steam engines, and electric telegraphs and rifled guns, and so forth." Not content with this, the author adds, to his little readers in the attached "Moral," ". . . do you learn your lessons, and thank God that you have plenty of cold water to wash in; and wash in it, too, like a true Englishman."

Lewis Carroll does not cloy in this way because he had a very sophisticated image of his audience. One may be highly specific about what the word child meant to Charles Lutwidge Dodgson. It meant first of all a girl; further, a girl between the ages of ten and thirteen, who belonged to an upper-middle class family; was beautiful; intelligent; well dressed and well behaved. Anything else was not a child. Now it is obvious that such a restricted view of children cannot be the same one which animates Lewis Carroll the author. Rather, this audience is conceived not in terms of chronology, but as a state of perceptual innocence and honesty. Children are the proper audience of nonsense only to the degree that they let strange things remain strange; to the degree they

14. Martin Gardner, *The Annotated Snark* (New York, 1962), p. 25.
15. *Ibid.*, p. 19.
16. *The Enchafèd Flood* (New York: Vintage Books, 1967), p. 63.
17. Letter cited in Roger Lanclyn Green, *Lewis Carroll* (New York, 1962), p. 52.

resist forcing old systems on new, and insist on differences rather than
similarities. The allegorists who have written about the *Snark* without
having *seen* it are obviously long past such a state of open potentiality.

The best argument against the *Snark*'s allegorization remains, of
course, the poem itself. The interpretation which follows is based not
only on the poem itself, but on the various ways in which it *is* itself.
That is, the poem is best understood as a structure of resistances to
other structures of meaning which might be brought to it. The meaning of the poem consists in the several strategies which hedge it off as
itself, which insure its hermetic nature against the hermeneutic impulse. Below are six of the many ways by which the poem gains coherence through inherence.

1.   The dedication poem to Gertrude Chataway appears at first
glance to be simply another of those treacly Victorian set pieces Dodgson would compose when he abandoned nonsense for what he sometimes thought was serious literature. But a second reading reveals that
the poem contains an acrostic: the first letter of each line spells out
Gertrude Chataway; a third reading will show that the initial word in
the first line of each of the four quatrains constitute another acrostic,
Girt, Rude, Chat, Away. This is the first indication in the poem that the
words in it exist less for what they denote in the system of English than
they do for the system Carroll will erect. That is, the initial four words
of each stanza are there less to indicate the four meanings present in
them before they were deployed by Carroll they at first convey (clothed,
wild, speak, begone) than they are to articulate a purely idiosyncratic
pattern of Carroll's own devising.

2.   Another index of the systematic arbitrariness of the poem is
found in the second quatrain of the first Fit: "Just the place for a Snark!
I have said it twice: / That alone should encourage the crew. / Just the
place for a Snark! I have said it thrice: / What I tell you three times is
true." The rule of three operates in two ways. First of all it is a system
for determining a truth that is absolutely unique to this poem. When
in Fit 5 the Butcher wishes to prove that the scream he has heard belongs to a Jubjub bird, he succeeds in doing so by repeating three times,
"'Tis the voice of the Jubjub!" Now, there will be those who say that
there is no such thing as a Jubjub bird. But in fact, in the system of the
Snark poem, there is—and his existence is definitively confirmed
through the proof which that system *itself* provides in the rule of 3. In

the game of nonsense that rule, and only that rule, works. The system itself provides the assurance that only it can give meaning to itself.

The rule of three also operates as a marker, indicating that the intrinsic logic of the poem is *not* that of extrinsic logic which operates in systems outside the construct of the poem. In other words, it is a parody of the three components of that core element in traditional logic, the syllogism. As an example of this, take an exercise from Dodgson's own book, *Symbolic Logic* (1896): "No one has read the letter but John; No one, who has *not* read it, knows what it is about." The answer is, of course, "No one but *John* knows what the letter is about." The third repetition "Tis the voice of the Jubjub," has the same effect in nonsense that the third part of the syllogistic progression has in logic. The *Oxford Universal Dictionary* defines a syllogism as a major and a minor premise, "with a third proposition called the conclusion, *resulting necessarily from the other two.*" If you begin with nonsense, and its conclusion, like the syllogism, results necessarily from the beginning, you also end with nonsense. The progression is closed to other systems. It is not, incidentally, without significance for Carroll's play with words that the etymology of syllogism is a portmanteau from the Greek *syllogizesthai* (to reckon together) and *logizesthai* (to reason) which has its root, *logos.*

3.   The same effect of an arbitrariness whose sense can be gleaned only from the poem itself is to be found in the various names of the crew members: Bellman, Boots, Bonnet-maker, Barrister, Broker, Billiard-marker, Banker, Beaver, Baker, and Butcher. They all begin with a B. And much ink has been spilled in trying to explain (from the point of view of the allegory a given critic has tried to read into the *Snark*) why this should be so. The obvious answer, if one resists the impulse to substitute something else for the text, is that they all begin with B *because they all begin with B.* The fact that they all have the same initial sound is a parallel that draws attention to itself because it is a parallel. But it is only a parallel at the level where all the crew members on this voyage will be referred to by nouns which have an initial voiced bilabial plosive. In other words, it is a parallel that is rigidly observed, which dramatizes itself, but only as a dynamic *process* of parallelism, and nothing else.

4.   Another way in which the poem sets up resistances which frustrate allegory is to be found in the fifth Fit. The butcher sets out to prove that two can be added to one. "Taking three as the subject to reason

about—/A convenient number to state—/We add seven and ten, and then multiply out/By one thousand diminished by eight.

The result we proceed to divide, as you see,/By nine hundred and ninety and two:/Then subtract seventeen, and the answer must be/Exactly and perfectly true."

And in fact the answer is perfectly true—but it is also what you begin with. The equation begins with 3—the number the Butcher is trying to establish—and it ends with 3. The math of the equation looks like this:

$$\frac{(X + 7 + 10)(1000 - 8)}{9922} - 17 = X$$

which simplifies to x, or a pure integer. The equation is a process which begins with no content and ends with no content. It is a pure process which has no end other than itself. It is thus perhaps the best paradigm of the process of the whole poem: it does what it is about. It is pure surface, but as Oscar Wilde once observed, "there is nothing more profound than surface."

5.   A fifth way in which the poem maintains its structural integrity is found in the many coinages it contains, words which Humpty Dumpty defines as portmanteau words, two meanings packed into one word like a portmanteau; words which Giles Deleuze, in the most comprehensive study of Carroll's significance for language, *Logique du Sens,* has so charmingly translated as "les mots-valises."[18] Carroll, in the introduction to the *Snark* writes, ". . . take the two words 'fuming' and 'furious.' Make up your mind that you will say both words, but have it unsettled which you will say first. Now open your mouth and speak. If your thoughts incline ever so little towards 'fuming' you will say 'fuming-furious;' if they turn by even a hair's breadth towards 'furious,' you will say 'furious-fuming;' but if you have that rarest of gifts, a perfectly balanced mind, you will say 'frumious.' "

"If you have that rarest of gifts, a balanced mind. . . ," in other words, you will find just the right word, and not some approximation. In the seventh Fit, when the Banker is attacked by the Bandersnatch, the bird is described as having "frumious jaws." And the Banker, utterly shaken, chants "in mimsiest tones," a combination of miserable and flimsy. For a bird which exists only in the system of nonsense, adjectives used to describe objects in other systems will not do; they are not precise enough, and so the system itself provides its own adjective

18. Paris: Editions de Minuit, 1969, p. 59; see also pp. 268–78.

for its own substantive. Since only the Banker has ever been attacked by a Bandersnatch, it is necessary to find a unique adjective adequate to this unique experience: thus "mimsiest." This attempt to find just the right word, and no other, resulting finally in coinages, is another way in which Carroll's search for precision, order, relates him to language as an innovative process in modern literature. Carroll speaks of "that rarest of gifts, a balanced mind" as the source of his experiment. In our own century it was a man remarkable for *not* possessing that gift who has best expressed the pathos of its absence in the face of language. In one of his fragments Antonin Artaud says "there's no correlation for me between *words* and the exact states of my being . . . I'm the man who's best felt the astounding disorder of his language in its relation to his thought."[19] Carroll's portmanteau words are revealing not only for the way they participate in the self-insuring autonomy of the poem. They also provide an illustration of how Carroll's nonsense is grounded in a logic of surface. The portmanteau word is not only a combination of two definitions, it is a combination of two systems, language and logic. Mention was made earlier of Saussure's insight into the way language *means* through *divergence.* The portmanteau word creates a new meaning by phonologically exploiting the divergence between two old meanings. It thus provides one of the most economical proofs of Saussure's insight into language. But the portmanteau word is also the third element of a three-part progression, from one, furious, to two, fuming, to three, frumious. Like the rule of three it results in a new "truth," and like the rule of three it is a unique kind of syllogism. In order to get a logical conclusion to the syllogism, it must grow out of a divergence between two prior parallel statements.

This is an important point if one is to see the logic which determines that Carroll's system is a *language* and not gibberish. In logic, not all pairs of apparent concrete propositions can result in a meaningful conclusion. Two examples, again taken from our poet's own textbook of *Symbolic Logic* will make the point. The two statements, "No riddles interest me if they can be solved"; and "All *these* riddles are insoluble," cannot lead to a conclusion due to the fallacy of like eliminads not asserted to exist. "Some of these shops are not crowded; no crowded shops are comfortable" cannot lead to a conclusion due to the fallacy of *un*like eliminads with an entity-premise. These and other possibilities for false syllogisms are generally subsumed under the fallacy of

19. *Artaud Anthology,* ed. Jack Hirschman (San Francisco, 1965), p. 37.

"post hoc, ergo propter hoc." That is, the invalidity of the conclusion is a result of incorrect premises. And the criterion for determining whether the primary and secondary propositions are *valid* or not is provided by the rules of logic itself. These rules make up one system. But if one were to create *another* system, which would state that the original premises were correct according to *its* rules, then the same conclusion which the system of logic would call invalid would, perceived as a result obtained according to the new rules, be correct. By extrapolation a true syllogism has been created out of what was in another set false.

The point this arcane diversion into eliminads and entity-premises seeks to make is that the system of Carroll's nonsense is just such an extrapolation, it is the transcendence of the post hoc, ergo propter hoc principle into an aesthetic. Carroll's portmanteaux are *words* and not gibberish because they operate according to the rule which says that all coinages in the poem will grow out of the collapse of two known words into a new one. Carroll can deploy words he invents and still communicate, because he does so according to rules. Whereas an expression of gibberish would be a sound pattern whose meaning could not be gleaned from its *use* according to rules: an expression of gibberish would be a sound pattern whose meaning could not be gleaned either from the syntactic or morphological principles provided by its use, or which would be deducible according to such principles in a known language system. Nonsense, like gibberish, is a violence practiced on semantics. But since it is systematic, the sense of nonsense can be learned. And that is the value of it: it calls attention to language. Carroll's nonsense keeps us honest; through the process of disorientation and learning which reading him entails, we are made aware again that language is not something we know, but something alive, in process— something to be discovered.

6.   The final structure of resistance I'd like to mention is contained in perhaps the most obvious feature of the poem, its rhyme. William K. Wimsatt, in a well-known essay, makes the point that in a poem the rhyme imposes "upon the logical pattern of expressed argument a kind of fixative counterpattern of alogical implication."[20] He goes on to say that "rhyme is commonly recognized as a binder in verse structure. But where there is need for binding there must be some difference or sepa-

20. *The Verbal Icon* (New York, 3rd Noonday edition, 1962), p. 153.

ration between the things to be bound. If they are already close together, it is supererogatory to emphasize this by the maneuver of rhyme. So we may say that the greater the difference in meaning between rhyme words the more marked and the more appropriate will be the binding effect." This important insight into verse is contained in a piece entitled "One Relation of Rhyme to Reason." Now, Lewis Carroll wrote a book entitled *Rhyme? and Reason?* (1883), and I suggest that the distinctive role which rhyme plays in the *Snark* is best caught by means of a titular portmanteau here. That is, it is precisely that one relation of rhyme to reason which Professor Wimsatt evokes in *his* title, which is put into question marks not only by *Carroll*'s title of 1883, but which is also put into question in the function rhyme serves in *The Hunting of the Snark*.

Professor Wimsatt suggests that "the words of a rhyme, with their curious harmony of sound and distinction of sense, are an amalgam of the sensory and the logical, or an arrest and precipitation of the logical in sensory form; they are the icon in which the idea is caught."[21] I read this to mean that two words which are disparate in meaning result, when bound by rhyme, in a new meaning which was not contained in either of them alone. In other words, you get a kind of rule of three at work. Like the syllogism, two disparate but related elements originate a third. Thus understood, the rhyme of traditional verse has the effect of meaningful surprise; two rhymes will constitute a syllogism resulting in a new association.[22]

But this is not true of nonsense verse. "They sought it with thimbles, they sought it with care;/ They pursued it with forks and hope;/ They threatened its life with a railway-share;/ They charmed it with smiles and soap." This stanza begins each of the last four Fits, and may stand as an example for what rhyme does throughout the poem. The rhyme words, "care, railway-share," and "hope, soap" would be very different from each other in traditional verse, and binding effects of the sort Professor Wimsatt has demonstrated in Pope or Byron would be possible. Because the language of most verse is simply a more efficiently organized means of making sense of the sort that language *outside* verse provides. Thus, while very different, some kind of meaningful association could be made of them capable of catching an idea.

21. *Op. cit.,* p. 165.
22. For a detailed study of sound/sense patterns in verse see: A. Kibedi Varga, *Les Constantes du poème* (The Hague, 1963), pp. 39–42, 91–121.

But "care," "railway-share," "hope" and "soap" in this quatrain have as their ambiance *not* the semantic field of the English language, but the field of Carroll's nonsense. In traditional verse "rhyme words . . . can scarcely appear in a context without showing some difference of meaning."[23] But if the whole context of a poem is *without* meaning, its separate parts will also lack it. There can be no differences in meaning between words because they are all equally meaningless in this context. So the reader who attempts to relate rhyme to meaning in Carroll's poem will be frustrated. The syllogism of rhyme, which in other verse has a new meaning as its conclusion, ends, in Carroll's verse, where it began. Instead of aiding meaning, it is another strategy to defeat it. Language in nonsense is thus a seamless garment, a pure cover, absolute surface.

But if *The Hunting of the Snark* is an absolute metaphor, if it means only itself, why read it? There are several answers, but the one I have chosen to give here is that it may help us to understand other, more complex attempts to do the same thing in modern literature. It is easy to laugh at the various casuistries by which readers have sought to make an allegory, something else, out of the *Snark*. But the same sort of thing is being done every day to Kafka or Nabokov. Possibly the example of Lewis Carroll may suggest how far we must go, how much we must forget, how much we must learn in order to see fiction as fiction.

For the moral of the *Snark* is that it has no moral. It is a fiction, a thing which does not seek to be "real" or "true." The nineteenth-century was a great age of system building and myth makers. We are the heirs of Marx and Freud, and many other prophets as well, all of whom seek to explain *everything*, to make sense out of *everything* in terms of one system or another. In the homogenized world which resulted, it could be seen that art was nothing more than another—and not necessarily privileged—way for economic or psychological forces to express themselves. As Robbe-Grillet says, "Cultural fringes (bits of psychology, ethics, metaphysics, etc.) are all the time being attached to things and making them seem less strange, more comprehensible, more reassuring."[24]

Aware of this danger, authors have fought back, experimenting with new ways to insure the inviolability of their own systems, to invite

23. Wimsatt, p. 156.
24. "A Path for the Future of the Novel," in Maurice Nadeau, *The French Novel Since the War*, tr. A. M. Sheridan Smith (London, 1967), p. 185.

abrasion, insist on strangeness, create fictions. Lewis Carroll is in some small degree a forerunner of this saving effort. To see his nonsense as a logic is thus far from being an exercise in bloodless formalism. That logic insures the fictionality of his art, and as human beings we need fictions. As is so often the case, Nietzsche said it best: "we have art in order not to die of the truth."

After having stressed at such length that everything in the *Snark* means what it means according to its own system, it is no doubt unnecessary, but in conclusion I would like to answer the question with which we began. What is a Boojum? A Boojum is a Boojum.

III. 1970–1979

ORA AVNI

Introduction: The Seventies

Yale in the seventies. It was an exciting moment, not only because a new world was opening up for us as graduate students in the Department of French, but because new venues were opening up for the study of French literature in the United States, and Yale was in the frontline.

A cursory, somewhat simplifying look will contextualize this last claim. New Criticism had marked a turning point in the fifties. Parting with literary history, it focused pointedly on the text and text only (the movement was amply represented at Yale—suffice it to name René Wellek, William K. Wimsatt, Cleanth Brooks, Maynard Mack, Robert Penn Warren, John Palmer, John Crowe Ransom). While New Criticism presented a turning point in departments of English, however, it didn't have the same impact on French studies, which, in the Lanson-Brunetière tradition had been practicing *explication de texte* for half a century and for whom close reading was old news. Only with the advent of structuralism in the late sixties did French literary criticism come into its own in American academe. Structuralism still drew on close analysis of texts in the French tradition, albeit with an eye toward structural and functional coherence that New Criticism and *explication de texte* were missing.

Structuralism soon became confining, however, as systems and structures grew increasingly more exacting, more rigorous, less supple, and above all, as they fell short of their lofty claims of total elucidation of texts. And here lies the paradox: the more structuralism raised scholars' hopes of attaining a total and comprehensive critical understanding of a literary work, the greater the disappointment was when any detail of a text remained unexplained, irregular, agrammatical, excluded from the neat workings of the system said to account for the whole. At the same time that structuralism flourished, however (arbitrary slicing

YFS 96, *50 Years of Yale French Studies: A Commemorative Anthology*, eds. Porter and Waters, © 1999 by Yale University.

by decades is doomed to be ridden with ifs, buts, and ands), other thinkers were moving away from *defending* semantic and structural clarity to *questioning* it. Barthes partially recovered the structuralist losses and attempted to reconcile the divergent voices with his *effet de réel* (1967) by bravely reassigning the stumbling block of one interpretive account to a more receptive structure: Madame Aubain's frivolous barometer thus became the telltale sign of realism. But the doubts and disappointments lingered and produced more criticism, more approaches, more methods. By the mid-seventies, a new mode of thinking had gained notable currency: whereas structuralist criticism had strived for clarity, certainty, knowledge, understanding, the new movement relished ambiguity, polysemy, uncertainty, hesitations, misreadings—all of which seemed to converge on a duplicitous rhetorical system best illustrated by metaphor.

This line of thinking was spearheaded simultaneously in France and in the United States, by Jacques Derrida and Paul de Man. It came to be known first as deconstruction, and later, as "theory" *tout court*. It was an exciting time at Yale. First because it put French literature and French departments in the avant-garde of criticism; second, because it took on a life of its own under our very eyes; third, and I apologize if it sounds parochial, because Yale (and *YFS*) was one of the centers in which the movement took place and, yes, we, the students, felt part of it.

In selecting the three essays for this decade, I have tried to convey this sense of excitement. Despite their differences in style and substance, each of these essays illustrates some of the magic—the innovations and the excesses—associated with the seventies. Take the first essay, by Jacques Erhmann, who, in 1970 edited the issue of *YFS* that made structuralism a household word in academe. By the time he died in 1972, Ehrmann had all but renounced the tenets of structuralism. As Michel Beaujour wrote in his introductory essay to "In Memory of Jacques Ehrmann" (*YFS* 58), "Conflicts and polemics had replaced the old dialectical whirligigs to which we had formerly attributed, under the influence of Sartre and *Les Temps modernes*, an oracular virtue. . . . J. E. was through with caution, the predictability of the inside-out game. He was seeking another kind of wit, a boundless, unruly discourse out of which proper meanings would be expelled by a proliferation of tropes, word-play, equivocation" (6). Times, tastes, and concerns may have changed since then, but the brilliance of Ehrmann's "boundless, unruly discourse" is still striking.

Or again, take Derrida's essay. Few literary debates have been as thought-provoking as the quarrels that pitched Derrida against Lacan, Foucault, or Austin. Whether each of these thinkers presented the thinking of the other correctly was irrelevant. What mattered were the questions that those debates raised, the *enjeux* they exposed, the arguments they used. Thus when Derrida criticized the structuralist legacy he read in Lacan's "Seminar on the 'Purloined Letter,' " his critique did not bear on the accidental interpretation of an errant text, but on a whole system of thought—which raised the stakes (and the level) of the discussion considerably. Both Lacan's and Derrida's essays made literary history not because they offered new readings of Poe's "Purloined Letter" (although they did), but because they were in fact manifestoes— brash, dogmatic, cutting, and, sometimes, prey to excessive claims.

And finally, Dragonetti's wonderful reading of Mallarmé's "Nénuphar blanc." A reading? Certainly. But a *close* reading? Just close enough to quote the poem profusely and offer an interpretive paraphrase, but not close enough to dampen imagination, speculative thinking, broad connections, and an unrelenting attention to the larger picture. Underlying this reading one can detect the attention to naming, to the signifier, to figurative language, to word play, and above all, to the semantic supremacy of the text over the reader—all of which were trademarks of the period.

These essays may not be the "best" *YFS* published, nor were they perhaps the most "visible." In light of the embarrassment of riches, I opted for essays that are "representative" of an approach whose main weaknesses were its spectacular success and the energy and haste with which it was advocated and followed.

JACQUES DERRIDA

The Purveyor of Truth* 1

Ils le remercient pour les grandes vérités qu'il vient de
proclamer,—car ils ont découvert (ô vérificateurs de ce qui ne peut
être vérifié!) que tout ce qu'il a énoncé est absolument vrai;—bien que
d'abord, avouent ces braves gens, ils aient eu le soupçon que ce
pouvait bien être une simple fiction. Poe répond que pour son compte,
il n'en a jamais douté.

—Baudelaire

PRETEXTS

Let us suppose there is psychoanalysis. (La psychanalyse, à supposer,
se trouve.)

When you think that you have got it, it is—to be supposed—that
psychoanalysis evidences itself. (Quand on croit la trouver, c'est elle,
à supposer, qui se trouve.)

When it is evidenced—to be supposed—it evidences itself—something. (Quand elle trouve, à supposer, elle se trouve—quelque chose.)

To limit oneself here to deforming the generative grammar—as it is
called—of these three or four statements.

---

*From Yale French Studies 52 (1975): Graphesis: Perspectives in Literature and Phi-
losophy.

1. The term "purveyor" has been chosen to render the French term "facteur." "Facteur" has retained the meaning of the Latin term "factor" ("maker"). It can thus designate the person who "makes" the mail arrive by delivering it, i.e. the mailman but also
refers to each term of a mathematical operation or product. In a way, Derrida is here playing with both senses: he takes Lacan up on the question of whether or not a letter can always arrive at a destination and he also examines all the "elements" or "terms" involved
in the unfolding of the story. Whenever there is a similar difficulty in translation, we have
attempted to explain it in a footnote or in the text itself through the use of parentheses.—
Ed. [Marie-Rose Logan]

YFS 96, 50 Years of Yale French Studies: A Commemorative Anthology, eds.
Porter and Waters, © 1999 by Yale University.

Where then? Where is psychoanalysis—already, still, always—evidenced?

Let us call text that in which it (ça) is evidenced, if it is evidenced. Not only for the purpose of recalling that the theoretical and practical inscription of psychoanalysis (in the text as "language," "writing," "culture," "mythology," "history of religion," of philosophy, literature, science, medicine, etc., in the text as a "historical," "economic," "political" realm, field of "drives," etc., in the heterogeneous and conflictual fabric of differance, defined elsewhere as *general text*—and, without boundaries) must have effects that have to be taken into account. But also for the purpose of defining the space of a determined question.

Unless one were to engage here in a particular kind of logic: the species would include the genus.

For example: what occurs in the psychoanalytical deciphering of a text when the deciphered (text), already explains itself? When it reveals a great deal more (a debt acknowledged more than once by Freud)? And above all when it also inscribes in itself the scene of deciphering?[2] When it deploys more force in staging and carries the process down to the very last word—for example, truth?

For example, truth. But is truth an example? What happens—and about what—when a text, for example a so-called literary fiction (but is this still an example?) stages truth? When it defines analytical reading, assigns the analyst his position, shows him in search of truth, and even finding it, holding a discourse about the truth of the text and then pronouncing in general terms the discourse of truth, the truth of truth? What happens then to a text allowing for such a scene and, excelling in its program, in situating the analytical bustle at grips with truth?

This excess does not express the mastery of an author, or, even less, the meaning of the fiction. It would be rather the standard effect of an energetic stance. Truth would play a certain part in it: drawn, by the philosopher or the analyst, from within a more powerful functioning system.

---

2. The expression "scene of deciphering" echoes on another major essay of Derrida where psychoanalysis in the text is put in question: "Freud and the Scene of Writing," *French Freud: Structural Studies in Psychoanalysis*, ed. J. Mehlman (Yale French Studies, N.° 48, 1972), pp. 73–117. The term "scene" is used by Derrida to emphasize the theatricality of literary representation. We have followed Jeffrey Mehlman's suggestion to translate "scène" as scene when there is emphasis on visibility and as stage when there is emphasis on conflict. See the Introductory Note in *ibid.*, p. 73,—Ed.

As an apologue or parabolic pretext, and for the purpose of first enounc-
ing the question of a certain multiplicative coefficient of truth, I open
The Interpretation of Dreams, somewhere near the middle.

Questioning the history of repression from *Oedipus Rex* to *Hamlet,* nullifying all the differences between 1) Oedipus, 2) the legend, and
3) Sophocles' tragedy, Freud formulates a rule: the "secondary revision
of the material" [*sekundäre Bearbeitung des Stoffes*] includes everything in a text that does not make up the semantic core of two "typical
dreams" that he has just defined (incest with the mother and murder of
the father), everything that is foreign to the absolute *nakedness* of these
dream-contents. The formal (textual, in the usual sense) differences
that, from the outside, affect thus this semantic structure, in this case
Oedipus, constitute secondary revisions. For example, whenever critics have considered *Oedipus Rex* to be a tragedy of fate, a conflict
between men and gods, a theological drama, etc., what they have considered to be the essential element of the play was actually an after-
thought, a garment, a disguise, a fabric added to the *Stoff* itself in order
to mask its nakedness.

The baring of this *Stoff,* the discovery of the semantic material: such
would be the terminus of the analyst's deciphering. Baring the meaning behind these formal disguises, undoing the work, this deciphering
exhibits the primary contents under the secondary revisions.

Is the nakedness of the meaning covered by the veiling forms a
metaphor? Or already a metaphor of a metaphor? A metaphor in order
to render metaphoricity? Here is Bouhours quoted by Condillac in *De
l'art d'écrire:* "Metaphors are transparent veils that permit us to see
what they cover, or the costumes beneath which we recognize the person masked."

After having opposed the (primary) semantic content to the (secondary) formal revision, Freud refers parenthetically to what he was
saying some pages earlier about dreams of exhibiting: "Its further modification [*Ihre weitere Gestaltung*] originates once again in a miscon-
ceived secondary revision of the material, which has sought to exploit
it for theological purposes. (Cf. the dream material in dreams of exhibiting, p. 243f.)" (*Gesammelte Werke* [henceforth G. W.], II/III, 271;
Standard Edition [henceforth S. E.], IV, 264).

Exhibiting, baring, stripping down, unveiling—this is an old routine: the metaphor *of* truth, which is as much as to say the metaphor of
metaphor, the truth of truth, the truth of metaphor. When Freud intends to bare the original *Stoff* beneath the disguises of the secondary

processing, he foresees the truth of the text. For him the text would be geared, from its original content, toward its naked truth, but also toward truth as nakedness.

The subchapter to which Freud refers us is very short: four pages. It deals with certain dreams of embarrassment [*Verlegenheitsträume*]. What embarrasses the dreamer is his nakedness [*Nacktheit*]. The four pages contain two or four literary references. Two or four since in each case a "first" text is revived and transformed by a "second": Homer by Keller, Andersen by Fulda; neither this fact nor the very fact of turning to literary material for *illustrations* arouses any question on Freud's part.

Dreams of nakedness, then, calling forth a feeling of modesty or shame [*Scham*]. They are in fact "typical," only by virtue of their association with embarrassment, confusion, discomfort. This "core of their content" can subsequently lend itself to all sorts of transformations, revisions, translations. Nakedness gives place to substitutes. The lack of clothing, the removal of one's clothes [*Unbekleidung, Entkleidung*] carries over to other attributes. The same typical nucleus structures the dream of the former officer thrust into the street without his saber, without a necktie, or dressed in the checkered trousers of a civilian. All the examples suggested by Freud concern men, and men exhibiting the lack of a phallic attribute, somewhat affected by this exhibitionistic activity. Even more precisely: their nakedness does not reveal the penis or the absence of the penis, but rather the absence of the phallus as an attribute to fill a possible gap, the absence of the colossal double. Already a certain chain is announced: truth—unveiled woman—castration—modesty. Schreber: "Besides, we know in our hearts that men's lust is aroused by the sight of female nudes, while on the contrary women's lust is aroused much less, if at all, by the sight of male nudes; yet female nudes arouse *both* sexes to the same degree."

Another typical invariant: the contrast between the unbearable shame of the dreamer and the apparent indifference of the surroundings. The dreamer is the only *one* to see himself naked. And in contemplating his nakedness, he is alone. This, Freud says, is "a suggestive point." Everything works as if two parts, two pieces [*Stücke*], did not fit properly in the dream. The other people *should* be staring and laughing or becoming angry, but they are not. There is a force or a movement in play with which the wish of the dreamer must have dispensed. Only the other movement, which leads to exhibiting, remains and keeps its power [*Macht*]. The typical feature of such a dream is precisely this "contradiction." To describe it, to explain it as well, Freud needs an example, a literary illustration, what he calls an "interesting testimony" which as it happens we "possess" [*Wir besitzen ein interessantes Zeugnis dafür*]. We possess an interesting testimony: this is the gesture [*geste*] and the word used by Benveniste to refer to the categories of Aristotle, which conveniently appear to illustrate his demonstration.[3] We shall see another example of this jubilation in illustrating which treats the very subject matter of its "scientific" discourse as a marvelous paradigm which is [*found*] *there*, happily available for instructive discourse: usually in the form of a fable, a story, a tale.

For it has come to be the basis [*Grundlage*] of a fairy tale [*Märchen*] which is familiar to us all in Andersen's version, "The Emperor's New Clothes," and which has quite recently been put into verse by Ludwig Fulda in his *Der Talisman*. Hans Andersen's fairy tale tells us how two impostors weave the Emperor a costly garment, which, they say, will be visible only to the good and loyal subjects. The Emperor walks out in this invisible garment, and all the spectators, intimidated by the fabric's power to act as a touchstone, pretend not to notice the Emperor's nakedness.

This is just the situation in our dream. It is hardly rash to assume that the unintelligibility of the dream's content [*der unverständliche Trauminhalt*] has provided the stimulus to create a disguise[4] in which the situation, as it is present in the memory, becomes rich in sense [*sinnreich*]. That situation, however, is deprived in the process [*beraubt*] of its original meaning [*ursprüngliche Bedeutung*] and put to extraneous uses. But, as we shall see later, it is a common thing for the conscious thought-activity of a second psychical system to misunderstand the content of a dream in this way, and this misunderstanding must be regarded as one factor [*Faktor*] in determining the final form assumed by dreams (G. W., II/III, 248f.; S. E., IV, 243, translation modified). Then Freud provides the key to the "transcription" [*Umdeutung*]:

3. I have attempted to analyze this pattern and the implications of this procedure in "Le supplément de copule," in *Marges* (Paris, 1972).

4. The word—*Einkleidung*—is here more important than ever: the French translation uses the word "fable" [and the *Standard Edition*, "form"—Tr.], reducing the metaphorical fold, the very one that I wish to emphasize here and that Freud, too, had begun by smoothing out. A disguise: a garment that conceals one's true identity and supplies a false one in its place.

The impostor is the dream and the Emperor is the dreamer himself; the moralizing tendency of the dream [the modesty of those who, as good subjects, are unwilling or unable to see the King's nakedness] reveals an obscure knowledge of the fact that the latent dream-content is concerned with forbidden wishes that have fallen victim to repression. For the context in which dreams of this sort appear during my analyses of neurotics leaves no doubt: they are based upon memories from earliest childhood. It is only in our childhood that we are seen in inadequate clothing [*in mangelhafter Bekleidung*] both by members of our family and by strangers—nurses, maid-servants, and visitors: and it is only then that we feel no shame at our nakedness.*

Note by Freud
* A child plays a part in the fairy tale as well; for it was a small child who suddenly exclaimed: "But he has nothing on!" (G. W., II/III, 249; S. E., IV, 244, translation modified).

Freud pays no attention to a fold in the text, a structural complication that envelops his discourse and within which his discourse must inevitably be situated.

What does he say first? That the literary narrative is a secondary revision and, as such, an *Einkleidung*, a formal garment, a coating, the disguising of a typical dream, of its original simple content. The tale dissimulates or disguises the nakedness of the *Stoff*. Like all stories, like all secondary revisions, it veils a nakedness.

Now what is the nature of the nakedness that it covers in this way? It is the nature of nakedness: the dream of nakedness itself and its esential affect, modesty. For the nature of nakedness thus veiled/unveiled is that nakedness does not belong to nature and that it has its truth in modesty.

The hidden theme in "The Emperor's New Clothes" is indeed the hidden theme. What the formal, literary, secondary *Einkleidung* veils and unveils is the dream of veiling/unveiling, the unity of the veil (veiling/unveiling), of disguising and baring. Such a unity is staged [*se trouve mise en scène*] in a no-snag structure, in the form of an invisible nakedness *and* an invisible garment, a fabric visible to some and invisible to others, a nakedness at once unapparent and exhibited. The same fabric conceals and shows the *Stoff* of the dream, i.e., also the truth of that which is present with no veil. If we take into account the more than metaphorical equation of veil, text, and fabric, Andersen's text has the text as its theme. More precisely, the determination of the text as a veil within the space of truth, the reduction of the text to a movement of *aletheia*. Freud's text is staged when he explains to us that the text, e.g. that of the fairy tale, is an *Einkleidung* of the nakedness of the dream of nakedness. What Freud states about secondary revision (Freud's explaining text) is already staged and represented in advance in the text explained (Andersen's fairy tale). This text, *too*, described the scene of analysis, the position of the analyst, the forms of his language, the metaphorico-conceptual structures of what he seeks and what he finds. The locus of one text is in the other.

Would there then be no difference between the two texts?

Well, there are many, many differences, to be sure. But their co-implication is undoubtedly more complex than one would think. One may say that Freud's text has scientific value or claims a scientific status, that it is not a literary fiction. But what is the ultimate criterion for such a division? Its obviousness seems to be guaranteed neither from the formal nor from the semantic point of view. It can be said that their content is equivalent, that they mean the same thing. As for the "form" of the Freudian text, it belongs no more clearly to the tradition of scientific discourse than to a specific genre of fiction. Is *The Interpretation of Dreams* to "The Emperor's New Clothes" as the formulation of a law is to the narration of an individual case? But the individual case is here language, and the event disappears there among the veils in which the discourse of science is implicated (the King, the Law, the truth, nakedness, etc.).

To distinguish science from fiction, one will finally have recourse to the criterion of truth. And to ask, "What is truth?" one will return very soon, beyond the stages of adequation or of *homoiosis*, to the value of unveiling, revelation, baring that which is, as it is, in its being. Who will then claim that "The Emperor's New Clothes" does not present a staging of truth itself—the possibility of truth as a process of baring—the baring of the King, the master, the father, the subjects? And if the shame of the baring had something to do with woman or with castration, the figure of the King would play all the roles here.

A "literature" can thus produce, stage, and advance something like truth. Its power thus extends itself beyond the truth of which it is capable. Can such a "literature" be read, consulted and even deciphered on the basis of psychoanalytic patterns that come under the jurisdiction of what it itself produces? The baring of baring, as Freud proposes, the baring of the motif of nakedness as secondarily revised or disguised [*eingekleidet*] by Andersen's fairy tale, will be exhibited/dissimulated in advance by the fairy tale in a piece of writing that therefore no longer belongs in the realm of decidable truth: exhibited/dissimulated according to an abyssal structure that we shall have to define. The realm of decidable truth is invaded by powers of dissimulation. The analytical scene, a baring and deconstitution of *Einkleidung*, is produced by "The Emperor's New Clothes" in a scene of writing which strips, without seeming to, the master sense, the master of sense, the King of truth and the truth of the King. Psychoanalysis finds—all that it finds—in the text that it deciphers. More than itself. What are the consequences of this, as far as truth and the text are concerned? Where does it lead us?

SUPPLEMENT TO THE INVESTIGATION

a little *too* self-evident . . .

The issue involved could be evaluated by way of any number of different standards. Within the cultural boundaries of my personal reference and because of analyses begun elsewhere,[5] I believe that the elaboration of this problematic must at the present time pause for the consideration of Jacques Lacan's proposed reading of Freud, or, more specifically, within the space of this article, of the "Seminar on 'The Purloined Letter.' "

Those "literary critics" in France who have been influenced by psychoanalysis have not yet posed the question of the text. Their interest as well as their fecundity lay elsewhere. It seems that the same applies equally and without injustice to Marie Bonaparte's psychobiography, any psychoanalysis of material imagination, existential psychoanalysis, psychocriticism, a thematic phenomenology colored by psychoanalysis, etc.

Quite the contrary as regards the "Seminar on 'The Purloined Let-

---

5. *Passim* and more specifically within the range of the maneuvers of a few notes active in their program of ambushing and pouncing upon some of Freud's shorter texts prudently left in corners, animal machines lying in wait in the shadows and menacing the security of a space and a logic. In this case I must especially presuppose "Freud and the Scene of Writing" (concerning the "Note Upon the Mystic Writing-Pad" (1925) in *Writing and Difference* (1966–67), *"La Double Séance"* (on *Das Unheimliche*, 1919 especially notes 25, 44 and 56), "Hors Livre" (on *Das Medusenhaupt*, 1922) in *La Dissémination* (1969–72). A note in *Positions* augured this reading of "The Seminar on 'The Purloined Letter'" which was originally the object of a lecture at Johns Hopkins University, Nov., 1971. As regards Freud, I refer throughout to the works of Sarah Kofman (*L'Enfance de l'art*, Payot, 1970; *Camera obscura de l'idéologie*, Galilée, 1973; *Quatre romans analytiques*, Galilée, 1974) and of Jean-Michel Rey (*Parcours de Freud*, Galilée, 1974). And for a rigorous reading of Lacan, to the fundamental and indispensable book by Jean-Luc Nancy and Philippe Lacoue-Labarthe (*Le titre de la lettre*, Galilée, 1973).

ter' "—at least apparently. Even though Lacan is not directly and systematically interested in so-called "literary" texts, and even though the problematic of *Das Unheimlich* does not, to my knowledge, occur in his discourse, the work of the *general* question of the text is generally present. In other words, the logic of the signifier tempers any naive semanticism. Lacan's "style," moreover, was such that for a long time it would hinder and delay all access to a *unique* content or a single unequivocal meaning determinable beyond the writing itself. Three additional claims on our interest: they are precisely to be found in the "Seminar on 'The Purloined Letter.'"

1. Its subject is Poe, a representative of the sort of "fantasy literature" which operates and overflows Freud's *Das Unheimlich.*

2. Although it is not the earliest of Lacan's *Écrits* chronologically, the Seminar comes at the head of this collection after its determinant strategic place has been prepared by an overture.[6] By the overture, furthermore, the horizon of the analysis of "The Purloined Letter" is drawn. This horizon is the problem of the relation of truth to fiction. After granting the Seminar "the privilege of heading off the other articles in spite of their own diachrony," Lacan names what is "no more feigned than the truth when it inhabits fiction." If the truth inhabits fiction, does this make fiction true or the truth fictional? Is that a real alternative, the true vs. the fictional?

3. Finally, the Seminar is part of a larger investigation of the repetition automatism [*Wiederholungszwang*] which, in the group of texts dating from 1919–1920 (*Jenseits, Das Unheimlich*) transforms, at least in principle (cf. *La Double Séance,* notes 44 and 56),[7] the rela-

---

6. Delivered in 1955, committed to paper in 1956 and published in 1957, only in 1966 does the Seminar receive its place *at the head* of *Écrits,* thus following an order which, not being chronological, does not arise in any simple way from his theoretico-didactic system. It might stage *Écrits* in a particular way. The necessity of this priority, in any event, happens to be confirmed, recalled and emphasized by the introduction to *Écrits* in the "Points" edition (1970): "... the text, which here keeps the entry post it possesses elsewhere ..." Anyone wishing to narrow the scope of the questions raised here can by all means keep those quetions in the "place" given to the Seminar by its "author": entry post. "This post [*le poste*] differs from another post [*la poste*] only in gender," according to Littré.

7. See Jacques Derrida, *La Dissémination* (Paris: Le Seuil, 1972), pp. 279–280 and pp. 300–301. Within a rather long text questioning the literary process through Plato and Mallarmé, Derrida tackles Freud's dealing with a work of art and notably the displacement in Freud's approach before and after *Das Unheimlich.* Derrida also points out there how Freud in *Das Unheimlich* is sensitive to the undecidable ambivalence, "the game of the double, the endless interplay between the fantastic and the real."—Ed.

tionship between psychoanalysis and literary fiction. All of Lacan's work presupposes the urgency of the problematic of *Jenseits* even though that very problem appears mythological, poetic and speculative to so many psychoanalysts. The point, therefore, is to take over the *Wiederholungszwang* and follow out its consequences in the logic of the signifier. "Our inquiry has led us to the point of recognizing that the repetition automatism [*Wiederholungszwang*] finds its basis in what we have called the *insistence* of the signifying chain. We have elaborated that notion itself as a correlate of the *ex-istence* (or: excentric place) in which we must necessarily locate the subject of the unconscious if we are to take Freud's discovery seriously."[8] These are the opening lines of the Seminar.

Which will, in effect, demonstrate "the preeminence of the signifier over the subject." No more than meaning, the subject is not the master or the author of the signifier. It is not what governs, emits or orients, gives rise [*donne lieu*], makes sense or originates. Any subject *of* the signifier is to be subjected to the law of the signifier. Its place is assigned by the route of the signifier, its literal topology and the rule of its displacements. First consequence: this analysis of a literary text foregoes[9] all reference to the author (whereas Freud never thought necessary to do without it), Poe, whose psychobiography structures Bonaparte's entire analysis. So much for any reference to the author of the text. But he is not "the author of the letter" whose *circulation* (italics mine) Lacan questions. An additional consequence is that "the author of the letter" "remains out of the game" as well. "From then on, the responsibility of the author of the letter takes second place to that of its holder" (SPL, p. 58). The letter is held but never possessed. Never, neither by its sender nor by its addressee. "We say: the *holder* and not the *possessor.* For it becomes clear that the addressee's proprietorship of the

8. Jacques Lacan, "Seminar on 'The Purloined Letter'," trans. J. Mehlman, *French Freud*, pp. 38–72. Hereafter cited in the text as SPL followed by the page number. The problematic set forth in *The Purveyor of Truth* can best be grasped through a rereading of Poe's *Purloined Letter* and of the *Seminar* as well as the editorial notes of Jeffrey Mehlman.—Ed.

9. We should make immediately clear that he foregoes almost all reference, that he foregoes it in appearance, as we shall see later.

Again and again, *Écrits* describes the "resistance" revealed in analysts' making a psychobiographical reference to the writer. If such a suspicion were to be granted, it could be extended to the point of being a formalist neutralization of any signature effect. That presupposes the opening of another (theoretical and more) space for the elaboration of these questions. We ourselves are locked within this other space.

letter may be no less debatable than that of anyone else into whose hands it comes" (SPL, p. 58).

The letter apparently has no owner. It is no one's property. It has no proper meaning, no proper content which bears on its trajectory. Structurally, therefore, it is in flight [*volante*] and purloined [*volée*]. Its flight would not have taken place if it had made sense or if it had been constituted by the content of its sense, i.e. if it were limited to making sense and being determined by the legibility of this sense. "And the mobilization of the elegant society whose frolics we are following would as well have no meaning if the letter itself were content with having one" (SPL, p. 56).

Lacan does not say that the letter makes no sense: it simply does not have just one sense. Which could mean: there are other things, more or less, besides making sense in this self-displacing and mobilizing letter. Or: there is more than one sense and this multiple possibility is responsible for the movement. In any event, sense, according to Lacan, is something the letter does not *just* have. What would happen if it were demonstrated that, according to Lacan, the letter *just* had a sense and just one? But we are getting ahead of ourselves.

The fact that the signifier cannot in appearance allow itself to be brought back to its transmitting origin, its sender, the fact that it depends neither on the signifier nor on the subject, which in fact its movements determine ("the displacement of the signifier determines the subjects' acts"), *would* have as a consequence that the signifier, in its letter, as a sealed text and locality, remains and finally falls. We *would* have, therefore, two remainders [*deux restes*]: 1) a remainder which could be destroyed precisely because it is excessive. The minister replaces the purloined letter with another. "*A remainder* that no analyst will neglect, trained as he is to retain whatever is significant, without always knowing what to do with it: the letter, abandoned by the Minister, and which the Queen's hand is now free to roll into a ball" (SPL, p. 42); 2) a remainder which is indestructible precisely because it steals away, i.e. the "unforgettable" insistence of the purloined letter which determines the repetition and the "persistence of conduct":

> The Minister then is not *altogether* mad in his insane stagnation, and that is why he will behave according to the mode of neurosis. Like the man who withdrew to an island to forget, what? he forgot—so the Minister, through not making use of the letter, comes to forget it. As is expressed by the persistence of his conduct. But the letter, no more than the neurotic's unconscious, does not forget him. It forgets him so little

that it transforms him more and more in the image of her who offered it to his capture, so that he will now surrender it, following her example, to a similar capture.

The features of that transformation are noted, and in a form so characteristic in their apparent gratuitousness that they might validly be compared to the return of the repressed (SPL, p. 65).

If the critique of a certain sort of semanticism constitutes an indispensable phase in the elaboration of a theory of the text, the Seminar exemplifies a clear progress beyond any post-Freudian psychoanalytic critique. It takes into account the organization, material as well as formal, of the signifier without throwing itself upon any semantic, not to say thematic, content of the text.

"Material" does not imply the empirical materiality of the perceptible [*sensible*] signifier (*scripta manent*), but that which retains, first, a certain *indivisibility* ("that materiality is *odd* [*singulière*] in many ways, the first of which is not to admit partition. Cut a letter in small pieces, and it remains the letter that it is—and this in a completely different sense than *Gestalttheorie* would account for with the dormant vitalism informing its notion of the whole" (SPL, p. 53), and, second, a certain locality. This locality itself is non-empirical and *non-ideal* because it gives rise to what is not where it is and hence "missing from its place" [*manque à sa place*]. It cannot be found where it is to be found, or else (but is this the same thing?) can be found where it cannot be found. The values of indivisibility (the barrier of the score) and of locality are themselves in this case indissociable and mutually selfconditioning, and we will eventually have to interrogate them all together. They may somewhere take charge of confronting us and riveting us again to what binds the sign-manual to singularity [*ce qui lie le seing au singulier*]. The unity of the signifier would bear witness to this in exchange for a certainty which this unity *receives* from it. But we are getting ahead of ourselves. Consider first of all what welds the indivisible and the local through the concept of *letter* or of the *materiality of the signifier:*

But if it is first of all on the materiality of the signifier that we have insisted, that materiality is *odd* in many ways, the first of which is not to admit partition. . . . For the signifier is a unit in its very uniqueness, being by nature symbol only of an absence. Which is why we cannot say of the purloined letter that, like other objects, it must be *or* not be in a particular place but that unlike them it will be *and* not be where it is, wherever it goes. . . . For it can *literally* be said something is missing from its place only of what can change it: the symbolic. For the real, whatever upheaval we subject it to, is always in its place; it carries it glued to its heel, ignorant of what might exile it from it (SPL, pp. 53–55).

The letter at issue, the materiality of the signifier at issue: perhaps only one letter need be changed, maybe even less than a letter in the expression: "missing from its place" [*manque à sa place*]. Perhaps we need only introduce a written "a," i.e. without accent, in order to bring out that if the lack has its place [*manque a sa place*] in this atomistic topology of the signifier, that is, if it occupies therein a specific place of definite contours, the order would remain undisturbed. The letter will always discover its proper place, a thwarted lack, which is certainly not empirical but transcendental (even better and more certain). It will be where it always was, always should have been, intangible and indestructible across the detour of a proper and properly circular trajectory. But we are getting ahead of ourselves.

Lacan, therefore, pays attention to the letter, i.e. to the materiality of the signifier. He is attentive also to its formality which, just as much as the place of the literal atom, determines the subject: "Subjectivity originally has no relationship to the real, but is of a syntax which engenders within it the signifying mark" (*Écrits*, p. 50).[10]

A break from naive semanticism and naive psycho-biographicism, an elaboration of a logic of the signifier (in its literal materiality and its syntactical formality), an appropriation of the problematic of *Beyond the Pleasure Principle*, these are the most general forms of what seems at first glance to be a legible advance on the part of the Seminar.

We must draw closer now, reread and question.

From the beginning we recognize the classical landscape of applied psychoanalysis. It is applied in this case to literature. The status of Poe's text is never challenged—Lacan simply calls it "fiction"—yet, Poe's text is summoned up as an example. It is an example for the sake of "illustrating" through a dialectical process a law and a truth which form the proper object of the Seminar. Literary writing occupies an illustrative position, which means making a general law legible through example, making clear the meaning of a law or a truth, manifesting them in a signal or exemplary way. The text is in the service of truth, and, what is more, this truth can be taught:

10. Jacques Lacan, *Écrits* (Paris: Le Seuil, 1966), p. 10. Hereafter cited in the text as *Écrits* followed by the page number.

Which is why we have decided to illustrate for you today the truth which may be drawn from that moment in Freud's thought under study—namely, that it is the symbolic order which is constitutive for the subject—by demonstrating in a story the decisive orientation which the subject receives from the itinerary of a signifier.

It is that truth, let us note, which makes the very existence of fiction possible (SPL, p. 40).

Again an illustration and again of a doctrine, this time Freud's own: "What Freud teaches us in the text we are commenting on is that the subject must pass through the channels of the symbolic, but what is illustrated here is more gripping still: it is not only the subject, but the subjects, grasped in their intersubjectivity, who line up" (SPL, p. 60).

The "truth which may be drawn from that moment in Freud's thought under study," the truth around which the most decorative and most pedagogical literary illustration will be organized, is not, as we will see, just any truth. It is truth itself, the truth of truth. Hence the most rigorously philosophical aspect of the Seminar.

This is, of course, the most classical way of doing things. It is typical of a certain kind of philosophical "literary criticism" but also of Freud himself every time he turns to literature for examples, illustrations, evidence or confirmation of a bit of knowledge or a truth which he arrives at differently elsewhere. Although the Lacanian statements concerning the relationship between fiction and truth are elsewhere not as clear and univocal, there can be no doubt in the present case. "Truth inhabits fiction" should not be understood in the somewhat perverse sense of a fiction which is more powerful than the truth which inhabits it and is inscribed in it. In truth, truth inhabits fiction as the master of the house, as the law of the house and as the economy of fiction. Truth brings about the economy of fiction. It directs, organizes and renders fiction possible. "It is that truth, let us note, which makes the very existence of fiction possible" (SPL, p. 40). The question is thus to ground fiction in truth to guarantee it within truth and to do so without stressing, as is the case of *Das Unheimlich*, this resistance, always renewed, of literary fiction to the general law of psychoanalytic knowledge. Lacan never poses the different question of what distinguishes different literary fictions. Even if all fiction were founded on a truth or made possible by a truth, the question may remain pertinent to the type of fiction from which something like literature, in this case "The Purloined Letter," arises, and to the effects literature might have on the very thing which seems to render it possible.

The first limit circumscribes the entire Seminar through which it scatters its mark in definite reimpression. What literary examples are supposed to deliver is a *message* which must be deciphered on the basis of the lessons of Freud. Reimpression: the *"Ouverture de ce recueil"* (Oct. 1966, ten years after the Seminar) speaks of "Poe's message deciphered and coming back from him, reader, in that, to read it, it says that it is no more feigned than the truth when it inhabits fiction" (*Écrits*, p. 10).

What Lacan analyzes, by decomposing it into its elements, origin and destination and discovering it in its truth is a *history* or *story* [*histoire*].

The word *"histoire"* appears at least four times on the first page alone. What serves as an example is a "story":

   a.   "Which is why we have decided to illustrate for you today the truth which may be drawn from that moment in Freud's thought under study—namely, that it is the symbolic order which is constitutive for the subject—by demonstrating in a story the decisive orientation which the subject receives from the itinerary of a signifier" (SPL, p. 40).
   b.   "It is that truth, let us note, which makes the very existence of fiction possible. And in that case, a fable is as appropriate as any other story for bringing it to light" (SPL, p. 40).
   c.   "Which is why, without seeking any further, we have chosen our example from the very *story* in which the dialectic of the game of even or odd—from whose study we have but recently profited—occurs (SPL, p. 40).
   d.   "It is, no doubt, no accident that this *tale* [*histoire*] revealed itself propitious to pursuing a course of inquiry which had already found support in it" (SPL, pp. 40–41: italics mine).

This is certainly the story of a letter, of a theft and of the displacement of a signifier. But the subject of the Seminar is merely the content of this history, precisely its story, what is related to the account, the internal and narrated side of the narration. Not the narration itself. Lacan's interest in the instance of the signifier in its letter seizes this instance insofar as it constitutes primarily the exemplary content and the meaning of Poe's fiction, i.e. what is written therein as opposed to the writing itself, the signifier and the narrating form. Hence the displacement of the signifier is analyzed as a signified, and as the recounted object in a short story.

At a certain point one could be led to believe that Lacan is preparing to deal with the (narrating) narration, to the complex structure of the scene of writing which is being played [*la scène de l'écriture qui s'y joue*], and of the quite curious place of the narrator. Once glimpsed, however, the narrator's place is excluded by analytical decipherment, neutralized, or more accurately, by a process we hope to follow, this decipherment acquiesces to the narrator's dictation of an effect of neutralizing exclusion ("narration" as "commentary") which transforms the entire Seminar into an analytical fascination with a content. In this way a scene is lacking. Where Lacan sees two ("There are two scenes" [SPL, p. 41]), there are at least three. And where he sees one or two "triads," there is always a supplementary square whose opening complicates the computation.

How does this neutralization work and what are its effects if not its aims?

At first we are led to believe that the position of the narrator and the narrating operation are going to intervene in the decipherment of "Poe's message." A number of distinctions allow us to hope for this at the moment the "tale" is introduced: "As you know, we are talking about the tale which Baudelaire translated under the title: *La lettre volée*. At first reading, we may distinguish a drama, its narration, and the conditions of that narration." The "drama" is the recounted action, the (narrated) *story* which forms the Seminar's specific object. But at the very moment the narration is evoked, it is immediately reduced to the level of "commentary" which "redoubles" the drama, staging and making visible, without any intervention of its own, as a transparent element, a general diaphaneity. Later the "general narrator" will come into question. "The narration, in fact, doubles the drama with a commentary without which no *mise en scène* would be possible. Let us say that the action would remain, properly speaking, invisible from the pit—aside from the fact that the dialogue would be expressly and by dramatic necessity devoid of whatever meaning it might have for an audience:—in other words, nothing of the drama could be grasped, neither seen nor heard, without, dare we say, the twilighting which the narration, in each scene, casts on the point of view that one of the actors had while performing it."

"There are two scenes. . . ." There follows the analysis of the two triangles, the content of the "tale," the object of analytical decipherment.

Afterwards narrator, narration and the process of "*mise en scène*" are all dropped. The unique place of the narrator on two sides of the narration, the specific status of his discourse—which is not neutral or the effect of whose neutrality is not neutral—his interventions and his very psychoanalytical position will never be interrogated through the rest of the Seminar which will remain an analysis of "intersubjective triads" which are supposed to constitute the inside of the narrated history, what Lacan calls the "story" or the "drama," the "real drama" ("each of the two scenes of the real drama is narrated in the course of a different dialogue"). All allusions to the narrator and to the act of narration are there simply for the sake of excluding them from the "real drama" (the two triangular scenes) and thus turning them over, once they have been clearly delimited, to the analytical decipherment of the message. This occurs in two moments in accordance with the *dialogues* which divide "The Purloined Letter."

First moment. The exclusion in this case is quite plain and facilitated by Poe's own text which seems to encourage it. This is the moment of what Lacan calls *exactness*. The narrator is called the "general narrator." He is like the neutral, homogeneous and transparent element of the narrative. He "adds nothing," says Lacan. As if something had to be added to a relation for an intercession to occur. In a narrative scene no less. And as if nothing were added through questions, remarks and exclamations—which are the "general" narrator's intercessions in what Lacan specifies as the "first dialogue." Even before the "first dialogue" begins, furthermore, the "general narrator" makes some comments which will be of interest later. Finally, the narrator who himself is staged in his staging is staged in turn in a text much broader than the so-called "general narration." Which is a supplementary reason not to consider the narrator as a neutral place of passage. The Seminar pays no specific attention to that extra text. Rather, it isolates as its essential object the two "narrated" triangular scenes, the two "real dramas," neutralizing at once that fourth personage (the "general narrator"), his narrative operation and the text which stages the narration and the narrator. In effect, as text and as fiction, "The Purloined Letter" begins neither with the triangular dramas nor with the narration which stages them by involving itself with them in a particular way which we will analyze later. Nor does it end there. "The Purloined Letter" stages a narrator and a stage director who—feigned by "The Purloined Letter"—feigns by "The Purloined Letter" to recount the "real drama" of the Purloined Letter, etc. So many supplements which engulf and damage [*abîment*] the triangle which is the subject of the narration. So many reasons to think that the "general narrator" always adds something and that, from the first dialogue on, he is not the general condition of the possibility of the narrative, but an actor of an extremely unusual status. So many reasons not to be satisfied with what Lacan says about the matter in what I called the first moment of exclusion. The filter of the general narrator is not "a fortuitous arrangement" and he does remind us that "the message" "indeed belongs to the dimension of language," simply because that fourth position cannot be excluded as an elementary generality from the triangular scenes which would form the object contained under the "real drama."

Second moment. Lacan refines out or delimits a "second dialogue," neglecting once again, this time between the two dialogues, a long period without dialogue during which the narrator makes comments to which we shall turn later. During this "second dialogue" we are supposed to pass from the register of "exactness" to that of "truth," "strictly speaking to the very foundation of intersubjectivity." This time we expect an analysis of the specific position of the narrator. Lacan writes in effect, "Thus the indirect telling sifts out the linguistic dimension, and the general narrator, by duplicating it, 'hypothetically' adds nothing to it. But its role in the second dialogue is entirely different" (SPL, p. 48).

No: The situation was already different in the first dialogue and Lacan in no way changes his treatment during the second. He describes the narrator as the receptacle or mediator or purely formal assistant whose sole function consists in permitting Dupin to lay a trap and thus trap us by trapping the passive narrator, to renew his trick "in a purer form" at the moment at which he pretends to expose his procedure, at that point "really" deceiving the narrator and us.

> What could be more convincing, moreover, than the gesture of laying one's cards face up on the table? So much so that we are momentarily persuaded that the magician has in fact demonstrated, as he promised, how his trick was performed, whereas he has only renewed it in still purer form: at which point we fathom the measure of the supremacy of the signifier in the subject.
> Such is Dupin's maneuver . . . (SPL, pp. 49–50).

But when did we find out that the narrator quite happily listened passively and really allowed himself to be deceived? Whoever allows himself to be really deceived whenever the narrator narrates himself? Etc.

How does this neutralization of the narrator affect the Seminar?

1. The narrator (himself redoubled into narrating narrator and nar-

rated narrator and never simply reporting the two dialogues) is obviously neither the author himself (whom we shall call Poe) nor, which is not so obvious, the inscriber of a story-telling text, or rather one which makes a narrator speak who himself, in many senses, makes several people speak. Inscriber and scription are original functions which may be confused neither with the author and his actions nor with the narrator and his narration and even less with that particular object, that narrated content which is the "real drama" and which the psychoanalyst precipitately identifies as "Poe's message deciphered." The fact that the entire surface of scription as a whole—the fiction called "The Purloined Letter"—should be enveloped by a narration whose narrator says "I" does not permit us to confuse fiction with narration. Even less, of course, with any given narrated passage, however long and overt it may be. We are faced with a problem of framing, bordering or delimiting which demands an absolutely precise analysis if the effects of fiction are to become evident. Without breathing a word, Lacan excludes the textual fiction within which he isolates "general narration." Such an operation is facilitated, too obviously facilitated, by the fact that the narration contains the entire fiction entitled "The Purloined Letter." But *that* is the fiction. There is an invisible but structurally irreducible frame around the narration. Where does it begin? With the first letter of the title? With the epigraph from Seneca? With the words, "At Paris, just after dark . . ."? It is much more complicated than that and will require reconsideration. Such complication suffices to point out everything that is misunderstood about the structure of the text once the frame is ignored. Within this invisible or neutralized frame, Lacan takes the borderless narration and makes another subdivision, once again leaving aside the frame. He sets apart two dialogues with the narration which form the narrated history, i.e. the content of a representation, the internal meaning of a story, the all-enframed which demands our complete attention, mobilizes all the Oedipal and psychoanalytic schemas available and draws all the effort of decipherment towards its center. Missing, however, is an elaboration of the problem of the frame, the signature and the *parergon*. This lack allows us to reconstruct the scene of the signifier as a signified (an ever inevitable process in the logic of the sign), writing as the written, the text as discourse or more precisely as an "intersubjective" dialogue (there is nothing fortuitous to the fact that the Seminar discusses the two dialogues in "The Purloined Letter").

2. It involves, first of all, a *formal* limit to the analysis. The for-

mal structure of the work is ignored, quite classically, as soon as, or perhaps whenever, one claims to decipher the "truth" or the exemplary message. The fictional structure is reduced as soon as it is related to the condition of its truth. In this way one practices bad formalism. Formalism is practiced because no interest is taken in the subject-author. In certain situations this could constitute progress and a legitimate requirement. But this formalism is rigidly inconsequential whenever, on the pretext of excluding the author, no account is taken of 1) the scription-fiction and the scriptor-fictor and 2) the narrating narration and the narrator. This formalism guarantees, as always, the surreptitious subdivision of a semantic content to which psychoanalysis devotes all of its work of interpretation. Formalism and hermeneutic semanticism always reinforce one another: it depends on the angle.

3. The limit, therefore, is not merely formal and for the moment of no interest to a science of poetic fiction or narrative structure. We are not trying to save something like literature or literary form from the grips of psychoanalysis. Quite the contrary. There is a profound historical and theoretical complicity between the formalist backtrack and psychoanalysis applied to literature, which it is supposed to avoid. We have just hit upon the principle. Noteworthy in this case is the fact that formal deficiency implies a semantic and psychoanalytic decision. Once distinguished from the author and thereafter from the scriptor, the narrator is not merely the formal condition of the narration which could be symmetrically contrasted with the content, such as the narrating and the narrated, for example. He intercedes in a specific way, at once "*too* self-evident" and invisible in a triangle which thus touches another triangle at one of its points. He intercedes in two "intersubjective" triangles. All of which singularly complicates the "intersubjective" structure, this time within the framed, twice framed, scenes, with the represented content. Not taking this complication into account is no fault of "formalist" literary criticism, but rather the operation of a psychoanalyst-semanticist. The narrator does not fade away [*s'effacer*] as a "general narrator" or rather, in making himself fade away into homogeneous generality, he moves forward as a uniquely singular character in the narrated narration, in the framed. He constitutes an instance, a position with which the triangle, through the intermediary of Dupin (who himself represents all the positions in turn), maintains an *extremely determinate and cathected* relationship. The violence of the Seminar's framing, the cutting off of the narrated figure from a fourth

side to leave merely triangles evades a certain, perhaps Oedipal, difficulty which makes itself felt in the scene of writing.

Before showing this more concretely, let us follow Lacan into the framed content in the analysis of the two triangles which constitutes the specific contribution of the Seminar. Let us begin from his own premises and with his own framework [*encadrement*]. Let us assume that the frame can be neutralized, both as a delimitation and as a precarious construction, a four-sided artefact at least.

The expressions, "trio," "triangles," "intersubjective triangle," occur quite frequently in order to describe the two scenes of the "real drama" thus deciphered. First of all, a long quotation in order to recall to memory and to testimony this logic of the excluded quarter. On Oedipus:

> There are two scenes, the first of which we shall straightway desinate the primal scene, and by no means inadvertently, since the second may be considered its repetition in the very sense we are considering today.
>
> The primal scene is thus performed, we are told [by neither Poe, nor the scriptor, nor the narrator, but by G, the Prefect of Police who is *mis en scène* by all those involved in the dialogues—J. D.], in the royal *boudoir*, so that we suspect that the person of the highest rank, called the "exalted personage," who is alone there when she receives a letter, is the Queen. This feeling is confirmed by the embarrassment into which she is plunged by the entry of the other exalted personage, of whom we have already been told [again by G—J. D.] prior to this account that the knowledge he might have of the letter in question would jeopardize for the lady nothing less than her honor and safety. Any doubt that he is in fact the King is promptly dissipated in the course of the scene which begins with the entry of the Minister D. . . . At that moment, in fact, the Queen can do no better than to play on the King's inattentiveness by leaving the letter on the table "face down, address uppermost." It does not, however, escape the Minister's lynx eye, nor does he fail to notice the Queen's distress and thus to fathom her secret. From then on everything transpires like clockwork. After dealing in his customary manner with the business of the day, the Minister draws from his pocket a letter similar in appearance to the one in his view, and, having pretended to read it, places it next to the other. A bit more conversation to amuse the royal company, whereupon, without flinching once, he seizes the embarrassing letter, making off with it, as the Queen, on whom none of his maneuver has been lost, remains unable to intervene for fear of attracting the attention of her royal spouse, close at her side at that very moment.

Everything might then have transpired unseen by a hypothetical spectator of an operation in which nobody falters, and whose *quotient* is that the Minister has filched from the Queen her letter and that—an even more important result than the first—the Queen knows that he now has it, and by no means innocently.

A *remainder* that no analyst will neglect, trained as he is to retain whatever is significant, without always knowing what to do with it: the letter, abandoned by the Minister, and which the Queen's hand is now free to roll into a ball.

Second scene: in the Minister's office. It is in his hotel, and we know—from the account the Prefect of Police has given Dupin, whose specific genius for solving enigmas Poe introduces here for the second time—that the police, returning there as soon as the Minister's habitual, nightly absences allow them to, have searched the hotel and its surroundings from top to bottom for the last eighteen months. In vain,—although everyone can deduce from the situation that the Minister keeps the letter within reach.

Dupin calls on the Minister. The latter receives him with studied nonchalance, affecting in his conversation romantic *ennui.* Meanwhile Dupin, whom this pretense does not deceive, his eyes protected by green glasses, proceeds to inspect the premises. When his glance catches a rather crumpled piece of paper—apparently thrust carelessly in a division of an ugly pasteboard card-rack, hanging gaudily from the middle of the mantelpiece—he already knows that he's found what he's looking for. His conviction is re-enforced by the very details which seem to contradict the description he has of the stolen letter, with the exception of the format, which remains the same.

Whereupon he has but to withdraw, after "forgetting" his snuff-box on the table, in order to return the following day to reclaim it—armed with a facsimile of the letter in its present state. As an incident in the street, prepared for the proper moment, draws the Minister to the window, Dupin in turn seizes the opportunity to seize the letter while substituting the imitation, and has only to maintain the appearances of a normal exit.

Here as well all has transpired, if not without noise, at least without all commotion. The quotient of the operation is that the Minister no longer has the letter, but, far from suspecting that Dupin is the culprit who has ravished it from him, knows nothing of it. Moreover, what he is left with is far from insignificant for what follows. We shall return to what brought Dupin to inscribe a message on his counterfeit letter. Whatever the case, the Minister, when he tries to make use of it, will be able to read these words, written so that he may recognize Dupin's hand: ". . . Un dessein si funeste/ S'il n'est digne d'Atrée est digne de Thyeste,"[11] whose source, Dupin tells us, is Crébillon's *Atrée.*

Need we emphasize the similarity of these two sequences? Yes, for the resemblance we have in mind is not a simple collection of traits chosen only in order to delete their difference. And it would not be enough to retain those common traits at the expense of the others for the slightest truth to result. It is rather the intersubjectivity in which the two actions are motivated that we wish to bring into relief, as well as the three terms through which it structures them.

The special status of these terms results from their corresponding simultaneously to the three logical moments through which the decision is precipitated and the three places it assigns to the subjects among whom it constitutes a choice.

That decision is reached in a glance's time. For the maneuvers which follow, however stealthily they prolong it, add nothing to that glance, nor does the deferring of the deed in the second scene break the unity of that moment.

This glance presupposes two others, which it embraces in its vision of the breach left in their fallacious complementarity, anticipating in it the occasion for larceny afforded by that exposure. Thus three moments, structuring three glances, borne by three subjects, incarnated each time by different characters.

The first is a glance that sees nothing: the King and the police.

The second, a glance which sees that the first sees nothing and deludes itself as to the secrecy of what it hides: the Queen, then the Minister.

The third sees that the first two glances leave what should be hidden exposed to whomever would seize it: the Minister and finally Dupin.

In order to grasp in its unity the intersubjective complex thus described, we would willingly seek a model in the technique legendarily attributed to the ostrich attempting to shield itself from danger; for that technique might ultimately be qualified as political, divided as it here is among three partners: the second believing itself invisible because the first has its head stuck in the ground, and all the while letting the third calmly pluck its rear; we need only enrich its proverbial domination by a letter, producing *la politique de l'autruiche,* for the ostrich itself to take on forever a new meaning.

Given the intersubjective modulus of the repetitive action, it remains to recognize in it a *repetition automatism* in the sense that interests us in Freud's text (SPL, pp. 41–44).[12]

11. "So infamous a scheme/ If not worthy of Atreus, is worthy of Thystes."

12. *La politique de l'autruiche* combines the policy of the ostrich (*autruche*), others (*autrui*) and Austria (*Autriche*).

We will analyze later the singular relationship between the "subject" (narrated narrator) of the narration and Dupin insofar as he complicates definitively and from the start the triangular structure. Let us consider for the moment what is implied in this exclusion of the fourth or of the third-plus-or-minus-one in this rush to truth. We should also consider how the demand for the truth leads to setting aside the scene of writing, to setting aside what almost (feigned) always itself allows (itself) to be set aside, set apart, such as the quarter, for example. The remainder, what can be dropped, not only in the narrated content of writing (the signifier, the writing, the letter) but also in the operation of writing, must be taken into account.

Lacan leads us back to the truth, but *this* truth does not get lost. He returns the letter and shows that it returns itself to its *proper* place by way of a *proper* trajectory, and, as he expressly mentions, this destination is what interests him. Destiny as destination. The signifier has its place in the letter which rediscovers proper meaning in its proper place. A certain reappropriation and re-adequation will reconstitute the proper, the place, the meaning and the truth which are self-distanced for the duration of a detour or a suspended delivery [*une souffrance*]. Algorithm. A whole, once more, has to be covered over: it need not be filled but its contour has to be seen and delimited.

We have read it: the signifier (in the letter, in the message) has no self-identical place. The signifier is *missing* from its place. Its meaning is of little importance since the signifier is not encapsulized therein. But what the Seminar would like to show in the end is that there is a single proper trajectory for the letter. The letter always returns to its own, ever the same and determinable place. The Seminar would show furthermore, that, although its meaning (what is written on the note in circulation) is (according to a hypothesis which is itself rigorously inadmissible) indifferent and unknown to us, the meaning of the letter and of its trajectory are necessary, unique and determinable in truth, just like the truth itself.

The place and the meaning of the letter are, of course, not at the disposition of the subjects who are subject to the moment of the signifier. But when Lacan says the letter has no proper place, we will have to take this as an objective place which is determinable in a naive and empirical topology. When he says that the letter has no proper meaning, we must assume this is meaning as content, completely contained by what is written on the note. The signifier-letter, according to the psychoanalytico-transcendental topology and semantics with which we are deal-

ing, has a proper place and meaning which form the condition, origin and
destination of the entire circulation, as of the entire logic of the signifier.

First, the proper place. The letter was sent from a place and arrived
at a place. It is not a subject but a void, the lack out of which the subject is constituted. The contour of this void is determinable and mag-
netizes the entire trajectory of the detour which leads from void to void
and from the void to itself and which has, therefore, a circular form.
This is a regulated circulation which organizes a return from the detour to the void, and a transcendental reappropriation and readequation
which accomplish an authentic contract. Lacan says quite literally that
the trajectory is proper and circular.

> Thus we are confirmed in our detour by the very object which draws
> us into it: for we are quite simply dealing with a letter which has been
> diverted from its path; one whose course has been *prolonged* (etymo-
> logically, the word of the title), or, to revert to the language of the post
> office, a *letter in sufferance* [*une lettre en souffrance*].
>
> Here then, *simple and odd*, as we are told on the very first page, re-
> duced to its simplest expression, is the singularity of the letter, which
> as the title indicates, is the *true subject* of the tale: since it can be di-
> verted, it must have a course *which is proper to it:* trait confirming its
> incidence as signifier. For we have learned to conceive of the signifier
> as sustaining itself only in a displacement comparable to that found in
> the electric news strips or in the rotating memories of our machines-
> that-think-like-men, this because of the alternating operation which is
> its principle, requiring it to leave its place, even though it returns to it
> by a circular path (SPL, pp. 59–60: Lacan's italics.)

"*Quitte*": "leave [*quitte*] its place, even though [*quitte*] it returns to
it by a circular path."[13] Circulation, the payment [*acquittement*] of a
debt, steps in to repair the dehiscence which, by opening the debt and
the contract, expelled for a time (the time of the signifier) the signified
from its proper origin. Circulation allows it to return. This readequation (the truth), therefore, implies a theory of the proper place which itself implies a theory of the letter as an indivisible locality. The signifier should never venture an unreturning loss, destruction or shredding
of itself.

Next, proper meaning. Since the letter has (a) place of origin and destruction, and remains what it is en route (but what guarantees this?),

---

13. The French "quitte" can mean both "leave" (*quitter*) and "even though" as in
(*quitte à*).

it has a proper meaning first in the law of its trajectory if not in its content, although the latter is sufficiently if minimally conditioned through decipherment. It must have a relationship with what constitutes the contract or the "pact," i.e. with the subjection of the subject and hence somewhere with the hole as the proper place of the letter. Its place has an essential relationship with its sense which must be such that the letter is constantly directed back to its place. We know in fact what the note contains. Indeed, Lacan must speak of and recall its sense, at least as that which threatens the pact by which it is constituted. It is the phallic law represented by the King and in the custody of the Queen, a custody which, according to the pact, she should share with the King but which she precisely threatens to divide, dissociate and betray.

> But all this tells us nothing of the message it conveys.
> Love letter or conspirational letter, letter of betrayal or letter of mission, letter of summons or letter of distress, *we are assured of but one thing:* the Queen must not bring it to the knowledge of her lord and master.
> Now these terms, far from bearing the nuance of discredit they have in *bourgeois* comedy, take on a certain prominence through allusion to her sovereign, to whom she is bound by pledge of faith, and doubly so, since her role as spouse does not relieve her of her duties as subject, but rather elevates her to the guardianship of what royalty according to law incarnates of power: and which is called legitimacy.
> From then on, to whatever vicissitudes the queen may choose to subject the letter, it remains that the letter is the symbol of a pact, and that, even should the recipient not assume the pact, the existence of the letter situates her in a symbolic chain foreign to the one which constitutes her faith. . . . Our fable is so constructed as to show that it is the letter and its diversion which governs their entries and roles. If *it* be 'in sufferance,' *they* shall endure the pain. Should they pass beneath its shadow, they become its reflection. Falling in possession of the letter— admirable ambiguity of language— its *meaning* possesses them (SPL, pp. 57–58, 60; italics mine).

A passage typical of Heidegger's formulations, as is most often the case in these decisive pauses.

The letter, therefore, has a proper meaning, a proper trajectory and a proper place. Which ones? In the triangle, only Dupin seems to know. Let us drop for the moment the problem of this knowledge and concern ourselves first of all with what is known therein: What in fact does

Dupin know? He knows that the letter *ends up* where it should *be* in order to return circularly and adequately to its proper place. This proper place (known to Dupin *and* the psychoanalyst who, as we shall see, occupies Dupin's place) is the place of castration. It is, woman, a place unveiled as that of the lack of the penis, as the truth of the phallus, i.e. of castration. The truth of the purloined letter is the truth itself, its meaning is meaning, its law is law, the contract of truth with itself in the logos. Subtending this value as pact (and thus adequation), that of veiling/unveiling brings the entire Seminar into harmony with Heidegger's discourse on truth. What is veiled/unveiled in this case is a hole, a non-being [*non-étant*]; the truth of being [*l'être*], as non-being. Truth is "woman" as veiled/unveiled castration. Here, at the place of the signifier and the letter, begins the departure of the signifier (its inadequation to the signified). But the trial begins here as well, the promise of reappropriation, of return and readequation "at the cost of restoring the object." The singular *unity* of the letter is the place of truth's contact with itself. That is why the truth *returns to* the woman (at least as long as she wants to keep the pact and hence what reverts to the king and to the phallus of which she has custody). That is why, as Lacan says elsewhere, the letter reverts to being [*la lettre revient à l'être*], i.e., to that nothingness which is to be openness [*l'ouverture*] as a hole between the woman's legs. Such is the proper place, where the letter can be found, where its meaning can be found and where the Minister believes it is the most protected, but where in fact, in its very hiding place, it is the most utterly exposed. As possessor of the sheltered letter, the Minister begins to identify with the Queen (but is not Dupin forced to do the same in turn, not to speak of the psychoanalyst within him? We are, however, getting ahead of ourselves).

Thus:

> . . . everything seems intended for a character, all of whose utterances have revealed the most virile traits, to exude the oddest *odor di femina* when he appears.
>
> Dupin does not fail to stress that this is an artifice, describing behind the bogus finery the vigilance of a beast of prey ready to spring. But that this is the very effect of the unconscious in the precise sense that we teach that the unconscious means that man is inhabited by the signifier: could we find a more beautiful image of it than the one Poe himself forges to help us appreciate Dupin's exploit? For with this aim in mind, he refers to those toponymical inscriptions which a geographical map, lest it remain mute, superimposes on its design, and which may

become the object of a guessing game: who can find the name chosen by a partner?—noting immediately that the name most likely to foil a beginner will be one which, in large letters spaced out widely across the map, discloses, often without an eye pausing to notice it, the name of an entire country. . . .

Just so does the purloined letter, like an immense female body, stretch out across the Minister's office when Dupin enters. But just so does he already expect to find it, and has only, with his eyes veiled by green lenses, to undress that huge body.

And that is why without needing any more than being able to listen in at the door of Professor Freud, he will go straight to the spot in which lies and lives what that body is designed to hide, in a gorgeous center caught in a glimpse, nay, to the very place seducers name Sant' Angelo's Castle in their innermost illusion of controlling the City from within it. Look! between the cheeks of the fireplace, there's the object already in reach of a hand the ravisher has but to extend . . . (SPL, pp. 66–67).

The letter—the place of the signifier—is in effect where Dupin and the psychoanalyst expect to find it: on the immense body of the woman, between the cheeks [*jambages*] of the fireplace. Such is its proper place, the terminus of its circular trajectory. It returns to the sender who is not the signatory of the note, but the place where it began to detach itself from its feminine possessor or inheritor, the Queen, seeking to reappropriate for herself that which (in virtue of the pact subjecting her to the King, namely, the Law) guarantees her the disposition of the phallus (of which she would otherwise be deprived, which she took the risk of dividing, multiplying and thus depriving herself of); this same Queen undertakes to reconstruct and reclose the circle of restrained economy [*l'économie restreinte*] and the circulatory pact. She wants to retrieve the letter-fetish and to that end begins by replacing or exchanging one fetish for another. She emits a quantity of money—without really spending it since there exists a certain equivalency—and this money is exchanged for the letter thus assuring the latter's circular return. Like the analyst, Dupin finds himself on the circumference in that circle of restrained economy which I have called elsewhere the constriction of the ring [*la stricture de l'anneau*] and which the Seminar analyzes as the truth of fiction. We should return later to this problem of economy.

This determination of the proper, of the law of the proper and of *economy* leads back, therefore, to castration as truth, to the figure of the woman as a figure of castration *and* of truth. Of castration as truth, which does not at all mean, as one might tend to believe, that we are led back to truth as essential dislocation and irreducible parcelling. On the contrary, castration is what contracts (constriction of the ring) to bring the phallus, the signifier, the letter or the fetish back to their *oikos*, their familiar dwelling, their proper place. In this sense castration-truth is the opposite, the very antidote, of parcelling. What is in this case missing from its place has its own fixed and central place, away from any substitution. Something is missing from its place but the lack itself is never missing. Because of castration, the phallus always remains in place in the transcendental topology we spoke of above, where it is indivisible and thus indestructible, like the letter which *takes its place*. Hence the undisinterested and never demonstrated presupposition of the materiality of the letter *as indivisibility* was indispensable to Lacan's restrained economy and his circulation of the proper.

The difference I am interested in here is that the lack has no place in dissemination—a formula to be understood however you will.

By determining the place of the lack (the topos of what is missing from its place), by constituting it as a fixed center, Lacan is in fact proposing at once a discourse-truth and a discourse on the truth of the purloined letter as the truth of "The Purloined Letter." In spite of the appearance of denegation, his is a hermeneutical decipherment. The link between Femininity and Truth is its ultimate signified. Fourteen years later, in re-introducing the Seminar at the head of *Écrits* by means of an "Unpublished Introduction" ("Points," 1, 1969), Lacan emphasizes above all this link and this meaning. He capitalizes Woman and Femininity, which elsewhere is often reserved for the Truth: "What Poe's tale shows in my hands is that the effect of the signifier's (in this case the purloined letter's) subjection bears primarily on its post-theft possessor, and that along its travels what it conveys is that very Femininity which it is to have taken into its shadow."

Femininity is the Truth (of) castration. It is the first figure of castration, because in the logic of the signifier it is always in a state of having been castrated and "leaves" something in circulation (the letter in this case), detached from itself, to bring it back to itself so that "it never had it: from where the truth comes out of the hole, but never only at mid-body."

This first castration (pre-castration) tends to castrate and thus feminize whoever holds the letter which signifies phallus and castration. "Here is no more than completed what first feminizes him [the Minister—J. D.] as by a dream. . . . Wherewith our Dupin shows his success to be equal to that of the psychoanalyst" ("Points," Introduction, p. 8).[14]

POINT OF VIEW: TRUTH IN (THE) PLACE OF FEMININE SEXUALITY

What of this success? Before answering this question, let us reconsider in all its complexity the relationship between the position of Dupin and that of the analyst, then between the analyst and the one who says Freud and I in the Seminar as well as in presentations of the Seminar. This calls for a long excursus.

Our questions up till now suggest that if there is such a thing as a purloined letter there might be an additional trap here. The letter would have no fixed place, not even that of a definable gap or void. The letter would not be found; it might always not be found; it would in any case be found less in the sealed writing whose "story" is told by the narrator and "deciphered" by the Seminar, less in the context of the story, than "in" the text escaping on a fourth side the eyes of both Dupin and the psychoanalyst. The rest, the remnant, would be "The Purloined Letter," the text that bears this title, and whose place, like the once more invisible large letters on the map, is not where one was expecting to find it, in the enclosed content of the "real drama" or in the hidden and sealed interior of Poe's story, but in and as the open letter, the very open letter, which fiction is. This, because it is written, implies at least a fourth avenue for appeal that escapes and manages the escape of the letter of the text from the decoder, the purveyor of truth [*facteur de la vérité*] who puts it back in the circle of its proper course: this is the operation of the Seminar, which repeats the operation of Dupin who, in no way contradicting the circularity of the proper course, "has succeeded in returning the letter to its proper course" (SPL, p. 69), in accordance with the Queen's wishes.

To return the letter to its proper course, supposing that its trajectory is a line, is to correct a deviation, to rectify a divergence, to recall a direction, an authentic line, so that it can serve as the good rule, i.e., as the norm. Dupin is clever: he knows his cleverness (*connaît son adresse*) and he knows the law.[15] The moment one believes that one

14. Jacques Lacan, *Écrits I* (Collection "Points"; Paris: Seuil, 1966), p. 8. Hereafter cited in the text as "Points," Introduction followed by the page number.—Ed.

15. The text plays with two possible meanings of the French term "adresse," i.e. "address" and "adroitness."—Ed.

can get hold of the letter by drawing triangles and circles and manipulating the opposition imaginary/symbolic, the moment one reconstitutes truth, self-adequation, "The Purloined Letter" escapes by a too-self-evident opening. Baudelaire bluntly reminds us of this. The purloined letter is in the text: not only as an object with its proper course described, contained in the text, a signifier that has become a theme or a signified of the text, but also as the text producing framing effects. At the very moment when Dupin and the Seminar find the letter, when they find its proper place and course, when they believe the letter is at one place or another as if on a map, a place on a map as if on the woman's body, they no longer see the map itself: not the map described by the text at one moment or another but the map that the text "is," that it describes, "itself," like the four-way divergence (*l'écart du quatre*) with no promise of topos or truth. The remaining structure of the letter, contrary to the final words of the Seminar ("what the 'purloined letter,' nay, the 'letter in sufferance' means is that a letter always arrives at its destination"), is that a letter can always not arrive at its destination. Its "materiality" and its "topology" result from its divisibility, its ever-possible partition. It can always be broken up irrevocably and this is what the system of the symbolic, of castration, of the signifier, of truth, of the contract, and so forth, try to shield it from: the point of view of the King and that of the Queen are here the same, bound together by contract in order to reappropriate the bit. Not that the letter never arrives at its destination, but part of its structure is that it is always capable of not arriving there. And without this danger (breach of contract, division or multiplication, irrevocable division, of the phallus mutilated for a moment by the Queen, that is, by every "subject"), the circuit of the letter would never have even begun. But with this danger, it may always not be completed. Here dissemination threatens the law of the signifier and of castration as a contract of truth. Dissemination mutilates the unity of the signifier, that is, of the phallus.

At the moment when the Seminar, like Dupin, finds the letter where it is to be found, between the legs of the woman, the deciphering of the enigma is anchored in truth. The sense of the story, the meaning of the purloined letter ("what the 'purloined letter,' nay, the 'letter in sufferance' means is that a letter always arrives at its destination"), is discovered. The hermeneutic discovery of meaning (truth), the deciphering (that of Dupin and that of the Seminar), arrives itself at its destination.

Why then does it find, at the same time that it finds truth, the same meaning and the same topos as Bonaparte when, leaping over the text, she proposes a psycho-biographical analysis of "The Purloined Letter?"[16] Is this a coincidence?

Is it a coincidence if, while claiming to break with psycho-biographical criticism ("La Science et la vérité," *Écrits*, p. 860), one rejoins it in its ultimate semantic anchoring—and after a possibly less rigorous textual analysis?

For Bonaparte, too, the castration of the woman (the mother) is the final meaning of "The Purloined Letter"; and, with it, truth, readequation, or reappropriation as the desire to plug the hole. But Bonaparte does what Lacan does not do: she establishes the connection between "The Purloined Letter" and other texts of Poe—and she analyzes how they function. Later, the *internal* necessity of this operation will become clear.

One example is "The Black Cat," in which "the castration fear, embodied in the woman as the castrated being, lies at the core of the tale" (Bonaparte, p. 481). "Nevertheless, all the primitive anxieties of the child, which often remain those of the adult, seem to be gathered here as if by appointment, in this story of extreme anxiety, as if at a crossroads" (Bonaparte, p. 481): at this crossroads [*quadrifurcum*], absentmindedly named, neglected as a frame, the representation of a circle or a triangle. The Seminar: "Here we are, in fact, yet again at the crossroads at which we had left our drama and its round with the question of the way in which the subjects replace each other in it" (SPL, p. 60). Bonaparte continues with a page of generalizations about castration anxiety that can be summed up in a statement of Freud's that she does not quote here: the realization of the mother's lack of a penis is "the greatest trauma"; or one of Lacan's: "Division of the subject? This is a nodal point. Let us recall how Freud spins it out [*où Freud le déroule*]: in terms of the mother's lack of a penis, in which the nature of the phallus is revealed" ("La Science et la vérité," *Écrits*, p. 877).

After having dealt with the Law and with fetishism as a process of rephallization of the mother (for the purpose of restoring to her what has been stolen—or detached—from her), Bonaparte writes the following passage, in which we recognize the crux of Lacan's interpretation, and a few other things as well:

16. Marie Bonaparte, *Edgar Poe: Etude analytique* (1933; rpt. in 3 vol. Paris, 1958). Translated by John Rodker as *The Life and Works of Edgar Allan Poe: A Psycho-analytic Interpretation* (London, 1949). References in the text are indicated by "Bonaparte," the page number corresponds to the English translation. In some cases, however, the translation had to be slightly modified.—Tr.

Finally, with the gallows theme, we see death-anxiety, or fear of death.

All these fears, however, remain subordinate to the main theme of fear of castration, with which all are closely interwoven. The cat with the white breast has also a missing eye; hanging represents not only death, but rephallization; the urge to confess leads to the discovery of a corpse surmounted by an effigy of castration; even the cellar and tomb, and the gaping aperture of the chimney, recall the dread cloaca of the mother.

Other tales by Poe also express, though in different and in less aggressive fashion, regret for the missing maternal penis, with reproach for its loss. First among these, strange though it seem, is "The Purloined Letter."

The reader will remember that, in this story the Queen of France, like Elizabeth Arnold, is in possession of a dangerous and secret correspondence, whose sinister writer is unknown. A wicked minister, planning political blackmail and to strengthen his power, steals one of these letters under the Queen's eyes, which she is unable to prevent owing to the King's presence. This letter must at all costs be recovered. Every attempt by the Police fails. Fortunately Dupin is at hand. Wearing dark spectacles with which he can look about him, while his own eyes are concealed, he makes an excuse to call on the Minister, and discovers the letter openly displayed in a card-rack, hung "from a little brass knob just beneath the middle of the mantelpiece." *

Here, then, a note of Bonaparte's:

*Baudelaire translates: *"suspendu . . . à un petit bouton de cuivre au-dessus du manteau de la cheminée."* The impression of Baudelaire's translation, as far as this sentence is concerned, is obvious: in particular, "beneath" is translated by *"au-dessus"* ("above"), which is completely wrong.

This note is not without importance. In the first place, it makes clear that Lacan had read Bonaparte, although the Seminar never alludes to her. As an author so careful about debts and priorities, he could have acknowledged an irruption[17] that orients his entire interpretation, namely, the process of rephallization as the proper course of the letter, the "return of the letter" restored to its "destination" after having been found between the legs of the mantelpiece. Or he could have suppressed it. But since footnotes represent, if not the truth, the ap-

17. The term "frayage" has been rendered here by "irruption" which is closer to the "directed disruption" involved in the process of *Bahnung* as viewed by Derrida.—Ed.

pendix in which is revealed that which is not to be said or that which as Schelling, quoted in "The Uncanny," says, "should remain hidden," the Seminar drops a note in response:

> Look! between the cheeks of the fireplace, there's the object already in reach of a hand the ravager has but to extend. . . . The question of deciding whether he seizes it above the mantelpiece as Baudelaire translates, or beneath it, as in the original text, may be abandoned without harm to the inferences of those whose profession is grilling [aux inférences de la cuisine].*

Here, then, a note of Lacan's:

> "*And even to the cook herself" (SPL, pp. 66f.).

Without harm? On the contrary, the harm would be decisive, within the Seminar itself: on the mantelpiece, the letter could not have been "between the cheeks of the fireplace," "between the legs of the fireplace." The stakes are thus important, even if one left aside (imagining it to be extraneous) the scornful irritability with regard to [à l'endroit de] a woman psychoanalyst and her legacy.[18] Why relegate the question to the kitchen, as if to contingency, and the woman who replies to it to the rank of cook? Certain "masters of truth," in Greece, knew how to hold the kitchen as a place for thinking.

A bit before this note, we recall, the Seminar named the "toponymical inscriptions," the "geographical map" of the "huge body" and the place of what Dupin "expects to find," because he repeats the action of the Minister who himself identifies with the Queen, whose

---

18. Legacy (legs) and rephallization:

   1. "Is it the letter that makes Woman the subject, at once all-powerful and in bondage, so that every hand to which she leaves the letter takes with it that which, by receiving it, she bequeaths (fait lais)? 'Legacy' means what Woman bequeaths by never having had it: hence, truth emerges from the well, but only at waist-level" ("Points" Introduction, pp. 7f.).

   2. "To the grim irony of rephallizing the castrated mother, by hanging, we must now add the irony that relactifies her dry breasts by the broad spattering of the splotch of milk . . . even though the main resentment comes from the absence of the penis on the woman's body" (Bonaparte, II, 572; 475).

   Later we shall return to the question implied here of the "part-object." As for the well, Dupin recalls in "The Murders in the Rue Morgue," after the discovery of the "fearfully mutilated" "body of the mother": "He [Vidocq] impaired his vision by holding the object too close. He might see, perhaps, one or two points with unusual clearness, but in so doing he, necessarily, lost sight of the matter as a whole. Thus there is such a thing as being too profound. Truth is not always in a well."

letter always occupies, properly, the same place: the place of detachment and attachment.

Bonaparte continues, after the note:

> By a further subterfuge, he possesses himself of the compromising
> letter and leaves a similar one in its place. The Queen, who will have
> the original restored to her, is saved.
>
> Let us first note that this letter, the very symbol of the maternal pe-
> nis also "hangs" over the fireplace, in the same manner as the female
> penis, if it existed, would be hung over the cloaca which is here repre-
> sented—as in the foregoing tales—by the frequent symbol of the fire-
> place. We have here, in fact, what is almost an anatomical chart, from
> which not even the clitoris (or brass knob) is omitted. Something very
> different, however, should be hanging from that body! (Bonaparte, p.
> 483).

After this brief allusion to the knob (which the Seminar does not
echo), Bonaparte links this interpretation to Oedipal behavioral and
clinical patterns. The interest in "the author's life" does not simplify
the reading of the text any more than disinterest, under other circumstances, would be enough to certify it. The accent is placed on an "ar-
chaic, pregenital, and phallic" Oedipal struggle for the possession of the
maternal penis, here determined as an incomplete object. Bonaparte is
never tempted to accord to Dupin the position of analyst, not even to
surpass him with a different sort of mastery. His lucidity comes from
the war in which he is engaged, the war that he declares himself at the
end of the story ("'But I had an object apart from these considerations.
You know my political prepossessions. In this matter, I act as a partisan of the lady concerned. For eighteen months the Minister has had
her in his power. She has now him in hers; since, being unaware that
the letter is not in his possession, he will proceed with his exactions as
if it was . . . D—, at Vienna once, did me an evil turn, which I told him,
quite good-humoredly, that I should remember.'") and that has never
ceased to motivate him—nor to place him on the circuit of debt, of the
phallus, of the signifier in its letter, of money, which Bonaparte, unlike
Lacan, does not consider here as neutralizing or "destructive of all signification." She writes:

> Small wonder that Dupin, the embodiment of the son, when speaking
> of his "political prepossessions," should declare himself "a partisan of
> the lady concerned." Finally, in return for a cheque of 50,000 francs,
> leaving to the Prefect of Police the fabulous reward, Dupin restores to

the woman her symbolic letter or missing penis. Thus, once more, we meet the equation gold = penis. The mother gives her son gold in exchange for the penis he restores.

So, too, in "The Gold Bug" . . . (Bonaparte, p. 484f.).

The circle of this restitution traces indeed the "very course" of the Seminar. What then of the movement sketched out there that would identify Dupin's position with that of the analyst? Bonaparte is never tempted by this movement. It is strangely divided or suspended in the Seminar. First, the signs of this identification.

1. The third glance, which involves no delusion, sees the triangle. Dupin, probably, occupies within it a position identical to the position of the Minister—the Minister in the first scene and not in the second, in which the Minister has assumed the place of the powerless Queen. Dupin would thus be the only one not letting himself be plucked like an ostrich. ("The third sees that the first two glances leave what should be hidden exposed to whoever would seize it: the Minister, and finally Dupin. . . . Three partners: the second believing itself invisible because the first has its head stuck in the ground, and all the while letting the third calmly pluck its rear" [SPL, p. 44].) Finally Dupin: at the end Dupin is thus considered to break off his temporary identification with the Minister and to remain the only one who sees everything, thus withdrawing from the circuit.

2. This is supposedly confirmed by a first interpretation of the money that Dupin demands in return for the letter, by "the business of Dupin's remuneration." The problem of indebtedness that it raises is examined by Lacan just after the note about the cook—and a supplementary blank space of a few lines.[19] The "we" refers to the community of analysts. The author of the Seminar seems at first to include himself among them:

Do we not in fact feel concerned with good reason when for Dupin what is perhaps[20] at stake is his withdrawal from the symbolic circuit of the letter—we who become the emissaries of all the purloined letters which at least for a time remain in sufferance with us in the transference. And is it not the responsibility their transference entails which we neutralize by equating it with the signifier most destructive of all signification namely: money (SPL, p. 68).

19. One of six divisional spacings in the French text of the Seminar; they are not indicated in the English-language edition.—Tr.
20. This "perhaps" will be forever suspended.

As the "perhaps" indicates, as these questions without question marks suggest, the "But that's not" opening the following paragraph, the question will not receive a clear answer. The very position of the question, in its form, in its terms, was elaborated to prevent this response: indeed, how could one establish the conceptual rigor of the expression "equal the signifier most destructive of all signification"? Is money destructive of all signification or not? The question is neither a formal one as it has been stated, nor simply one to know who is playing the ostrich by wielding an annihilating plus or minus. If money is not totally destructive of all signification, if it is only "the most destructive," it cannot "equal" a "neutralization." And money is not sufficient for "withdrawal" from the "symbolic circuit of the letter."

3. A confirmation again in the new introduction to the *Écrits* (in the collection "Points"), which we have already quoted:

> This is why the Minister comes to be castrated: castrated, the word for the fact that he continues to believe he has it: that letter which Dupin has been able to spot in its obvious location, dangling between the legs of his high mantelpiece [*Cheminée de haute lisse*]. . . . Wherewith our Dupin shows his success to be equal in his success to that of the psychoanalyst. . . . ("Points," Introduction, p. 8).

Under cover of the indetermination that we have just noted ("perhaps," "the most destructive"), these signs of identification between Dupin and us psychoanalysts will thus become complicated: not merely to refuse Dupin admission into the institution of analysts, which would neutralize "the responsibility [that] transference entails," but to split the we of the psychoanalysts into two Dupins, the fool, the one who remains a participant in the triangle, believing himself the master, and the other one, who sees everything, from the place from which all psychoanalysts are addressed who understand nothing of Dupin, of his "real strategy," i.e., of the author of the Seminar who is capable of returning to the letter of Freud, of finding it where it is found for the purpose of restitution, and by whose efforts both Freud's teaching and Poe's demonstration are meted out: the entire Seminar opens with the project, repeated a hundred times elsewhere, of "taking Freud's discovery seriously" and of organizing "the lesson of this seminar" accordingly, this in opposition to the re-routing from which Freud's letter has suffered in the institution of Lacan's colleagues; and "what Poe's story demonstrates as the result of my efforts" contributes to this return of Freud's text to its proper place. From this position one ridicules the too rapid identification of (all) the other psychoanalysts with Dupin, with a certain Dupin: they do not see that as keeper of the letter he continues to resemble the Minister, is henceforth in the place of the latter and begins like him to become feminine, to identify with the Queen. The author of the Seminar cuts himself off from the community of analysts. "We" means from now on Freud, Poe, one of the Dupins, and "I":

> In which our Dupin demonstrates himself to be equal in his success to that of the psychoanalyst, who cannot function without an unexpected slip of the other. Ordinarily, his message is the only real failure of his treatment: just like Dupin's it must remain concealed, even though it closes the case.
>
> But if I were to explain—since the text that retains here the entry post that it has elsewhere will be judged on this basis—these terms which are always more, they would be understood that much less.
>
> Less understood by the psychoanalysts, by virtue of the fact that these terms are for them as plain to see as the purloined letter, that they see the letter even in themselves, but that on that basis they believe themselves to be its masters, as does Dupin.
>
> They are actually masters only of using my terms without rhyme or reason—by which several of them have made themselves look ridiculous. These are the very ones who assure me that what produces skepticism in the others is actually a rigor to which they know they could never measure up ("Points," Introduction, p. 8).

The ridiculous disciples or heirs thus divert, without rhyme or reason, the master's own terms, and he reminds them that they must not take themselves for masters by identifying with the naive Dupin. And to use the master's terms properly, to bring them back to him, is also to remember the right way, to remember that the master, like Dupin (which one?) is master of the return to Freud of Freud's own letter.[21] To be continued.

21. Freud's letter, itself also in sufferance, awaited restoration. The community of analysts is organized like a general-delivery service keeping sealed the threatening power of a legacy. As we know, the return to the literality of Freud's letter is the motive of the entire course of the Écrits. This is declared throughout, particularly under the title "D'un dessein" (this word will later appear in quotation marks within quotation marks), in an introduction proposed after the fact (1966) to the "Introduction au commentaire de Jean Hyppolite sur la Verneinung de Freud." This foreword on the subject of negation begins by insisting: above all, don't expect a "sanctification" of the letter of Freud, or some sort of "appointment" arranged in advance to meet there: "The two specimens of our seminar that follow move us to communicate to the reader some idea of the intention of our teaching. . . .

There is a double benefit to be gained by identifying Dupin with the psychoanalyst from the beginning: first, the lucidity of the one who can see what no one else can: the place of the thing, between the legs (the author of the Seminar then says we-psychoanalysts, we withdraw from the symbolic circuit and neutralize the scene in which we do not participate); second, the possibility, in creating the impression that Dupin continues to be a participant (and how), and in maintaining the identification of Dupin with the psychoanalyst, of denouncing the naiveté of the community of analysts, of saying: you psychoanalysts, you delude yourselves at the very moment when, like Dupin, you think you are the masters.

Indeed. After the paragraph whose indecisiveness we detected ("perhaps," "the signifier most annihilating," etc.), a cunning game is played, but one which, in order to show the extent to which Dupin's ruse—the greatest in the Oedipal scene—introduces *motivation* into his own trap, goes here so far as to be carried away itself.

This concerns the final pages of the Seminar, set off by a "But that's not all" (SPL, p. 68) and an "Is that all . . ." (SPL, p. 72). From that point onward when the remuneration demanded by Dupin is interpreted as an analytic procedure for the purpose of withdrawing from the circuit by means of the "signifier most destructive of all signification: money," it is difficult to keep track of all the signs of non-neutrality that build up at the end of "The Purloined Letter." Isn't this a shocking paradox?

> "But that's not all. The profit Dupin so nimbly extracts from his exploit,
> if its purpose is to allow him to withdraw his stakes from the game,

---

For to let oneself be guided thus by the letter of Freud to the flash of illumination that it entails, without making an appointment with it in advance; not to recoil before the ultimate residuum of one's enigmatic outset; and even not to release oneself, at the end of the process, from the astonishment by which one entered into it—this is how an established logician brought us the warranty of what formed our quest when, as long as three years ago, we sought to found our authority upon a *literal commentary* of Freud.

This *necessity of reading* is not the vague cultural demand for which it might be taken.

The privilege accorded to the letter of Freud is for us in no way superstitious. It is when one takes it lightly that one brings to it a sort of sanctification entirely compatible with its degradation to merely routine application.

Every text, whether it presents itself as sacred or profane, experiences an increase in literality as it implies properly a greater confrontation with truth: the discovery of Freud indicates the structural reason for this relationship.

Precisely in what the truth that this discovery provides, the truth of the unconscious, owes to the letter of language, to what we call the "signifier" ("D'un dessein," *Écrits*, pp. 363ff.). Cf. also, e.g., "Réponse au commentaire de Jean Hyppolite," *Écrits*, p. 381.

makes all the more paradoxical, even shocking, the partisan attack, the underhanded blow, he suddenly permits himself to launch against the Minister, whose insolent prestige, after all, would seem to have been sufficiently deflated by the trick Dupin has just played on him" (SPL, p. 68).

So that was not all. And we must call attention to Dupin's "explosion of feeling" at the end of the story, his "rage of manifestly feminine nature" at the moment when he says he is settling up with the Minister by signing his blow. Thus he reproduces the so-called process of feminization: he conforms to the (wishes of the) Minister whose place he occupies from that point on when, holding the letter—the place of the signifier—he accommodates himself to the wishes of the Queen. Here, because of the pact, it is no longer possible to distinguish between the place of the King (marked by blindness) and that of the Queen, the place where the letter, in its "proper course" must return circularly. Since the signifier has only one proper place, there is ultimately only one place for the letter, and it is occupied successively by all those who hold the letter. Thus it must be recognized that Dupin, once he has entered the circuit, having identified with the Minister in order to take the letter away from him and return it to its "proper course," cannot leave. He must traverse the circuit in its entirety. The Seminar asks a strange question about this:

> He is thus, in fact, fully participant in the intersubjective triad, and, as such, in the median position previously occupied by the Queen and the Minister. Will he, in showing himself to be above it, reveal to us at the same time the author's intentions?
>
> If he has succeeded in returning the letter to its proper course, it remains for him to make it arrive at its address. And that address is in the place previously occupied by the King, since it is there that it would reenter the order of the Law.
>
> As we have seen, neither the King nor the Police who replaced him in that position were able to read the letter because that *place entailed blindness* (SPL, p. 69).

If Dupin now occupies the "median position," has he not always occupied it? And is there any other position in the circuit? Is it only at this moment in the story, when he holds the letter, that he finds himself in this position? This hypothesis does not take us far enough. Dupin acts from the beginning with an eye to the letter, to getting hold of it for the purpose of giving it to whoever has the right to it (neither the King nor the Queen but the Law that binds them) and thus being preferable to his enemy(-brother), his younger or twin brother (Atreus/ Thyestes), the Minister, who pursues fundamentally the same object, with the same acts. Thus if he is in a "median position," the distinction made above among the three glances is no longer pertinent. There are only ostriches, no one escapes being plucked, and the more one is the master, the more one presents one's rear. This is thus the case of whoever identifies with Dupin.

On the subject of Dupin, as we were saying, a strange question: "Will he, in showing himself to be above it, reveal to us at the same time the author's intentions?"

This is not the only allusion to the "author's intentions" (SPL, p. 41). Its form implies that the author, in his intention, is in a situation of general mastery, his *superiority* with respect to the triangles he stages (supposing that he stages only triangles) being representable by the superiority of the actor: Dupin. Let us abandon this implication: a whole conception of "literature."

Does Dupin demonstrate himself to be superior? The Seminar, proceeding from what Dupin sees where he expects to find it, repeating the operation of the restoration of the letter, cannot reply "no." Nor can it reply "yes," for Dupin, too, is an ostrich. Thus the "true" position of Dupin will be left in the obscurity of a non-revelation or in the suspense of a hypothesis, without this hampering, however, the "decipher[ing of] Dupin's real strategy" (here there is no more obscurity or hypothesis). This is the unrevealed: "Wherewith our Dupin shows his success to be equal in his success to that of the psychoanalyst, who cannot function without an unexpected slip of the other. Ordinarily his message is the only real failure of his treatment: just like Dupin's, it must remain concealed, even though it closes the case" ("Points," Introduction, p. 8).

This is the hypothesis in suspension: "But if [the Minister] is truly the gambler we are told he is, he will consult his cards a final time before laying them down and, upon reading his hand, will leave the table in time to avoid disgrace" (SPL, p. 72). Does he do so? Nothing in the Seminar says so, although it sojourns in this territory long enough to make sure, despite the unrevealed or the hypothesis, that it has in its possession the cipher of the letter, Dupin's real strategy, and the true meaning of the purloined letter. The "yes" is here "doubtless." Just as Dupin, to whom the narrator leaves the last word at the end of the story, seems sure to have won. The end of the Seminar:

. . . [he] will leave the table in time to avoid disgrace.

Is that all, and shall we believe we have deciphered Dupin's real strategy above and beyond the imaginary tricks with which he was obliged to deceive us? Yes, doubtless, for if "any point requiring reflection," as Dupin states at the start, is "examined to best purpose in the dark," we may now easily read its solution in broad daylight. It was already implicit and easy to derive from the title of our tale, according to the very formula we have long submitted to your discretion: in which the sender, we tell you, receives from the receiver his own message in reverse form. Thus it is that what the "purloined letter," nay, the "letter in sufferance" means is that a letter always arrives at its destination (SPL, p. 72). (These are the last words of the Seminar).

FIRST SECOND: THE TRUTH (OUT) OF THE LETTER FROM FREUD'S HAND

In seeing what Dupin sees (unseen by the others), even what Dupin himself does not see or, double as he is (in and out of circulation, being both recipient and non-player),[22] only half sees (like all the others, finally), the Seminar is enunciated from the place where everything is seen, "easily," "in broad daylight."

Somewhat, like Dupin, at the moment when, not taking into account his blindness as "recipient," he was described as "the third [which] sees that the first two glances . . . etc." And like Dupin, the Seminar delivers the letter at (to) its destination after having recognized its place and its course, its law and its destiny, namely destination (as such): the arrival at (one's) destination.

But Dupin, the lucid one, could only be so by entering into the circuit so far as to occupy in it successively all the positions, including, unwittingly, those of the King and of the Police. Like all the others, whom he has perfectly doubled, he is put in motion by the desire of the Queen and by the pact contracted therein. And for him "proving oneself superior," even in relation to all the other masters, his rivals, twins, brothers or colleagues [confrères] (Atreus/Thyestes), meant repeating the trick without being able to look back. Which did not necessarily deprive him of pleasure at the time when somebody else keeps the pen in hand.

---

22. "Recipient" translates "partie prenante," designating the party who receives a pecuniary benefit. Besides keeping the legal connotation of the term, "recipient" with its Latin etymology (it is a component of capio-ere, to take) stresses also the active aspect implied here.—Ed.

Hence Dupin repeats. By dint of being able to "read easily now its solution in broad daylight," the author of the Seminar, let us not forget, stages a quarrel with his colleagues, ill keepers, and unfaithful, of Freud's legacy. He wants at least, with the passional explosion whose signs we have spotted, to re-discover the direction: to rectify, to redress, to put back on the right track, "to correct a deviation too manifest not to avow itself as such at all of its turns" (*"D'un dessein,"* in *Écrits*, p. 366). He reproaches his male colleagues [*confrères*] but also his female colleagues [*consœurs*] who seem to have appropriated his terms ("like Dupin," see above), to have diverted them, his own terms, but he too in order to return them, to render them unto Freud the restitution of whose true teaching, the right doctrine, is here in question.[23] Just as Dupin, in calling himself "the lady's partisan," obliges the Queen and mimics the contract which binds her to the King, so there is supposed to be something like a pact between Freud—who, having died too soon to know anything, like the King, about the outcome—and the author (the place of the author) of the Seminar. But is a King bound by a pact? Is a dead person? The question must wait.

The most remarkable attack, let us say the most insidious "blow below the belt," "the rage of a manifestly feminine nature," is unleashed against him or her among his colleagues, Bonaparte, who, for a long time, believed him [her] self to be in France the most authorized depositary, the legatee of Freud's authority, maintaining with him a correspondence, ties of personal confidence, even representing him in France as a sort of minister of whose both betrayal and blindness the author of the seminar is aware. This minister has even wanted, in his [her] book, to lay hands[24] on "The Purloined Letter." First on Freud's di-

---

23. More literally, "the Freudian experience along its authentic lines" ("The Insistence of the Letter in the Unconscious," in *Structuralism*, ed. Ehrmann, *Yale French Studies*, N.° 36–37, 1966, p. 132) [*"dans sa ligne authentique"* (*Écrits*, p. 523)].

24. *Question de main:* as the self-styling detainer of the Freudian message, Bonaparte was destined to receive blows. In an insistent, repetitive, automatic manner. The footnote coming down hard on the cooking-woman [*la cuisinière*] where one had *simply* scorned the kitchen was added, in the *Écrits*, some ten years after the first publications of the Seminar in *La psychanalyse*. But from Rome already the speech of that name, five years before, hurls at Bonaparte a major accusation: second hand! Her texts have not got Freud's letter first hand. Such and such is "little alert" to the Freudian theory "since he approaches it through the work of Marie Bonaparte, which he quotes incessantly as an equivalent of the Freudian text and with nothing to inform the reader of this fact, relying perhaps, not without reason, on the latter's good taste not to confuse them, but proving thereby no less that he sees nothing of the true level of the second hand" (*Écrits*, p. 247). And as it is necessary to keep to oneself the first and not to generalize too much

verted letter. And she has used the front of her book on Poe, an affidavit signed by Freud, a kind of letter which seals at the same time the pact and the betrayal (depending on the place), putting the father of psycho-analysis *simultaneously* in the place of the King, of the Queen (to whom one must restitute "her" letter in order to reconstitute the pact, to stamp out the betrayal and "correct the deviation") and of the mysterious signatory of the purloined letter, the Queen's friend or fellow conspirator. As it will be said later of the truth (*causa sui* is to be at once cause and effect), Freud is the only one (and on account of his death, since he also occupies the place of the dead [king]) to contract with none but himself.

This affidavit, signed by Freud's hand, must be read here. For the fun of it, but also in order to gauge how much the King will have seen that, by removing the pen from the last handwritten document, he has mobilized since his death, while awaiting for the restitution if not for the restoration. In a position of having died too soon, *a priori*, he will have never prefaced the Seminar which has taken this task upon itself several times over. But one can dream of what a foreword by Freud would have looked like. In order to encourage daydreaming, here is the foreword which he signs, in his very own hand, solely for Bonaparte herself (from the *Pretexts* on, the theory of factors [*facteurs*] is there only to be continued):

> In this book my friend and pupil, Marie Bonaparte, has shone the light of psycho-analysis on the life and work of a great writer with pathological trends.
>
> Thanks to her interpretative effort, we now realize how many of the characteristics of Poe's works were conditioned by his personality, and can see how that personality derived from intense emotional fixations and painful infantile experiences. Investigations such as this do not claim to explain creative genius, but they do reveal the factors which awaken it and the sort of subject matter it is destined to choose. Few tasks are as appealing as enquiry into the laws that govern the psyche of exceptionally endowed individuals. Sigm. Freud (Bonaparte, p. XI.)

---

about the second, there are two "levels," a good and a bad second hand. The "good" one, we shall see, takes the letter of the Freudian text as "a text vehicle of a word [speech, *parole*], inasmuch as it constitutes a new emergence of the truth," it knows "to treat it as true word," "to experience it in its authenticity" of "a full word [*parole pleine*]" (*Écrits*, p. 381): it is Freud's text which is in question. And the obstinacy to keep off Bonaparte's "second hand" could be read a few lines before the chapter to the glory of the "full word."

This seal is handed down first in Bonaparte's translation, let it be noted, not to cast doubt on its exactitude, but to concede that it does not appear in an authenticity of an absolute first hand.

At the very moment he cuts short the identification with the Dupin who is the recipient in order to keep only the other one; when he deciphers "the true strategy" of this latter at the instant of his getting up from the table; when "yes, no doubt," he exhibits in broad daylight the true meaning [*vouloir-dire*] of "the purloined letter," it is at that very moment that the analyst (which one? the other one) most resembles Dupin (which one? the other one) when the chain of identifications has sent him in the opposite direction, through the whole circus, has made him repeat automatically, compulsively, the minister, the Queen, the King (the Police). As each one occupies, at one time or another, the King's place, there are at least four kings (to be continued) in the game.

What then of the truth according to Lacan? Is there *a* Lacanian doctrine, a Lacanian *doctrine* of the truth? Two reasons might make this seem doubtful. The first is general and has to do with the terms of the question. That a purely homogeneous systematics is an impossibility of structure has appeared to us elsewhere. The second reason has to do with the mobility of the discourse which interests us here. In the publications of a later date than the *Écrits*, in the indications they give of an ongoing oral teaching, one perceives a certain retreat muting the incantation of the *aletheia*, the *logos* (live) speech, the word, etc. An even more noticeable effacing of the connotations, if not of the post-War Existentialist concepts. Nonetheless a certain type of statement, the truth, has given itself out, has multiplied itself, at a precise moment, in a systematic form. And it involved all the features necessary for that effect. As the Seminar belongs to this system (this is at least my hypothesis), as well as a certain number of other essays to which I shall refer (so as not in turn to engulf all of the *Écrits* in the Seminar), it must be disengaged if one is to understand the reading of "The Purloined Letter." This can and must be done even if, after 1966, in a transformed theoretical field, the Lacanian discourse on truth, on text or on literature has lent itself to a certain number of alterations in size or of decisive retouchings, which is not even certain.[25] Its chronological and the-

25. The doctrine of the truth as cause (*Ursache*), as well as the expression "truth effects," can accord with the system in which we are going to be interested. Truth effects are the effects of the truth and as "La direction de la cure" (where the question is "to direct the subject towards the full word," in any case to leave him "free to try his hand at it" (*Écrits*, p. 641)) has already said, "the point is the truth, the only one, the truth about

oretical ordering would still remain rather suspect, given the remote time-lag of publication.

Whatever the case after 1965–1966, all the texts situated, more accurately, published, between 1953 (the so-called Rome Speech) and 1960 seem to belong to the same system of the truth. That is, quantitatively, almost the totality of the *Écrits*, including, therefore, the Seminar (1955–1957); "works of the early Lacan," might say future academics in a hurry to separate what cannot stand partition.

We are not going to expose this system of the truth, the condition of a logic of the signifier. It consists precisely of that which is non-exposable in exposition. We shall simply attempt to recognize those of its features which are pertinent to the Seminar, to its possibility and to its limits.

It is first of all a question of "emphasis," the authentic excellence of talking, of speech, of the word: of the *logos* as *phonè*. One must *explain* this emphasis, account for its necessary link to a theory of the signifier, of the letter and of the truth. It is necessary to explain why the author of "The Insistence of the Letter in the Unconscious" and of "The Seminar on 'The Purloined Letter' " incessantly subordinates writing, the letter and the text. Even when he repeats Freud on rebus, hieroglyphs, engravings, etc., he always resorts ultimately to a writing sublated [*relevée, aufgehoben*] by the voice. This would be easy to show. One example among many: "A writing [*écriture*], like dream itself, may be figurative, (yet) it is always like language symbolically articulated, that is (it is) just like, phonemic, and phonetic in fact, as soon as it is read[able]" ("Situation de la psychanalyse en 1956," *Écrits*, p. 470). This fact is a fact only within the boundaries of the so-called phonetic systems of writing. At the most, for there are non-phonetic elements in such systems of writing. As to the non-phonetic field of writing, its factual enormity no longer needs demonstration. But this does not matter much. What matters here, and even more than the relation of fact to right, is the implied equivalence ("that is") between the symbolic articulation and *the phoneticity*. The symbolic passes through the voice, and the law of the signifier unfolds only in vocalizable letters. Why? And what relation does this phonematism (which does not go back to Freud and hence is lost in the attempt to return to Freud) entertain with a certain truth value?

---

the effects of the truth" (p. 640). The circulation (traffic; *circulation*) will always be that of the truth: towards the truth. Cause and effect of the circle, *causa sui*, proper course and destiny of the letter.

Both scopes [*portées*] of the truth value, as we have seen, are present in the Seminar: 1. *Adequation,* in the circular return and the proper course, from the beginning to the end, from the place of the detachment of the signifier to the place of its re-attachment. This circuit of ade-quation guards and regards the circuit of the pact, of the contract, of the pledged faith. It restores it against the threat and as the symbolic order. And it takes shape itself at the moment the guarding of the phallus is entrusted as the guarding *of* the lack. By the King to the Queen, but from there on in a play of alternation without end. 2. *Veiling/unveiling* as the structure of lack: castration, the *proper* place of the signifier, origin and destination of the letter, shows nothing while unveiling. It thus veils itself while unveiling. But this truth operation has a proper place: the contours *being*—the place of the *manque à être* from which the signifier is detached for its literal circuit. These two truth values prop each other up [*s'étaient*].[26] They are indissociable. They require speech or the phonetization of the letter as soon as the phallus must be *kept* [*gardé*], must return to its point of departure, must not be disseminated on the way. Now for the signifier to be kept [*pour que le signifiant se garde*] in its letter and thus make a (safe) return, it is necessary that in its letter it should suffer no "partition," that it should be impossible to say some letter, only a letter, letters, the letter (SPL, pp. 53–54). Were the signifier divisible it might always be lost on the way. It is against this possible loss that is erected the statement of the "materiality of the signifier," that is to say of its indivisible singularity. *This "material-ity," deduced from an indivisibility which is not found anywhere, cor-responds in fact to an idealization.* Only the ideality of a letter resists destructive division. "Cut a letter in small pieces, and it remains the letter it is" (SPL, p. 53), as this may not be said of empirical material-ity, an ideality (intangibility of a self-identity travelling without alter-ation) must be implied therein. It alone permits the singularity of the letter to preserve itself [*se garder*]. If this ideality is not the meaning-content [*contenu de sens*], it must be either a certain ideality of the sig-nifier (the identifiable [aspect] of its form inasmuch as it is distinct from its empirical events and re-editions) or the point of stability [*point de capiton*] which pins the signifier onto the signified. The latter hypoth-esis conforms better to the system. This system is in fact that of the

26. "Prop up" represents an attempt to translate the French "s'étaient." The verb echoes on the Freudian notion of anaclisis [*étayage*]. See J. Laplanche and J. B. Pontalis, *The Language of Psycho-Analysis,* intro. Daniel Lagache and trans. D. Nicolson-Smith (London: The Hogarth Press and the Institute of Psycho-Analysis, 1973), p. 52.

ideality of the signifier. The idealism which resides in it is not a theoretical position of the analyst, it is a structure-effect [*effet structurel*]
of *signification* in general, whatever transformations or adjustments
are practiced on the space of *semiosis*. It is understandable that Lacan
finds this "materiality" "unique": he retains only its ideality. He considers the letter only at the point where, determined (whatever he says
about it) by its meaning-content, by the ideality of the message which
it "vehiculates," by the (spoken) word [*parole*] which, in its meaning,
remains out of the reach of partition, it can circulate, intact, from its
place of detachment to the place of its re-attachment, that is to say, to
(at) the same place. In fact, this letter does not elude only partition, it
eludes movement, it does not change place.

This presupposes, besides a phonematic limitation of the letter, an
interpretation of the *phonè* which spares it divisibility as well. The latter provokes this of itself, is made so as to lend itself thereto: it has the
phenomenal characters of spontaneity, of presence unto itself, of the
circular return to itself. The *phonè* keeps all the better for the belief
that it may be kept without external accessory, neither paper nor envelope: it is, so it tells us, always available, wherever it is. That is why
it is believed to remain longer than writings (*écrits*). "May it but please
heaven that writings remain, as is rather the case with spoken words"
(SPL, p. 56). It would be rather different were one to become more attentive to writing within the voice, namely *avant la lettre*.

The same problem indeed recurs concerning the voice or concerning what can be called, in order to preserve the concept's Lacanian definition, its letter (the indivisible materiality or locality of the signifier). This vocal "letter" would then be also indivisible, always
identical to itself no matter how its body is dismembered. It can be guaranteed of this integrity only through its link to the ideality of meaning
within the unity of the spoken word.

We are always led back, step by step, to this contract of contracts
which guarantees the unity of the signifier to the signified through all
the points of stability, thanks to the "presence" (see below) of the *same*
signifier (the phallus), of the "signifier of signifiers" underneath all the
signified-effects [*effets de signifié*]. This transcendental signifier is
therefore also the signifier of all signifieds and it is the one which finds
protection in the indivisibility of the letter (graphic or oral). Protection
from this threat, but also from that disseminating power which, in *De
la grammatologie*, I have proposed to call "Writing before the Letter"
(*"L'écriture avant la lettre,"* title of the first part): the privilege of the

"full word" [*la "parole pleine"*] is there questioned (cf. for example p. 17 ff.). The insistence of the Lacanian letter is the sublation of writing in the system of speech.

"The drama" of the purloined letter begins at the moment—which is not a moment—in which the letter *is presented*. At the motion of the minister who acts in order to preserve the letter (he might have torn it to pieces, and it then would indeed have been an ideality which would have remained available [*disponible*] and, for a while,[27] effective), of course, but even before that, when the Queen wants to keep the letter or to recover it: as a double of the pact which binds her to the King, a threatening double but one which as long as it is in her keeping cannot betray the "pledged faith" (*"foi jurée"*). The Queen wants to be able to play both contracts. This analysis cannot be pursued here; it is to be read elsewhere.

What matters here is that what is indestructible in the letter resides in that which elevates it toward the ideality of a meaning. Little as we know of the content of the letter, it must be related to the original contract which it indicates and subverts at the same time. And this knowledge, this memory, this retention (conscious or unconscious) makes up its property and assures its proper course towards its proper place. As the ultimate content of the letter is that of a pact binding two "uniquenesses," it implies an irreplaceability, it excludes, as threat and unmasterable anxiety, all simulacra of the double. The impact of life, presence of the word (*parole*), guarantees, in the last instance, the indestructible and unforgettable uniqueness of the letter, the taking-place of a signifier which does not get lost, does not ever go astray. The subject is very divided, but the phallus is never shared [*ne se partage jamais*]. Dismemberment is an accident which does not concern it. At least according to the insurance built up by the symbolic. And through a discourse on the assumption of castration which erects an ideal philosophy against dismemberment.[28]

27. Only for a while: till the moment when, incapable of returning a "material," divisible, effectively "unique" letter which is subject to partition, he would have had to let go of the hold which only a destructible document could assure him on (of) the Queen.

28. What we are analyzing here is supposed to be the most rigorous philosophy of psychoanalysis today, more precisely the most rigorous Freudian philosophy, undoubtedly more rigorous than Freud's and more strictly controlled in its exchanges with the history of philosophy.

It would be hard to exaggerate here the scope of this proposition on the indivisibility of the letter, or rather in its identity to itself inaccessible to dismemberment ("Tear a letter into little pieces, it remains the letter that it is"), as well as on the so-called materi-

Such would be, in its principle, the articulation of this logic of the signifier on a phonocentric interpretation of the letter. From here on the two values of the truth (adequation and process of veiling) can no longer be dissociated from the word, from present, living, authentic speech. The final word is that there is, when all is said, at the origin or at the end (proper course, circular destination), a word which is not feigned, a meaning [*vouloir-dire*] which, through all the imaginable fictional complications, does not mislead or else *truly* misleads, still teaching us the truth of decoy [*leurre*]. At this point the truth permits the analyst to treat the fictional characters as real people, and to resolve at the depth of the Heideggerian meditation on the truth, this problem of the literary text where Freud (more naively but more certainly than Heidegger and Lacan) would sometimes admit being at a loss. And it is still a literature with characters which is in question. Let us first quote the Seminar. A suspicion has just been aroused in the Seminar that the author's purpose was perhaps not to state, as Baudelaire calls it, *le vrai.* Which does not always mean, by the same token, that his purpose is to have fun. Here:

No doubt Poe is having a good time. . . .

But a suspicion occurs to us: might not this parade of erudition be destined to reveal to us the key words of our drama? Is not the magician repeating his trick before our eyes, without deceiving us this time about divulging his secret, but pressing his wager to the point of really explaining it to us without our seeing a thing. *That* would be the summit of the illusionist's art: through one of his fictive creations to *truly delude* us.

And is it not such effects which justify our referring, without malice, to a number of imaginary heroes as real characters?

As well, when we are open to hearing the way in which Martin Heidegger discloses to us in the word ἀληθής the play of the truth, we rediscover a secret to which truth has always initiated her lovers, and through which they learn that it is in hiding that she offers herself to them *most truly*" (SPL, pp. 50–51).

The *effets d'abyme* are here severely controlled, [as] a scientifically irreproachable precaution: it is science itself, at least ideal science and

---

ality of the signifier (the letter) [a materiality which is] intolerant to partition. A torn-up letter may be purely and simply destroyed, it happens (and if it is considered that the unconscious effect called here *letter* is never lost, that repression keeps everything and never allows any lowering of insistence, then this hypothesis—nothing is ever lost or mislaid—must be granted too with *Beyond the Pleasure Principle*), or produce other letters, whether the question is of characters or of messages.

even the truth of the science of the truth. From the statements which I have just quoted it should not be induced that truth is a fiction but that through fiction truth properly asserts itself (i.e. manifestation). *Dichtung* (*le dit poétique* or fiction, the term used by Goethe and Freud: as in Heidegger, it is literary fiction as *Dichtung* which is in question) is the manifestation of the truth, its being-confirmed (*être avéré*):

> There is so little opposition between this *Dichtung* and the *Wahrheit* in its nakedness, that the fact of poetic operation should rather make us stop at this feature which is forgotten in every truth, which is that it is confirmed [*s'avère*] in a structure of fiction (*Écrits*, pp. 741–2).

Truth commands the fictional substance of its manifestation which allows it to be or become what it is, to be confirmed. It commands this substance from its origin or from its telos, which ultimately subordinates this concept of literary fiction to a rather classical interpretation of *mimesis:* [as] detour towards the truth, more truth in fictive representation than in reality, increased faithfulness, "superior realism." The previous quotation called for a note:

> The propriety of this reminder in our subject would be sufficiently confirmed if that were necessary by one of these numerous unpublished texts which Delay's work brings to us shedding upon them the most appropriate light. Here, from the *Unpublished Diary* so-called of la Brévine, where Gide stayed during October 1894 (note on p. 667 of his volume II).
> The novel will prove that it can paint something other than reality— emotion or thinking directly; the novel will show to what extent it can be composed—that is to say a work of art. It will show that it may be a work of art, completely composed, of a realism not of little facts and contingent, but superior.

Follows a reference to the mathematical triangle, then:

> It is necessary that in their very relation each part of a work should prove the truth of each other part, there is no need of another proof. Nothing so irritating as the testimony given by Monsieur de Goncourt for everything he advances—he saw! he heard! as if the proof by the real were necessary.

Lacan concludes: "Need it be said that no poet ever thought otherwise . . . but that no one has followed through on this thought." And it is confirmed in the same article that it is a "person" who "brings" the "truth of fiction." This person is the "seducer" of the "young boy" (*Écrits*, p. 753).

Once the distinction has been made, as the whole philosophical tradition does, between truth and reality, it is self-evident that the truth "is confirmed in a structure of fiction."[29] Lacan insists much on the opposition truth/reality which he advances as a paradox. This opposition, as orthodox as can be, facilitates the passage of truth through fiction: common sense will always have made the distinction between reality and fiction.

But once again, why should the (spoken) word be the privileged entity of this truth confirmed *as* fiction, in the mode or in the structure of fiction, of this verified fiction, of what Gide calls "superior realism"?

As soon as truth is determined as adequation (to an original contract: the acquittal of a debt) and as unveiling (of the lack which gives rise to the contracting of the contract in order to reappropriate symbolically what has been detached), the master value is indeed that of propriation, hence of proximity, presence and preserving: the very same provided by the idealizing effect of speech. If this demonstration is granted it will not be surprising to find it confirmed. Were it not so, how would one explain this massive complication, in Lacan's discourse, between the truth, the word [*parole*], the present, full and authentic word? If it is taken into consideration one understands better: 1. that fiction for Lacan should be numbed with truth inasmuch as it is spoken and hence as it is non-real. 2. that this should lead to coping no longer, in the text, with whatever remains irreducible to the word [*parole*], to speech [*au dit*] and to meaning [*vouloir-dire*]: the irreducible ill-keeping [or inadvertence, *mé-garde*], the theft without return, the destructibility, the divisibility, the failure [*manque*] to reach destination (definitively rebellious to the destination of failure [or lack, *manque*]: unverifiable non-truth).

When Lacan recalls "this passion to unveil which has one object: the truth,"[30] and that the analyst "remains above all the master of the

29. For example: "Thus it is from elsewhere than the Reality which it concerns that the Truth draws its guarantee: it is from the Word. As it is from the latter that it receives this mark which institutes it in a structure of fiction.

The primal word [*le dit premier*] decrees, legislates, aphorizes, is oracle, it confers upon the reality of the other its obscure reality" (*Écrits*, p. 808).

30. "You have heard me, in order to locate the inquiry, refer with dilection to Descartes and to Hegel. It is somewhat in vogue these days 'to go beyond' the classical philosophers. I might just as well have started from the admirable dialogue with Par-

truth," it is always in order to link the truth to the power of the word [*parole*]. And of communication as contract (pledged faith) between two presents. Even if communication does not communicate anything, it communicates (itself): and even better, in this case, as communication, that is as truth. For example: "Even if it communicates nothing, the discourse represents the existence of communication; even if it denies the obvious, it affirms that the Word constitutes the Truth; even if it is destined to deceive, here the discourse speculates on faith in testimony."[31]

---

menides. For one cannot 'go beyond' Socrates, nor Descartes, nor Marx, nor Freud, inasmuch as they conducted their inquiry with this passion to unveil which has one object: the truth.

As wrote one of those princes of the word, and under whose fingers seem to glide of themselves the threads of the mask of the Ego, I have named Max Jacob, poet, saint and novelist, yes, as he wrote in his *Cornet à dés,* if I am not mistaken: the true is always new" ("Propos sur la causalité psychique," in *Écrits,* p. 193). It always is true. How can we not agree?

31. Jacques Lacan, *The Language of the Self: The Function of Language in Psychoanalysis,* trans. and ed. Anthony Wilden (Baltimore: Johns Hopkins, 1968), p. 13. Hereafter cited as *The Language of the Self* followed by the page number. The "true word" is the word authenticated by the other in the given or pledged faith. The other renders it adequate to itself—and no longer to the object—by returning the message in an inverted form, by making it true, by identifying from then on the subject with himself, by "announcing that he is the same." Adequation—as authentification—proceeds through intersubjectivity. The word "is therefore an act, and as such, presupposing a subject. But it is not enough to say that, in this act, the subject presupposes another subject, for much rather he founds himself in it as being the other, but in this paradoxical unity of both the one and the other, by means of which, as has been shown above, the one relies on the other in order to become identical to himself.

It may then be said that the word [*la parole*] manifests itself as a communication in which not only the subject, because expecting of the other that he render his message true, will utter it in an inverted form, but in which this message transforms him by anouncing that he is the same. As it appears in any given word, where the declarations 'you are my wife,' or 'you are my master' mean 'I am your husband,' 'I am your disciple.'

The word then appears all the more truly a word as its truth is less founded in what is called adequation to the thing: the true word is thus paradoxically opposed to true discourse, their truth being distinguished in this, that the former constitutes the recognition by subjects of their beings in that they are interested in it, while the latter is constituted by the cognition of the real, inasmuch as it is seen by the subject in objects. But each one of the truths here distinguished is altered by crossing the other in its way" ("Variantes de la cure-type," in *Écrits,* p. 352). In this crossing, the "true word" appears always as truer than "true discourse" which always presupposes its order, that of the intersubjective contract, of symbolic exchange and hence of debt. "But the true word, upon questioning the true discourse about what it signifies, will find therein that signification always refers to signification, no thing being capable of being shown except by a sign, and henceforth will make it appear as destined to error" (*ibid.,* p. 352). The ulti-

What is neither true nor false is reality. But as soon as there is speech, one is in the order of the unveiling of the truth as of its contract of property: presence, speech and testimony:

> The ambiguity of the hysterical revelation of the past does not depend so much on the vacillation of its content between the Imaginary and the Real, for it locates itself in both. Nor is it exactly error or falsehood. The point is that it presents us with the birth of Truth in the Word, and thereby brings us up against the reality of what is neither true nor false. At any rate, that is the most disturbing aspect of the problem.
>
> For the Truth of this revelation lies in the present Word which testifies to it in contemporary reality and which grounds it in the name of that reality. Yet in that reality, it is only the Word which bears witness to that portion of the powers of the past which has been thrust aside at each crossroads where the event has made its choice (*The Language of the Self*).

This passage has been closely preceded by a reference to Heidegger, and that is not surprising; it carries the *Dasein* back to the subject, and that is more surprising.

From the moment that the "present word" "testifies" to "the truth of this revelation" beyond true and false, beyond what is truthful or

---

mate adequation of the truth as true word therefore has the form of acquittal, "singular adequation" "which finds its answer in the symbolic debt of which the subject is responsible as subject of the word" (p. 434). These are the last words of *"La chose freudienne."* The adequation to the thing (true discourse) therefore has its foundation in the adequation of the word to itself (true word) so to the thing itself: that is to say *the Freudian thing to itself:* "The thing speaks of itself" (p. 403) and it says "I, the truth, am speaking." The thing is the truth: as cause, of itself and of the things of which the true discourse speaks. These propositions are less new, particularly in relation to the "Rome Speech," to "Variantes de la cure-type" and to the texts of the same period, than their author says: "It is to reintroduce through a totally different access the incidence of the truth as cause and to force a revision of the process of causality. Hence the first stage would seem to recognize what the heterogeneity of this incidence would have in it that's inherent. [This paragraph remakes, antedates, a line of thought which we have opened since (1966)" (p. 416).]

The "true word" (adequate to itself, conforming to its essence, destined to acquit itself of a debt which in the last instance binds it only to itself) permits the contract which permits the subject to "become identical to itself." It reconstitutes then the ground of Cartesian certitude: the transformation of the truth into certitude, subjectivization (determination of the Being [*l'être*] of being [*l'étant*] into subject), intersubjectivization (the chain Descartes-Hegel-Husserl). This chain catches incessantly, in the *Écrits*, Heideggerian motions which give themselves out as being, in all rigor, allergic to it, and as having "destructive" effects on it. Let us abandon for the moment this type of questions— the most decisive ones—which are never articulated in Lacan's discourse.

mendacious in such and such a statement or such and such a symptom in their relation to such and such a content, the values of adequation or of unveiling no longer even have to await their verification or their accomplishment from the outside of any object. They are intrinsically self-guaranteed. What matters is not what is communicated, be it true or false, but "the existence of communication," the present revelation made therein of the word testifying to the truth. Hence the necessary relay via the values of authenticity, of plenitude, of property, etc. The truth, that which must be recovered, is therefore not an object beyond the subject, the adequation of the word to an object,[32] but the adequation of the full word to itself, its own authenticity, the conformity of its act to its original essence. And the telos of this *Eigentlichkeit*, the proper focus of this authenticity shows the "authentic way" of analysis (*The Language of the Self*, p. 15), of didactic analysis in particular. "But what in fact was this appeal from the subject beyond the void of his speech? It was an appeal to Truth in its ultimate nature, through which other appeals resulting from humbler needs will find faltering expression. But first and foremost it was the appeal of the void . . ." (*The Language of the Self*, p. 9).

From this very appeal of emptiness towards the accomplishment of the full word, towards its "realization" through the assumption of desire (of castration), such is then the ideal process of analysis:

> I have tackled the function of the Word in analysis from its least rewarding angle, that of the empty Word, where the subject seems to be talking in vain about someone who, even if he were his spitting image, can never become one with the assumption of his desire. . . . If we now

---

32. This responsibility is defined soon after and since the exchange of the "full word" with Freud, in its "true educational [*formatrice*] value": "For in question is nothing less than its (his) adequation to (at) the level of man where he gets hold of it (himself), whatever he may think of it (himself)—at which point he is called upon to respond to him, whatever he may want—and of which he assumes, although he has it, the responsibility" (*Écrits*, p. 382).

Concerning the "level of man" the place is lacking to verify the essential link, in this system, of metaphysics (some of whose typical features we are tracing here) and of humanism. This link is more visible, if not better seen, in the mass of statements on "animality," on the distinction between animal language and human language, etc. This discourse on the animal (in general) no doubt coheres with all the categories and all the oppositions, bi- or tripartitions of the system. It does, nonetheless, condense for it the greatest obscurity. The treatment of animality, as of everything which is *submitted* by a hierarchical opposition, has always revealed, in the history of (humanist and phallogocentric) metaphysics the obscurantist resistance. Its interest is evidently capital.

turn to the other extreme of the psychoanalytic experience—if we look into its history, into its casuistry, into the process of the cure—we shall discover that to the analysis of the *hic et nunc* is to be opposed the value of anamnesis as the index and as the source of the progress of the therapy; that to obsessional intrasubjectivity is to be opposed hysterical intersubjectivity; and that to the analysis of resistance is to be opposed symbolic interpretation. Here it is that the realization of the full Word begins" (*The Language of the Self*, pp. 15–16).

The word here is not full of something which would be, beyond itself, its object: but from that very moment, the more so and the better, (full) of itself, of its presence, of its essence. This presence, as in the contract and the pledged faith, requires irreplaceable property, inalienable uniqueness, living authenticity, all those values whose system we have signaled elsewhere. The double, the repetition, the recording [*enregistrement*], the mimeme in general are excluded therefrom, with all the graphemic structure involved in them, through direct interlocution, and as inauthentic alienation. For example: "But precisely because it comes to him through an alienated form, even a retransmission of his own recorded discourse, be it from the mouth of his own doctor, it cannot have the same effects as psychoanalytic interlocution" (*The Language of the Self*, p. 20).

The disqualification of recording or of repetition in the name of the act of the living and present word folds itself to a well-known pattern. The system of the "true word," of the "word in action" (*Écrits*, p. 353) cannot do without condemning, as has been done from Plato to a certain Freud, the simulacrum and the hypomnesis: in the name of the truth, of that which links *mneme, anamnesis, aletheia*. Etc.

Only a word, with its effects of presence in act [*en acte*] and of authentic life, may keep the "pledged faith" which binds to the desire of the other. If "the phallus is the privileged signifier of this mark where the share of the logos [*la part du logos*] is conjoined to the advent of desire" ("La signification du phallus," *Écrits*, p. 692), the privileged locus of this privileged signifier, its letter then, is the voice: the spokesman [*porte-parole*]. It alone admits, as soon as the point of stability of the signified assures it its repeatable identity, the ideality or the idealization power necessary to safeguard (this is at any rate what it means) the indivisible, unique, living, non-mutilable integrity of the phallus, of the privileged signifier to which it gives rise. The *transcendental* position of the phallus (in the chain of signifiers to which it at once belongs and makes possible)[33] would thus have its proper locus—in Lacanian terms its letter exempt from any partition—in the phonemic structure of language. No protestation against metalanguage is opposed to this phallogocentristic transcendentalism. Especially if in metalanguage language focuses on the voice, that is to say on the ideal locus of the phallus. Had the phallus been per (mal)chance divisible or reduced to

33. This is the strict definition of the *transcendental position:* the privilege of a term within a series of terms which it makes possible and which presupposes it. In this manner a category is said to be transcendental (transcategorial) when it "transcends any genus" [*transcendit omne genus*] that is the list of categories of which however it is a part while accounting for it. It is therefore also the role of the hole and the lack in their determinable outline: "the phallus of his mother, that is for that eminent failure-to-be the privileged signifier of which Freud has revealed" ("The Insistence of the Letter," in *Structuralism,* p. 131). The transcendental eminence of this privilege is then put in perspective in its height, from the horrified viewpoint of the child—more precisely of the little boy and of his sexual theory.

This omnipresence of a condition of possibility, this permanent implication, in every signifier, of the "signifier of signifiers" ("La direction de la cure," *Écrits,* p. 630), of the "peerless signifier" (p. 642) can only have as the element of its presence a milieu of ideality: whence the eminence of the transcendental eminence which has the *effect* of keeping the presence, namely the *phonè.* This is what made it possible and necessary, at the cost of certain rearrangements, to integrate the Freudian phallocentrism into a fundamentally phonocentric Saussurian semio-linguistics. The "algorithmic" transformation does not seem to me to break this bond. Here is the best definition of the transcendental phallus, in regard to which all the protestations of anti-transcendentalism keep their value of negation: "For the phallus is a signifier, a signifier whose function, in the intra-subjective economy of the analysis, raises perhaps the veil of that which it held in mysteries. For it is the signifier destined to designate as a whole the signified-effects (as the stumbling yet directed work of Mrs. Klein makes obvious enough), but to the pregenital stages inasmuch as they are arrayed in the retroaction of the Oedipus" ("Du traitement possible de la psychose," *Écrits,* p. 554). "In fact what has he [Jones] gained in normalizing the function of the phallus as a partial object, if he needs to invoke its presence in the mother's body as an internal object, which term is a function of the phantasies revealed by Melanie Klein, and if he cannot to that extent separate himself from the doctrine of this latter, assigning these phantasies to the recurrence up to the limits of early childhood, of the Oedipal formation.

"One would make no mistake to take up the question again by asking oneself what could have forced upon Freud the evident paradox of his position. For one would be constrained to admit that he was guided better than anyone in his recognition of the order of unconscious phenomena of which he was the inventor, and that, for want of a sufficient articulation of the nature of these phenomena, his followers were destined to go more or less astray in it.

"It is from the starting-point of this wager—which we put at the basis of a commentary of Freud's work which we have been pursuing for the last seven years—that we have been led to certain results: chiefly, to promote as necessary to any articulation of the analytical phenomenon the notion of signifier, inasmuch as it is opposed to the notion of signified in modern linguistic analysis" ("La signification du phallus," *Écrits,* p. 688).

the status of a partial object,[34] the whole edification would have crumbled down, and this is what has to be avoided at all cost. This may still occur if its taking-place does not have the ideality of a phonemic letter (which the Seminar so strangely calls "the materiality of the signifier" alleging that it survives the burned or torn-up paper, and endures by dint of not letting itself be divided). This always *does* occur but the voice is there to decoy us onto this strange event and to leave us the ideal keeping of what is reduced to the status of a partial or divisible object: a disseminable bit [*mors disséminable*].

"It must be retained that Jones in his address to the Vienna Society which seems to have burned the ground for any contribution since then, has already found no more to produce than his rallying pure and simple to the Kleinian concepts in the perfect brutality wherein their author presents them: we mean the neglect in which Melanie Klein persists—the inclusion of the most primal Oedipal phantasies in the maternal body—of their source in the reality which the Name-of-the-Father presupposes" ("Propos directifs pour un Congrès sur la sexualité féminine," *Écrits*, pp. 728–729).

34. "The meaning of castration takes on its effective import (*clinically manifest*) as to the formation of symptoms, with its discovery as the castration of the mother" (*Écrits*, p. 686), that is of her lack of a penis and not of a clitoris. "That the phallus should be a signifier, imposes that it should be at the Other's place that the subject has access to it. But this signifier being there only as veiled and as reason of the Other's desire, it is this desire of the Other as such which it is imposed upon the subject to recognize. . . . If the mother's desire *is* the phallus, the child wants to be the phallus in order to satisfy it . . . *Clinical work shows us* that this ordeal of the desire of the Other is not decisive inasmuch as the subject learns in it whether or not he himself has a real phallus, but inasmuch as he learns that his mother does not have it . . . a man finds in effect satisfaction of his love demand in the relation to a woman because the signifier of the phallus constitutes her indeed as giving in love what she does not have . . ." (*Écrits*, pp. 693–694).

I underline *Clinically manifest, clinical work shows us*, and without the least suspicion as to the truth of these statements. Rather in order to question all the imports of a situation of psychoanalysis in XXXX.

"What she doesn't have . . ." "heiress of never having had it"; one remembers that it is "the Woman" and the queen who are here in question; the proper place orienting the *proper* course of the letter, its "destination," what it "means to say" and which is deciphered from a situation theorizing about what "clinical work shows us."

This situation (a theoretical discourse and an institution edified on a phase of the experience of the male child and on the corresponding sexual theory) sustains both in Bonaparte and in Lacan the interpretation of "The Purloined Letter." It corresponds rigorously, no unfaithfulness on the part of the legatees here, to the description given of it by Freud in the propositions disputed during the "battle" mentioned a moment ago. But by way of a reminder: "the main characteristic of this 'infantile genital organization' is its *difference* from the final genital organization of the adult. The fact is that, for both sexes, only one genital, namely the male one, comes into account. What is present, therefore, is not a primacy of the genitals, but a primacy of the *phallus.*

Unfortunately we can describe this state of things only as it affects the male child; the corresponding processes in the little girl are not known to us. . . . [Little boys] disavow the fact [of the absence of a penis] and believe that they *do* see a penis, all the same.

The decoy [*leurre*]—but the word no longer suffices—would no longer be that of the imaginary but of the so-called limit between the imaginary and the symbolic. Consequence: to be continued. The systematic and historical link between idealization, sublation [*Aufhebung*] and the voice, if it is now considered as demonstrated, insists then in "La signification du phallus." The raising to the function of a signifier is an *Aufhebung* of the "signifiable" (*Écrits*, p. 692): this is then

---

They gloss [Fr. tr. has *ils jettent un voile*, they throw a veil] over the contradiction between observation and preconception by telling themselves that the penis is still small and will grow bigger presently; and they then slowly come to the emotionally significant conclusion that after all the penis had at least been there before and been taken away afterwards. The lack of a penis is regarded as a result of castration, and so now the child is faced with the task of coming to terms with castration in relation to himself. The further developments are too well known generally to make it necessary to recapitulate them here. But it seems to me that *the significance of the castration complex can only be rightly appreciated if its origin in the phase of phallic primacy is also taken into account....*

"At the ... stage of infantile genital organization ..., *maleness* exists, but not *femaleness*. The antithesis here is between having *a male genital* and being *castrated*" ("The Infantile Genital Organization" [1923], Standard Edition, vol. XIX, pp. 142–145). One might be tempted to say: Freud, like those who follow him here, does nothing else but *describe* the necessity of phallogocentrism, explain its effects, which are as obvious as they are massive. Phallogocentrism is neither an accident nor a speculative mistake which may be imputed to this or that theoretician. It is an enormous and old root which must also be accounted for. It may then be described, as an object or a course are described, without this description taking part in what it operates the recognition of. To be sure. But this hypothesis, which one would then have to extend to all the texts of the tradition, encounters in these latter, as in Freud, as in those of his heirs who refuse to transform here anything of his legacy, a very strictly determinable limit: the description is a "recipient" when it induces a practice, an ethic and an education hence a politics assuring the tradition of its truth. The point then is not simply to know, to show, to explain, but to stay in it and reproduce. The ethico-educational purpose is declared by Lacan: the motif of authenticity, of the full word, of the pledged faith and of the "signifying convention" showed this sufficiently. It regulates itself systematically by a phallogocentric doctrine of the signifier. "Analysis can have for its goal only the advent of a true Word and the bringing to realization of his history by the subject in his relation to a future" (*The Language of the Self*, p. 65). "Just before the peaks of the path which I have established of its reading [the reading of Freud's work] before reaching transference, then identification, then anxiety, it is not chance, the idea of it would occur to no one, if this year, the fourth before my seminar should come to an end on Saint Anne, I thought it our duty to ascertain the ethic of psychoanalysis.

"It seems in effect that we risked forgetting in the field of our function that an ethic is at its basis, and that from then on, whatever he may think [*se dire*], and without my approval as well, about the end of man, our chief torment concerns a formation which may be qualified as human.

"Any human formation in essence, and not by accident, curbs pleasure [*refréner la jouissance*]" ("Discours de clôture des Journées sur les psychoses chez l'enfant," *Recherches, spécial Enfance aliénée,* 11, décembre 1968, pp. 145–146).

true by the privilege of the "privileged signifier" (the phallus) and of its literal locality *par excellence* (the voice). Hence the complicity of structure between the motif of the veil and that of the voice, between the truth and phonocentrism, phallocentrism and logocentrism. Which exposes itself thus:

> All these remarks still do nothing but veil the fact that it cannot play its role except veiled, that is to say as itself sign of the latency with which anything signifiable is stricken as soon as it is raised (*aufgehoben*) to the function of signifier.
>
> "The phallus is the signifier of this *Aufhebung* itself which it inaugurates (initiates) by its disappearance" (*Écrits*, p. 692).

It would appear that the Hegelian movement of *Aufhebung* is here reversed since it sublates [*relève*] the sensory signifier in the ideal signified. But as the best zone defense [*garde locale*] of the phallus (of the privileged signifier) is recognized by Lacan to be *verbal* language (the preconscious, even the conscious for Freud), the excellency of the voice annuls the reversal. It is common to both dialectics and idealizes the signifier.

The same thing always takes (the same) place. The point is still not to abandon the proper place in question.

Phallogocentrism is one thing. And what is called man and what is called woman might be subjected to it. The more so, we are reminded, since the phallus is neither a phantasy ("imaginary effect") nor an object ("partial, internal, good, bad"), even less the organ, penis or clitoris, which it symbolizes (*Écrits*, p. 690). Androcentrism ought therefore to be something else.

Yet what is going on? The entire phallogocentrism is articulated from the starting-point of a determinate *situation* (let us give this word its full impact) in which the phallus *is* the mother's desire inasmuch as she does not have it.[35] An (individual, perceptual, local, cultural, historical, etc.) situation on the basis of which is developed something called a "sexual theory": in it the phallus is not the organ, penis or clitoris, which it symbolizes; but it does to a larger extent and in first place symbolize the penis. The sequel is familiar: phallogocentrism as an-

---

35. *Écrits*, p. 695. As to the system-link between the logic of the signifier and phallogocentrism, everything in the Lacanian discourse responds here—indeed—to the question he poses in "Propos directifs pour un Congrès sur la sexualité féminine": "Is it then this privilege of the signifier which Freud aims at in suggesting that there is perhaps only one libido and that it is marked by the male sign?" (*Écrits*, p. 735).

drocentrism with the whole paradoxical logic and the reversals which it engenders: for example that "in the phallocentric dialectic, she [the woman] represents the absolute Other" (*Écrits*, p. 732). This consequence had to be traced in order to recognize the meaning [the direction, *sens*] of the purloined letter in the "course *which is proper to it.*" This is the end of "La signification du phallus" and the twice-repeated allegation of profundity:

> In a correlative manner is glimpsed the reason of this never-elucidated stroke [*trait*] in which once again the profundity of Freud's intuition can be measured: namely why he advances that there is only one libido, his text showing that he conceives it as of masculine nature. The function of the phallic signifier opens here [*débouche*] upon its most profound implication: that by which the Ancients embodied the Nous and the Λόγος.[36]

36. Culinary questions: when Baudelaire translates "coincidence" as *analogie* at the beginning of the story, at the precise moment of the two other "affairs" ("The Murders in the Rue Morgue" and "The Mystery of Marie Rogêt"), he misses, with the full force of the word *manque*, the fact that "The Purloined Letter" itself is presented in a series of coincidences, as one of them, their network already worked out before this third fiction. One detail among the many that now can be analyzed in an open reading of the trilogy: the epigraph of "The Mystery of Marie Rogêt," a quotation from Novalis, in German and in English translation, beginning: "There are ideal series of events which run parallel with the real ones. They rarely coincide. . . ." Baudelaire simply omits these last three words. The word "coincidences" then appears three times in two pages, italicized in each case. The last time, with reference to the interconnection [*embranchement*] of the three cases: "The extraordinary details which I am now called upon to make public, will be found to form, as regards sequence of time, the primary branch of a series of scarcely intelligible [*à peine imaginables*] coincidences, whose secondary or concluding [*finale*] branch will be recognized by all readers in the late murder of MARY CECILIA ROGERS, at New York." The subtitle of the "Mystery": "a sequel to 'The Murders in the Rue Morgue.' "

These reminders, of which countless other examples could be given, make us aware of the effects of the frame, and of the paradoxes in the parergonal logic. Our purpose is not to prove that "The Purloined Letter" functions within a frame (omitted by the Seminar, which can thus be assured of its triangular interior by an active, surreptitious limitation starting with a metalinguistic overhang), but to prove that the structure of the framing effects is such that no totalization of the border is even possible. The frames are always framed: thus by some of their content. Pieces without a whole, "divisions" without a totality—this is what thwarts the dream of a letter without division, allergic to division. From this point on, the seme "phallus" is errant, begins by dis-seminating, not even by *being* disseminated.

The naturalizing neutralization of the frame permits the Seminar, by imposing or importing an Oedipal outline, by finding it (self there) in truth—and it is there, in fact, but as a piece, even if a precisely central one, within the letter—to constitute a metalanguage and to exclude all of the general text in all of the dimensions we began here by recalling (return to the "first page"). Without even going into greater detail, the trap of metalan-

Profundity equals height. It opens [*débouche*] upwards, the mouth [*bouche*] precisely in which is "embodied" the *Nous*, the *Logos*, and which says profoundly: there is only *one* libido, hence no difference, even less opposition within it of masculine and feminine, besides it is masculine in nature. The reason for this never elucidated stroke [*trait*] can be but "glimpsed": it is not the reason for this stroke, it is reason itself. Before Freud, under Freud and since Freud. The drawn line of reason [*le trait tiré de la raison*]. Drawn by it, for it, under it. In the logic known as "kitchen logic" [*logique du "chaudron"*], (bill of exchange of reason) [*traite tirée de la raison*], reason will always outreason. Itself. [*La raison aura toujours raison. D'elle-même.*] It speaks up for itself. "The thing goes without saying" [*La chose parle d'elle-même*]. It speaks up to say what it cannot hear.

MEETING PLACE: FOUR OF A KIND, KINGS—DOUBLE

But it (reason) *cannot read* the story which it makes up. Nor the scene of writing—*avant la lettre*—in which the story is inscribed. Let us return to the "Purloined Letter" to get a "glimpse" there of the disseminal structure, i.e., the no-possible-return of the letter, the other scene of its remnance [*restance*].

Because there is a narrator on the scene, the "general" scene is not limited to a narration, a "tale," or a "story." We have already recognized the effects of the indivisible framing, from frame to frame, *from within which* psychoanalytical interpretations (semantico-biographical or triado-formalist) drew their triangles. By overlooking the narrator's position, the narrator's involvement in the content of what he seems to be recounting, one omits from the scene of writing anything going beyond the two triangular scenes.

And first of all (one omits that) in question is a scene of writing—its access or border undeterminable—whose boundaries are blurred [*abîmés*]. From the simulacrum of an overture, of the "first word," the narrator, as he narrates himself, advances a few statements which carry

---

guage, which, ultimately, is set up by no one, for the sake of no one, involving no one as the result of a mistake or weakness, this trap belongs to writing *avant la lettre* and discloses and conceals itself in the revealed/concealed elements of its affected title: "The Purloined Letter" is the title of the text and not only of its object. But a text never names itself, never writes: I, the text, write or write myself. It has, lets, or rather brings another to say: "I, truth, speak." I am always the letter that never arrives. At the destination itself.

the unity of the "tale" into an endless drifting-off-course: a textual drifting not at all taken into account in the Seminar. But if one were to take it into account, one ought not to turn it into the *"real subject* of the tale." Who would not have done it!

1. Everything begins "in" a library: among books, writing, references. Hence nothing begins. Simply a drifting or a disorientation from which one never moves away.

2. There is explicit reference, moreover, to two other stories to which "this one" is grafted. The "analogy" between the three stories is the core of "The Purloined Letter." The independence of the tale, as presumed in the Seminar, is thus the effect of an ablation, even if it is considered in its totality, with its narrator and narration. This ablation is all the more faint as the "analogy" is recalled from the very first paragraph on. It is true that the word "analogy," or, more precisely, "coincidence," authorizes, invites the ablation, and thus functions as a trap. The work of the Seminar begins only after the arrival of the Prefect of the Parisian police. Before this, however, the title, the epigraph, the first paragraph provided something to read (in silence, the silence).

> *The Purloined Letter*
>
> Nil sapientiae odiosius acumine nimio.
>
> Seneca

> At Paris, just after dark one gusty evening in the autumn of 18—, I was enjoying the twofold luxury of meditation and a meerschaum, in company with my friend C. Auguste Dupin, in his little back library, or book-closet *au troisième, Nº 33 Rue Dunôt, Faubourg St. Germain.* For one hour at least we had maintained a profound silence; while each, to any casual observer might have seemed intently and exclusively occupied with the curling eddies of smoke that oppressed the atmosphere of the chamber. For myself, however, I was mentally discussing certain topics which had formed matter for conversation between us at an earlier period of the evening; I mean the affair of the Rue Morgue and the mystery attending the murder of Marie Rogêt. I looked upon it, therefore, as something of a coincidence, when the door of our apartment was thrown open and admitted our old acquaintance, Monsieur G—, the Prefect of the Parisian police.
>
> . . . We had been sitting in the dark, and Dupin now arose for the purpose of lighting a lamp, but sat down again, without doing so. . . .

Thus everything "begins" by obscuring this opening in "silence," the "smoke" and the "dark" of this library. The casual observer sees only the smoking meerschaum: in short, a literary setting, the ornamental frame of a story. On this border, negligible for the interpreter interested in the center of the painting and the interior of representation, it was already possible to read that the whole thing was a matter of writing, and of writing off its course, in a writing-space unboundedly open to grafting onto other writing, and that this matter of writing, the third of a series in which the "coincidence" between the first two is noticeable, breaks suddenly into the text with its first word "au troisième, No. 33 Rue Dunôt, Faubourg St. Germain": in French in the original.

Fortuitous remarks, eddies of smoke, contingencies of framing? The fact that they go beyond "the author's intention," about which the Seminar is tempted to turn to Dupin for information, the fact that they are even purely accidental "coincidence," chance events, can only render them of greater interest for the reading of a text that makes of chance as writing what we shall be careful not to call "the *real subject* of the tale."

Rather, its remarkable ellipsis. Indeed, if, as we are invited to do even in the internal boundary of the frame, we go back before "The Purloined Letter," the same remarkable elements persist: scene of writing, library, chance events, coincidences. At the beginning of "The Murders in the Rue Morgue," what could be called the meeting place between the narrator (narrating-narrated) and Dupin is *already an obscure library*, the *coïncidence* (this is the word, rather than *analogie*, with which Baudelaire translates "accident")[37] of the fact that they are "in

---

37. Before dropping them, as everyone does with prefaces, or holding them up as the properly instructive theoretical concept, the truth of the story, I should like to draw from them a few statements. These are not necessarily the best of them; one should also recall each word of the title, and again the epithet about Achilles' name when he hid among women. "The mental features discoursed of as the analytical, are, in themselves, but little susceptible of analysis. . . . The analyst [glories] in that moral activity which *disentangles.* He derives pleasure from even the most trivial occupations bringing his talents into play. He is fond of enigmas, of conundrums, of hieroglyphics. . . . Yet to calculate is not in itself to analyze. A chess-player, for example, does the one without effort at the other. . . . I will, therefore, take occasion to assert that the higher powers of the reflective intellect are more decidedly and more usefully tasked by the unostentatious game of draughts [*jeu de dames*] than by all the elaborate frivolity of chess. . . . To be less abstract—Let us suppose a game of draughts where the pieces are reduced to four kings [*quatre* dames (in the game of draughts, or checkers, the "kings," like the game itself, are called in French "ladies," *dames*)], and where, of course, no oversight is to be expected. It is obvious that here the victory can be decided (the players being at all equal) only by some *recherché* movement, the result of some strong assertion of the intellect. Deprived of ordinary resources, the analyst throws himself into the spirit of his opponent, identifies himself therewith, and not unfrequently sees thus, at a glance, the sole methods

search of the same very rare and very remarkable volume." And the relationship formed then in this meeting place will, to say the least, never allow the so-called general narrator the position of a neutral, transparent reporter who does not intervene in the transaction going on. For example—but this time the example, read from the frame, is not at the beginning of the text. The frame describing the "meeting" cuts across the narration, so to speak. The frame is preceded, before Dupin appears in the story, by a feint in the form of an abandoned preface, a false short-treatise on analysis. "I am not now writing a treatise, but simply prefacing a somewhat peculiar narrative by observations very much at random." Not a treatise, a preface (to be dropped, of course).[38] At the end of the preface, the narrator simulates the Seminar:

(sometimes indeed absurdly simple ones) by which he may seduce into error or hurry into miscalculation . . . But it is in matters beyond the limits of mere rule that the skill of the analyst is evinced . . . Our player confines himself not at all; nor, because the game is the object, does he reject deductions from things external to the game." Etc. One must read the complete text, in both languages. I have taken some liberties [*Je me suis livré à quelque cuisine*] with Baudelaire's translation, which I do not always follow.

Méryon asked Baudelaire whether he believed "in the real existence of this Edgar Allan Poe"; Méryon attributed Poe's tales "to a group of highly skilled and most powerful men of letters, acutely aware of everything that was going on." The said group, then, does not specify whether the "things external to the game" border on a game recounted in the text or constituted by the text, nor whether *the game* that *is the object* is (in) the story or not. Nor whether the seduction seeks its prey among the characters or among the readers. The question of the narratee, and that of the receiver, which is not the same question.

38. The Seminar completely disregards the very definite involvement of the narrator in the narrative. Ten years later, in an addition made in 1966, Lacan writes as follows:

"An effect [of the signifier] as obviously graspable here as in the fiction of the purloined letter.

"Whose essence is that the letter has been able to carry its effects into the interior—to the actors in the tale, including the narrator—as well as to the exterior—to us readers and also to its author—without anyone ever having been concerned about what it meant. This is the usual outcome of everything that is written" (E, pp. 56f.).

Thus while subscribing up to a certain point, we still must point out that the Seminar said nothing about the effects on the narrator, *neither in fact nor in principle.* The structure of the interpretation excluded it. And about the nature of these effects, about the structure of the involvement of the narrator, the note of repentance still says nothing, limiting itself to the frame constructed by the Seminar. The claim that in this matter everything has happened "without anyone ever having been concerned about what it [the letter] meant," is incorrect for several reasons:

　　1. Everyone, as the police Prefect reminds us, knows that the letter contains at least something that would "bring into question the honor of a personage of most exalted station" and her "peace": a sturdy semantic mooring rope.
　　2. This knowledge is repeated by the Seminar and bolsters it on two levels:

The narrative which follows will appear to the reader in the light of a commentary upon the propositions just advanced.

Residing in Paris during the spring and part of the summer of 18—, I there became acquainted with a Monsieur C. Auguste Dupin. This young gentleman was of an excellent—indeed of an illustrious family, but, by a variety of untoward events, had been reduced to such poverty that the energy of his character succumbed beneath it, and he ceased to bestir himself in the world, or to care for the retrieval of his fortunes. By courtesy of his creditors, there still remained in his possession a small remnant of his patrimony; and, upon the income arising from this, he managed, by means of a rigorous economy, to procure the necessaries of life, without troubling himself about its superfluities. Books, indeed, were his sole luxuries, and in Paris these are easily obtained.

With a remnant of his paternal inheritance, apparently surrendered without calculation to the debtor who knows how, by calculating ("rig-

---

(a) as for the minimal, active meaning of this letter, the Seminar reports and transcribes the information of the police Prefect:

"But all this tells us nothing of the message it conveys.

"Love letter or conspiratorial letter, letter of betrayal or letter of mission, letter of summons or letter of distress, we are assured of but one thing: the Queen must not bring it to the knowledge of her lord and master" (SPL, p. 57). This tells us the essentials of the message it conveys: the variations proposed on this subject are not indifferent, even if they seek to make us believe that they are. In all the imagined hypotheses, the message of the letter (not only the fact that it is sent) must imply the betrayal of a pact, of a "pledge of faith." It was not forbidden for any person to send any letter at all to the Queen, nor for her to receive letters. The Seminar contradicts itself when a few lines later it radicalizes the logic of the signifier and of its literal place while pretending to neutralize the "message," then arrests or anchors this logic in its meaning or its symbolic truth: "It remains that the letter is the symbol of a pact." Contrary to what the Seminar says (an appalling proposition by virtue of the blindness that it could induce, but indispensable for the demonstration), it is indeed necessary that everyone "be concerned about what it (the letter) meant." Ignorance or indifference about this remains minimal and concerns details. Everyone knows, everyone is concerned, the author of the Seminar first of all. And if it did not have a fully determined meaning, no one would care about having a different one palmed off on him, which is what happens to the Queen and then to the Minister. Everyone makes certain, from the Minister to Lacan, including Dupin, that it is the letter in question and that it does indeed say what it says: the betrayal of the pact, and what it says, "the symbol of the pact." Otherwise there would be no "abandoned" letter: abandoned either by the Minister first or by Dupin and finally by Lacan. They all make sure of the content of the letter, of the "right one," they all mime the police Prefect, who, taking the letter from Dupin's hands in exchange for remuneration, checks its content: "This functionary grasped it in a perfect agony of joy, opened it with a trembling hand, cast a rapid glance at its contents, and then scrambling and struggling to the door, rushed at length unceremoniously from the room. . . ." The exchange of the check and the letter takes place over an *escritoire* (in French in the original) in which Dupin had the document locked up.

orous economy"), to draw from it a *rente,* an income, the surplus-value of a capital that works all alone, Dupin allows himself one extra, one luxury, in which the initial remnant reappears, passing through the restricted economy like a one-way gift. This luxury ("his sole luxuries": this is the word which appears again in the second line of "The Purloined Letter," but this time in the singular: "the twofold luxury of meditation and a meerschaum") is writing: the books that will structure the locus of the meeting and the *mise en abyme* of the whole so-called general narration. The locus of the meeting for the meeting between the narrator and Dupin is a result of the meeting of their interests in the same book, which they are never said to have found. This is literally the accident:

> Our first meeting was at an obscure library in the Rue Montmartre, where the accident of our both being in search of the same very rare and very remarkable volume, brought us into closer communion. We saw each other again and again. I was deeply interested in the little family history which he detailed to me with all that candor which a Frenchman indulges whenever mere self is the theme.

The narrator thus lets himself be narrated: that he is "deeply interested in [Dupin's] little family history," that particular one which leaves a remnant of income with which to purchase the luxury of books; then, as we shall see, that it is above all else Dupin's capacity for reading which astonishes the narrator, and that the society of such a man is therefore to him "a treasure beyond price." The narrator will thus purchase for himself Dupin's being-without-a-price, who purchases for himself writing's being-without-a-price, which is without-price in that very way. For the narrator, confiding openly in Dupin—or, as Baudelaire puts it, *se livrant* frankly to him, must pay for the privilege. He must rent the analyst's office—and furnish the economic equivalent of what is without-price. The analyst—or rather the narrator's own financial situation, almost the same as Dupin's, merely "somewhat less embarrassed"—authorizes him to do so: "I was permitted to be at the expense of renting. . . ." The narrator is thus the first one to pay Dupin to assure himself the availability of the "letters." Let us then follow the movement of the chain. What the narrator is paying for is also the locus of the narration, the writing in which the entire story will be told and offered for interpretations. And if he pays to write or speak, he also makes Dupin speak, makes him give his letters back and gives him the last word, in the form of a confession. In the economics of this office [*cabinet*], since the narrator himself appears on the scene in a function that is indeed that of a "corporation" (*société anonyme*) of capital and desire, no neutralization is possible, no general point of view, no overhang, no "destruction" of meaning by money. Not only Dupin but also the narrator is a "recipient." As soon as he makes Dupin give up his letters—and not only to the Queen (the other Queen)—the letter is divided, it is no longer atomic (atomism, Epicurean atomism, is also, as we know, one of Dupin's topics in "The Murders in the Rue Morgue") and thus loses any assurance of destination. The divisibility of the letter—this is why we insisted on this key or theoretical safety bolt [*verrou de sûreté théorique*] of the Seminar: the atomystique of the letter—is what puts in jeopardy and leads astray, with no guarantee of return, the remnant of anything whatever: a letter does *not always* arrive at its destination, and since this belongs to its structure, it can be said that it never really arrives there, that when it arrives, its possibly-not-arriving [*son pouvoir-ne-pas-arriver*], torments it with an internal divergence.

The divisibility of the letter is also the divisibility of the signifier to which it gives rise, and thus of the "subjects," "characters," or "positions" that are subject to them and that "represent" them. Before showing this in the text, let us recall a quotation:

> I was astonished, too, at the vast extent of his reading; and, above all, I felt my soul enkindled within me by the wild fervor, and the vivid freshness of his imagination. Seeking in Paris the objects I then sought, I felt that the society of such a man would be to me a treasure beyond price; and this feeling I frankly confided to him. It was at length arranged that we should live together during my stay in the city; and as my worldly circumstances were somewhat less embarrassed than his own, I was permitted to be at the expense of renting, and furnishing in a style which suited the rather fantastic gloom of our common temper, a time-eaten and grotesque mansion, long deserted through superstitions into which we did not inquire, and tottering to its fall in a retired and desolate portion of the Faubourg St. Germain.

Thus we have two (gloomy) fantastics, one of whom does not tell us who his "former associates" are, from whom he will now conceal the "secret" of the "locality." The entire space is now enclosed in the speculations of these two "madmen":

> Had the routine of our life at this place been known to the world, we should have been regarded as madmen—although, perhaps, as madmen

of a harmless nature. Our seclusion was perfect. We admitted no visitors. Indeed the locality of our retirement had been carefully kept a secret from my own former associates; and it had been many years since Dupin had ceased to know or be known in Paris. We existed within ourselves alone.

From this point on, the narrator lets himself narrate his progressive identification with Dupin. And in the first instance in "loving" the night, the "sable divinity" whose "presence" they "counterfeit" when she is not there:

> It was a freak of fancy in my friend (for what else shall I call it?) to be enamored of the Night for her own sake; and into this *bizarrerie,* as into all his others, I quietly fell; giving myself up to his wild whims with a perfect *abandon.* The sable divinity would not herself dwell with us always; but we could counterfeit her presence.

Thus the narrator, already positionally double, *identifies* with Dupin, whose "particular analytical ability" he "cannot help remarking and admiring" and who gives him countless proofs of Dupin's "intimate knowledge" of the narrator's own "bosom" [*personne*]. But Dupin himself, at these very moments, appears double. And this time it is a "fantasy" [*une fantastique*] of the narrator which sees Dupin as double:

> His manner at these moments was frigid and abstract, his eyes were vacant in expression; while his voice, usually a rich tenor, rose into a treble which would have sounded petulantly but for the deliberateness and entire distinctness of the enunciation. Observing him in these moods, I often dwelt meditatively on the old philosophy of the Bi-Part Soul, and amused myself with the fancy of a double Dupin—the creative and the resolvent.

The fancy of an identification between two doubles themselves double, the powerful cathexis [*investissement*] of the binding relationship [*liaison*] that involves Dupin *outside* of the "intersubjective triads" of the "real drama" and involves the narrator *in* what he narrates, the circulation of wishes and capital, of signifiers and letters before and beyond the two "primal" and secondary "triangles," the chain-fission of positions, beginning with the position of Dupin, who, like *all* the characters, inside and outside the narrative, occupies *all* the places— all this makes triangular logic a very limited part of the drama [*une pièce très limitée dans la pièce*]. And if the dual relationship between the two doubles (which Lacan would reduce to the imaginary) includes all of the space referred to as "symbolic," surpasses it and simulates it, engulfs it and breaks it down endlessly, then the opposition of the imaginary and the symbolic, and above all its implicit hierarchy, seem to be of very limited relevance: at least if it is measured within the scope of [à la carrure de] a scene of writing like this one.

We have seen that *all* the characters of "The Purloined Letter," particularly those of the "real drama," including Dupin, occupied successively and structurally *all* the positions, that of the King/dead man/blind man (and that of the police Prefect at the same time), after that of the Queen, and then of the Minister. Each position identifies with the other and is fragmented, even that of the dead man and of a supplementary fourth. The distinction of the three glances proposed by the Seminar to determine the proper course of the circulation is thus compromised. And above all the opening (duplicitous and identificatory) turned aside, toward the narrator (narrating, narrated), makes one letter come back only to send another astray.

And the phenomena of the double, hence of the "Unheimlichkeit," belong not only to the trilogical "context" of "The Purloined Letter." The question is indeed asked, in a conversation between the narrator and Dupin, whether the Minister is himself or his brother ("There are two brothers," "both have attained reputation"; where? "in letters"). Dupin affirms that the Minister is both "poet and mathematician." The two brothers are almost indistinguishable in him. Rivals within him, one playing and foiling [jouant et déjouant] the other. "'You are mistaken; I know him well; he is both [il est les deux]. As poet *and* mathematician, he would reason well; as mere mathematician, he could not have reasoned at all, and thus would have been at the mercy of the Prefect.'"

But at the Minister who "'is well acquainted with my MS.,'" Dupin strikes a blow signed brother or confrère, twin or younger or older brother (Atreus/Thyestes). This rival and duplicitous identification of the brothers, far from fitting into the symbolic space of the family triangle (the first, the second, or the one after), carries it off infinitely far away in a labyrinth of doubles without originals, of facsimile without an authentic, an indivisible letter, of casual counterfeits [contrefaçons sans façon], imprinting the purloined letter with an incorrigible indirection.

The text entitled "The Purloined Letter" imprints/is imprinted in these effects of indirection. I have only indicated the most conspicuous of these effects in order to begin to unlock their reading: the game of doubles, the endless divisibility, the textual references from facsimile to facsimile, the framing of frames, the interminable supplementarity of quotation marks, the insertion of "The Purloined Letter" in a purloined letter that begins with it, throughout the narratives of narrative of "The Murders in the Rue Morgue," the newspaper clippings of "The Mystery of Marie Rogêt" ("A Sequel to 'The Murders in the Rue Morgue' "). Above all else, the *mise en abyme* of the title: "The Purloined Letter" is the text, the text in a text (the purloined letter as a trilogy). The title is the title of the text, it names the text, it names itself and thus includes itself while pretending to name an object described in the text. "The Purloined Letter" functions as a text that escapes all assignable destination and produces, or rather induces by deducing itself, this inassignability at the exact moment in which it narrates the arrival of a letter. It pretends to mean [*vouloir-dire*] and to make one think that "a letter always arrives at its destination," authentic, intact, and undivided, at the moment and the place where the simulation, as writing *avant la lettre,* leaves its path. In order to make another leap— to the side. At this very place, of course.

Who signs? Dupin wants to sign, no matter what. And indeed the narrator, after having made or let him speak, gives him the last word,[39] the last word of the last of the three stories. So it seems. This is not an attempt to put the narrator, in turn, much less the author, in the position of the analyst who knows how to keep silent. There may not be here, measured in terms of [*à la carrure de*] this scene of writing, a possible enclosure for an analytic situation. There may not even be a pos-

39. One can even consider that he is the only one who "speaks" in the story. His discourse dominates with loquacious, didactic braggadocio, truly magisterial, handing out directives, giving directions, righting wrongs, teaching everyone. He spends his own time and that of others making corrections and reminding them of the rules. He assumes his post and speaks up. Only the address matters, the right one, the authentic one. It devolves, according to the law, to the proper quarter. Thanks to the man of the law and the rector of the proper course. All of "The Purloined Letter" is written so that he finally brings it back through the proper course. And since he proves himself to be cleverer than the others, the letter plays one more trick on him just as he spots its locus and its true destination. The letter eludes and deceives him (literature on stage left [*côté cour*] just at the time when, speaking up, he hears that he deceives while explicating deception, just at the time when he returns the blow and the letter. He agrees to every demand without knowing it; he doubles, or rather replaces, the Minister and the Police, and if there were only one dupe—hypothesis not taken up—he would be the most splendid one in the "story" [*de l' "histoire"*]. Yet—what about the lady [*quoi—de la belle*]. *Il l'adresse-la Reine-l'adresse-la-dupe.*

sible analyst, at least in the situation of psychoanalysis in X—. Only four kings, hence four queens, four police prefects, four ministers, four analysts Dupin, four narrators, four readers, four kings, etc., all more insightful and more foolish than the others, more powerful and more powerless.

Thus Dupin wants to sign, indeed, doubtless, the last word of the last message of the purloined letter. First by being unable to resist leaving his own mark—the seal, at least, with which he must be identified—on the facsimile that he leaves for the Minister. He fears the facsimile and, insisting on his utterly confraternal vengeance, he demands that the Minister know where it came from. Thus he limits the facsimile, the counterfeit exterior of the letter. The interior is authentic and properly identifiable. Indeed: at the moment when the madman ("'the pretended lunatic'" who is "'a man in my own pay'") distracts everyone with his "frantic behavior," what does Dupin do? He adds a note. He leaves the false letter, that is, the one that interests him, *the real one*, which is not a facsimile *except for the exterior*. If there were a man of truth, a lover of the authentic, in all this, Dupin would indeed be the model: "'In the meantime, I stepped to the card-rack, took the letter, put it in my pocket, and replaced it by a *fac-simile*, (so far as regards externals [*quant à l'extérieur*]), which I had carefully prepared at my lodgings; imitating the D—cipher, very readily, by means of a seal formed of bread.'"

Thus D—will have to decipher, on the inside, what the decipherer meant and whence and why he deciphered, with what end in mind, in the name of whom and what. The initial—the same, D, for the Minister and for Dupin—is a facsimile on the outside *but on the inside it is the thing itself.*

But what is this thing itself on the inside? This signature? This "last word" of a doubly confraternal war?

Again, a quotation by means of which the signer is dispossessed, whatever he may have: "I just copied into the middle of the blank sheet the words—

—Un dessein si funeste,
S'il n'est digne d'Atrée, est digne de Thyeste."

A play on quotation marks. In the French translation, there are no quotation marks, and the lines from Crébillon appear in small type. The sentence that follows ("Vous trouverez cela dans l'*Atrée* de Crébillon," "They are to be found in Crébillon's 'Atrée'") can be attributed equally well to the author of "The Purloined Letter," or the narrator, or the author of the letter left behind (Dupin). But the American edition at my disposal no longer leaves this doubt. It is, however, faulty in that it appears as follows, leaving interior quotation marks, suspended quotation marks called in French *"guillemets anglais."*

> "... He is well acquainted with my MS., and I just copied into the middle of the blank sheet the words—
>
> "'—Un dessein si funeste,
> S'il n'est digne d'Atrée, est digne de Thyeste.
> They are to be found in Crébillon's 'Atrée.'"

Thus it is clear that this final sentence is to be attributed to Dupin, Dupin saying to the Minister: I, the undersigned, Dupin, inform you of the fate of the letter, of what it means, of my purpose in stealing one from you in order to render it to its receiver, and why I am replacing it by this one, remember.

But, beyond the quotation marks that surround the entire story Dupin is obliged to quote this last word in quotation marks, to recount his signature: that is what I wrote to him and how I signed it. What is a signature within quotation marks? Then, within these quotation marks, the seal itself is a quotation within quotation marks. This remnant is still literature.

Two times out of three, the author of the Seminar transforms the word *"dessein"* (design) into *"destin"* (destiny), thus perhaps rendering a meaning [*vouloir-dire*] to its destination: deliberately, probably— there is no reason to rule out design anywhere. (These last words are dedicated of their own accord to Father Peter Coppieters de Gibson, who did not overlook the matter: the alteration coming to steal a letter in order to achieve its destiny along the way.)

"Whatever the case, the Minister, when he tries to make use of it, will be able to read these words, written so that he may recognize Dupin's hand: ... *Un dessein si funeste/S'il n'est digne d'Atrée est digne de Thyeste* whose source, Dupin tells us, is Crébillon's *Atrée* (SPL, p. 43).

Then: "The commonplace of the quotation is fitting for the oracle that face bears in its grimace, as is also its source in tragedy: '... *Un destin si funeste,/S'il n'est digne d'Atrée, est digne de Thyeste'"* (SPL, p. 71).

And finally: "... and I add (p. 52) that there is no chance that the crowing with which this Lecoq would like to waken him [*'un destin si funeste'*] in the little love note [*poulet*] he leaves for him [*qu'il lui destine*]—that there is no chance that that crowing will reach his ears" ("Points," Introduction, p. 8).

—Translated by Willis Domingo, James Hulbert,
Moshe Ron and M.-R. L.

ROGER DRAGONETTI

"Le Nénuphar blanc": A Poetic Dream with Two Unknowns*

It is a strange adventure that joins the fiction of a voyage with a more essential immobility!

Thus could one sum up the adventure that is traced by the writing of the poem and erased in the same gesture.

The title of the poem does not seem to allude to this imaginary voyage and appears only to retain the metaphoric goal of this "quest for water flowers" [*quête de floraison d'eau*]: a water-lily whose hollow whiteness envelopes a "nothingness."

The voyage described is made in a "yole," a light boat whose obsolete name, if we are to believe Mallarmé, ought to furnish a clue to the comprehension of the poem: "Notice the fact that the least used words often act as guides, unexpected and precious, between a distant double meaning of two considerable terms."[1]

The passage we have just quoted is part of the text which serves as an introduction to the *Table* of word families in the *Mots anglais.* Strangely enough, in looking over this *Table*, we find, under the letter *F*, and in particular in the group headed by *Far*, the word "wherry" which Mallarmé translates by "yole" (skiff [yawl]).

This discovery permits us to glimpse in the phonic nature of the word *nénuphar* the promise of a trip to distant places (to fare). Understood thus, the title would condense remarkably the course of the quest and its object. Besides, this trip which seems to deny itself twice (at any rate if one interprets as a double negation the first two syllables of the word *né-nu-phar*) supports admirably, as an imaginary voyage—whose appearances only would be preserved—the adjective "blanc" (white or

*From *Yale French Studies* 54 (1977): *Mallarmé.*

1. *Œuvres complètes*, Pléiade, "Les Mots anglais," p. 919. All quotations from Mallarmé's texts are taken from this edition, and cited here in the text.

YFS 96, *50 Years of Yale French Studies: A Commemorative Anthology*, eds. Porter and Waters, © 1999 by Yale University.

blank), in the sense it has in the expression "mariage blanc" (uncon-summated marriage).

Mallarmé hesitated for quite a while about the spelling of the word, *nénuphar* or *nénufar* (*Notes*, p. 1560), but the poet's opting in favor of the splitting of the letter *f* into *ph* establishes perhaps a supplementary relationship with the words wherry and yole, whose initial letters admit graphic division (v→w; i→ÿ).

Note that Mallarmé extracts the sense of an oscillation from the splitting of the letter *W:*

> The senses of oscillating (which would seem due to the vague doubling of the letter, then of floating, etc. . . . of water and humidity; of fainting and flight; then, of weakness, of charm and of imagination) melt in astonishing diversity . . . (*Table*, p. 932).

In reading this passage, would not one think he was in the atmosphere of the poem whose location is figured by a point of suspension on the water, the site of the oscillation of the *yole?* And does not this doubled initial reflect both the doubling in the word *wherry* as well as that of the initials engraved on the *two* oars?

> Je ne vérifiai l'arrêt qu'à l'étincellement stable d'initiales sur les avirons mis à nu, ce qui me rappela à mon identité mondaine (*Nénuphar blanc*, pp. 283–284).[2]

This halt in the navigation is thus doubled by the stopping of a flight, and the oars, like wings, transpose "into the region of luminous phenomena" the oscillation and the aquatic stability both metamorphosed into a "steady glittering."

Here one thinks of the possibilities of meaning which Mallarmé attributes to the letter *F* when added to the letter *L:*

> It forms with *L* most of the sounds representing the act of flight or beating the air, even transposed by rhetoric into the area of light phenomena, as well as the act of flowing, as in the classical languages (p. 935).

Evidently, it is the English language which is in question here, but the signifying impulses of isolated letters could constitute the basis of onomatopeia, a process in which, according to Mallarmé, the power of invention has taken refuge: "[onomatopeia] perpetuates in our idioms

---

2. "I only verified the halt by the steady sparkling of the initials on the raised oars, which called me back to my worldly identity."

a process of creation which was perhaps the first of them all" (*Mots anglais*, p. 920).

In other respects, when Mallarmé declares that the letter *F* "indicates in itself a strong and fixed embrace" (p. 935), how can we not see another analogue to the grasp of the rower entirely turned in upon himself, "les yeux au dedans fixés sur l'entier oubli d'aller" (*Nénuphar*, p. 283)?

Thus, the words "yole" and "nénuphar" seem to have inherited from their immemorial past "a thousand certain and mysterious intentions of language" that one rediscovers within the context of the poem and which "too much [philological] rigor," as Mallarmé again emphasizes, would have "transgressed" (*Mots anglais*, p. 919).

The following text proves that Mallarmé's reflections are valid as much for English as for French:

> More than one criticism will aim at the translation of this vocabulary into French: sometimes giving the primitive and now least used meaning or molding a thousand every-day nuances into a strict generality; it had to be done. It is even common, in order to relate a known word to some distant relative, to show only an almost accessory nuance of the meaning of this first word (p. 923).

Our analysis will take Mallarmé's reflections into account. They have bearing in a more general way on a new science which opposes to the rigor of traditional philology the poetic instinct of language, thanks to which success can be measured by an *impression* more than by the correctness of an etymology: "A link, so perfect between the meaning and form of a word that it seems to cause only one impression, that of its success, on the mind and the ear" (p. 920). This is why Mallarmé despairs of reaching certain readers, "already too accustomed to the habits of the philologists for this suggestion to reach them" (p. 922), when it will be necessary, for example, to warn his listeners to guard against the historical explanation of certain apparently arbitrary parallels: "no historical relation, in English (at least) and it is to an immemorial common origin that we must look for resemblances authorizing an apposition" (p. 922). This chimerical science (p. 921), into which Mallarmé ventures gropingly, aims at the "absolute meaning" of letters of the alphabet, "sometimes guessed, sometimes misunderstood" by men, whereas the poet, endowed with a superior instinct, has more of a chance to approach it:

> It will be the lot of the poet or even the knowing prosateur, by a superior and free instinct, to bring together terms united with so much more

advantage to compete with the charm and music of language as they come as from more fortuitous distances: this is the process inherent in the northern genius, and of which so many famous lines show us so many examples: ALLITERATION (p. 921).

Certainly, a reading of the "Nénuphar blanc" will be enriched if one takes into account these fortuitous pairings in which chance takes the place of knowledge. It is thus, for example, that the phonic intensities of the stressed syllable of *fiole, viole, yole* will lead us to discover affinities of meaning despite the difference in kind of these objects; in each of the three cases, there is a hollow envelope containing an essence, be it a perfume, a rhythm, or the intimate being of the rower-magician who identifies himself with the *yole*, as the "soul" of the instrument merges with the viola [*viole*]:

> Courbé dans la sportive attitude . . . je souris au commencement d'esclavage . . . que ne signifiaient pas mal les courroies attachant le soulier du rameur au bois de l'imbarcation, comme on ne fait qu'un avec l'instrument de ses sortilèges (*Nénuphar*, p. 284).[3]

A whole analogical network is organized about the idea of a hollow which leads us to other "exquisite emptinesses" [*vacances*][4] like that of the water lily or of the bubble of foam which could reveal the presence of the marauder:

> . . . partir avec: tacitement, en déramant peu à peu sans du heurt briser l'illusion ni que le clapotis de la bulle visible d'écume enroulée a ma fuite ne jette aux pieds survenus de personne la ressemblance transparente du rapt de mon idéale fleur (p. 286).[5]

And is it not from the disappearance of this wake of foam that the verse appears in its radical negation?

> "Rien, cette écume, vierge vers" (*Salut*, p. 27).

---

3. "Bent over in the sportive stance . . . I smiled at the beginning of enslavement . . . which the straps attaching the shoe of the rower to the wood of the boat signified fairly well, as a man becomes one with the instrument of his enchantments."

4. *Vacances* also gives us the sense of "leisure," "availability," which is associated in the text to the theme of the relaxation of the pleasure trip.

5. ". . . to leave with it: silently, by rowing backwards little by little, without by the shock breaking the illusion and without the lapping of the visible bubble of foam enrolled in my escape throwing up at anyone's arriving feet the transparent likeness of the abduction of my ideal flower."

These metaphors are basically only variations of a hollowness in the work of writing whose "cast of the die" [*dés*] (or of the "d," pronounced in French) will produce, by a successful effect, the relationship between *ramer* and *déramer, row* and *row backwards*. For it is really by the poetic game of language that Mallarmé makes us hear the negative force of the cast of the "die" [*dés*] in such oppositions as *astre/désastre, livre/délivre,* and here *ramer* and *déramer,* two words whose contrary action is the pure product of a poetic invention.

Taken in the context of the "Nénuphar blanc," *ramer* and *déramer* designate respectively the setting out on and return from the trip, whereas the *Littré* only mentions *déramer* (a word which has disappeared from the *Larousse*) in the sense of the "action of removing a cocoon of a silkworm from the branches." With respect to this meaning, fallen into disuse, the other appears manifestly as a happy "coup de dés" of Mallarmean invention and all the more fortunate in that it allows the opposite sense of *déramer,* that is, to spin a cocoon, to flow over onto *ramer.*

The poem thus presents itself as the secretion of a thread [*fil*] of silk [*soie*] (or of oneself) [*soi*] which the poet produces in a state of half-sleep. It is the work of the silkworm [*ver(s)*] (or line of verse) into whose envelope the true identity of the poet has disappeared, as the other identity, from which the steady *sparkling* of the letters frees itself, is only exterior, worldly. In this context of "spinning" [*filature*], the skiff, miniscule boat [*navire*] which carries the *rameur* or the *dérameur*, is metamorphosed into a shuttle [*navette*], and the back and forth of its shuttling imitates a movement of incessant return to the point of oblivion between two imaginary courses:

> J'avais beaucoup ramé, d'un grand geste net assoupi, les yeux au dedans fixés sur l'entier oubli d'aller, comme le rire de l'heure coulait alentour. Tant d'immobilité paressait que frôlé d'un bruit inerte *où fila jusqu'à moitié la yole,* je ne vérifiai l'arrêt qu'à l'étincellement stable d'initiales sur les avirons mis à nu, ce qui me rappela à mon identité mondaine (*Nénuphar,* pp. 283–284).[6]

It is thus that the poem of the "Nénuphar" begins. It paradoxically takes its departure from its arrival, which results in a confusion of the signs and a scintillation, which blurs the contours of things and letters:

---

6. "I had rowed much, with a great, clean, sleepy gesture, my eyes within fixed on the entire forgetting of motion, as the laughter of the hour flowed about me. So much immobility idled about that brushed by a dull noise *into which the boat half veered,* I only verified my stopping by the steady sparkling of initials on the raised oars, which brought me back to my worldly identity." (My italics.)

Je ne vérifiai l'arrêt qu'à l'étincellement stable d'initiales sur les avi-
rons mis à nu, ce qui me rappela à mon identité mondaine (pp. 283–
284).

Whether it be a question of his worldly identity or the other, through
the luminous or aquatic vibrations, depth is only perceptible in the confused shimmer of the surfaces.

The stream of revery which has carried the rower to this crucial
point is itself only an *interval* between dormant vegetation:

> Il fallut, pour voir clair en l'aventure, me remémorer mon départ tôt, ce
> juillet de flamme, sur l'intervalle vif entre ses végétations dormantes
> d'un toujours étroit et distrait ruisseau . . . (p. 284).[7]

As soon as the images doubled by their own reflection have arisen,
the "impartial oar-stroke" destroys their ephemeral consistency:

> Sans que le ruban d'aucune herbe me retînt devant un paysage plus que
> l'autre chassé avec son reflet en l'onde par le même impartial coup de
> rame . . . (p. 284).[8]

Forward stroke of the rower [*rameur*], which aims to make the vegetation and the branches[9]—where the thread of silk or self of the
dreamy worm or line of verse [*vers rêveur*] could spin itself—disappear,
and consequently *return stroke of the rower*, desirous of erasing its
traces down to the least vestige of this seam, bubble of foam, which
could have taken on the consistency of a cocoon:

> . . . partir avec: tacitement, en déramant peu à peu sans du heurt briser
> l'illusion ni que le clapotis de la bulle visible d'écume enroulée à ma
> fuite ne jette aux pieds survenus de personne la ressemblance transpar-
> ente du rapt de mon idéale fleur . . . (p. 286)

This is really the fundamental mark of the Mallarmean poem whose
projection safeguards in its trace the movement of its own disappear-

7. "It was necessary, to see the adventure clearly, to recall my early departure, this
flaming July, on the bright interval between the dormant vegetation of an always narrow
and distracted stream . . ."
8. "Without the ribbon of any grass holding me in front of one landscape more than
another dispelled with its reflection in the water by the same impartial oar-stroke . . ."
9. Mallarmé appears to allow the play in the word *rame* of its homonym (*rame* in Old
French means "branch of a tree"). In retaining this sense, the rower's stroke (*coup de
rame*), which erases the ephemeral branches reflected in the pool, produces the effect of
a narcissistic gesture. Another homonym, *ramer*, means in Old French, "to return (reci-
procate) love."

ance. As in "Igitur," the poet "proffers the word to plunge it back into its inanity" (*Igitur*, p. 451).

As with the oar-stroke, the rhythm in the poem punctuates the discourse of this destruction by the blank spaces in the text: intervals of silence with which the writing composes and imitates the play of its oscillation about the critical point. A series of questions brings together the blanks which scan this musical partition in three moments. The first introduces a development on the early part of the trip:

Qu'arrivait-il, où étais-je?

The second marks the rhythmic punctuality of the present:

Le pas cessa, pourquoi?

The third bears upon the return trip:

Conseille, ô mon rêve, que faire?

The initial question is double: it concerns as much the event (what was happening) as the place (where was I?), practically making time and space concurrent, as well as the present and the past, for, if the first imperfect has the value of a present, the other "where was I" which precedes the remembering of the departure, retains the ambiguity of these two poles of temporality.

Split and reassembled by this question which appears from this stopping-point on the water, time and space will produce, under other forms, the extremes of poetic fluctuation, and not without an effect of confusion. From the *present* to the *past* and vice-versa, the oscillation from "being" [*étant*] to "been" [*été*] engenders first the image of a season, summer [*été*], "this flaming July," temporal point of departure and then the spatial image of a pond [*étang*] as an arrival point.

As an effect of these interferences, the *pond*, end-point of the trip, confuses its image with that of a source:

Je venais échouer dans quelque touffe de roseaux, terme mystérieux de ma course, au milieu de la rivière; où tout de suite élargie en fluvial bosquet, elle étale un nonchaloir d'étang plissé des hésitations à partir qu'a une source (p. 284).[10]

10. "I had just run aground in a clump of reeds, mysterious end of my trip, in the middle of the stream, where immediately enlarged into a watery thicket, it spreads out the nonchalance of a pond rippled with a spring's hesitations at departure."

One reads almost by transparency the metaphorization of writing's double movement, both linear and undulating: the stream, *interval* between two banks, becomes an interval between two points and reabsorbs them like a flow of ink in this spot which in spilling over hides the true point of origin, that is, the purpose of the quest.

As always, the failure of writing translates itself into hesitations to start out again, but the repetition of the trip will not eliminate for all that the interferences of a new fluctuation.

Whatever the oscillation may be, it plays itself out more fundamentally between the *chance* of the adventure of the marauder "searching for water flowers" and the *calculation* of the rower who left with

> un *dessein* de reconnaître l'emplacement occupé par la propriété de l'amie d'une amie à qui [il] devait improviser un bonjour (p. 284. My italics).[11]

Two movements intertwine: on the one hand, the desire of the marauder (or the narrator) to wander, which supposes an openness favorable to the turns and detours; on the other hand, the desire to arrive at the goal to *explore* the place. The indeterminateness which affects the identity of the two friends corresponds to this disjunction of desire.

Indeed, how are we to know who is the recipient of the greeting, the unknown or the other? By virtue of its ambiguous position, the relative pronoun *qui* (whom) makes any identification problematic: "la propriété de l'amie d'une amie à qui je devais improviser un bonjour."

Here again, *improvisation* is mixed with the *calculation of the project* as the both dreamy and precise gesture of the rower is compounded into one:

> J'avais beaucoup ramé, d'un grand geste *net assoupi* (My italics.)

In the same way the fixity of the rower or the lazy immobility of the atmosphere, by contrasting themselves to the passing of the hour and the gliding of the boat, participate in the same counterpoint which underlies the entire poem:

---

11. "A *plan* to explore the emplacement occupied by the property of the friend of a friend to whom [he] was supposed to improvise a greeting."

... comme le rire de l'heure coulait alentour. Tant d'immobilité pares-sait que frôlé d'un *bruit inerte* où fila jusqu'à moitié la yole . . . (p. 283. My italics).[12]

For whom is this poem, verse of circumstance or this greeting both improvised and premeditated? For Madame X or for the unknown Y?

The figures of these two letters, as well as that of the two friends, scarcely come to the surface of the poem. In the silence of the three dots, the worldly identity of the known friend has erased itself so well that the same incognito surrounds the two women:

Simplement le parc de Madame . . . l'inconnue à saluer (p. 283).[13]

The unknown woman opposed and made parallel to the other be-comes by this fact a differentiation of the same.

Correlatively the respective places are presented as a "pretty neigh-borhood" whose "obstacle of greenery" occupies the undecipherable interval and precisely that point which assures the contiguity and sep-aration of an X spread out on the surface and a Y which plunges its root into the depths of the water like a water lily:

L'inspection détaillée m'apprit que cet obstacle de verdure en pointe sur le courant, masquait l'arche unique d'un pont prolongé, à terre, d'ici et de là, par une haie clôturant des pelouses. Je me rendis compte. Sim-plement le parc de Madame . . . l'inconnue à saluer.

Un joli voisinage . . . (p. 283).[14]

Now, this obstacle, against which the edge of the boat has just brushed, is, as the text says, the "mysterious end of [the] trip" (p. 284). The exploration of the place will be done by a measuring glance which joins in the poet's eyes the level of the surfaces to that of the depth. And everything takes place as though the "dormant vegetation," "the rib-bons of any grass" reassembled in the rippling of the stream stood up

12. ". . . the hour's laughter flowed about me. So much immobility idled about that brushed by the *dull noise* where the boat half drifted . . ."
13. "Simply the park of Madame . . . , the unknown to be greeted." One could say of these three dots what Mallarmé says about the text's blank spaces in that they replace the transitions "where the subject shimmers" (p. 1576).
14. "Detailed inspection taught me that this tapering obstacle of greenery on the cur-rent masked the single arch of a bridge prolonged on land on both sides by a hedge en-closing lawns. Then it became clear. Simply the park of Madame . . . , the unknown to be greeted.
A pretty neighborhood . . ."

in a "watery thicket" [*bosquet*], in this "clump of weeds" [*roseaux*], or even better in a "bouquet of water rushes" [*ros(e)/eau*], first image of the "ideal flower," water lily or *rose*, uniquely present in the vibration of the noun "roseaux" whose bouquet is stripped of "known calyxes":

> I say: a flower! and out of the oblivion where my voice relegates any contour, as something other than the calyxes that are known, musically arises an idea itself and fragrant, the one absent from all bouquets (*Crise de vers*, p. 368).

Both known and unknown, the friend, or the ideal flower, hides itself behind this *thicket* or in the watery depths of its root. That is why the eye of the rower, now a marauder, oscillates between the horizontality of the space projected by this point until it meets the divergent prolongation of the "hedges closing the lawns" and the depth which opens into the "single arch" [*arche*], privileged location of the arcana of this "feminine possibility" that the poet would prefer completely "lustral," or which he hopes to find unexpectedly inhabiting the area.

One obtains thus a constant wavering between the two friends and in such a manner that the frequency of the movement flowing back upon itself as soon as it has touched one of the extremities will prevent our fixing on one or the other.

This is why the limpid look of the two inhabitants of the "damply impenetrable" dwellings, *chilling* the willow leaves, transforms them into a mirror *clouded* with this same look which proceeds from inhabited surfaces or their depths:

> Un joli voisinage, pendant la saison, la nature d'une personne qui s'est choisi retraite aussi humidement impénétrable ne pouvant être que conforme à mon goût. Sûr, elle avait fait de ce cristal son miroir intérieur à l'abri de l'indiscrétion éclatante des après-midi; elle y venait et la buée d'argent glaçant les saules ne fut bientôt que la limpidité de son regard habitué à chaque feuille.

> Toute je l'évoquais lustrale (*Nénuphar*, p. 284).[15]

---

15. "A pretty neighborhood, during the season, the nature of a person who has chosen a retreat so damply impenetrable only being more to my taste. Surely, she had made this crystal her inner mirror, protected from the glaring indiscretion of the afternoons; she came there, and the silver mist chilling the willows was soon merely the limpidity of her glance accustomed to each leaf.

All I evoked her lustral."

The whole *pond* [*étang*] metamorphosed into a crystal mirror protected from the *summer* [*été*] becomes a point of convergence, haunted by the double presence, both positive and negative, of a *person*. Through the "steady glistening" of these reflections, the two unknown women are co-present, as two letters X and Y superimposed, in this point from which the guiding lines, which open the fictive space of the *impenetrable* landscape, diverge.

Tucked in his boat, and even more than in the beginning, in an almost total immobility, the rower leaning toward the bottom of the boat comes to join his own reflection at this unifying point, and seems with the *yole* to make a double screen for the "joli voisinage":

> Courbé dans la sportive attitude où me maintenait de la curiosité, comme sous le silence spacieux de ce que s'annonçait l'étrangère, je souris au commencement d'esclavage dégagé par une possibilité féminine: que ne signifiaient pas mal les courroies attachant le soulier du rameur au bois de l'imbarcation, comme on ne fait qu'un avec l'instrument de ses sortilèges (p. 284).[16]

By the use of a remarkable modulation, the poet here effectuates a transition from seeing to hearing. If the *yole* was able to suggest the idea of a place, receptacle of essences, it appears at present as an instrument, a sort of viola whose soul, in the technical and other sense of the term, has identified itself with the soul of the rower attached to the depths of the wood.

From interferences of space and time, we pass over, imperceptibly even here, to a crossing-over of space and of rhythm which is announced in the expression "spacious silence." The attention first given to the appearance of figures is displaced after the fact toward the sudden appearance of a rhythm, in sum toward this "step" [*pas*] of the stranger, and of which we do not know, moreover, if it really comes from elsewhere or from this "nudge with the thumb" or we should say with the "toe," well protected in the shoe of the rower, which becomes one with "the instrument of his enchantments." Chance, or, as Mallarmé implies elsewhere, trickery? "No sense, consequently, of trick-

16. "Bent over in the sportive stance in which curiosity kept me, as if under the spacious silence of the stranger's announcing herself, I smiled at the beginning of enslavement loosed by a feminine possibility: which the straps attaching the shoe of the rower to the wood of the boat signified fairly well, as a man becomes one with the instrument of his enchantments."

ery, and introduce, the gentle nudge, which rather, remains the statu-
ary caress, creator of the idea" (*Confrontation*, p. 412).

Just as in the "Démon de l'analogie" the wire breaks on the "zero
sound," (*Démon de l'analogie*, p. 273) here this "step" [*pas*] of "any
one" [*personne*], brusquely interrupted, seems to actualize that virtual
negativity that the two noun substantives have in common with the
homonymous negations: "ne . . . pas," "personne . . . ne." Thus the in-
terruption excludes the appearance of any "feminine possibility" driv-
en up from the edges or the depths:

> Aussi bien une quelconque . . . allais-je terminer. Quand un impercep-
> tible bruit me fit douter si l'habitante du bord hantait mon loisir, ou in-
> espérément le bassin.

> Le pas cessa, pourquoi? (*Nénuphar*, p. 285).[17]

The game of poetic repetition begins again, starting from a halt. If,
at the beginning of the poem, the rower, roused from his half-sleep *verified* by a glance rather than *heard* the halt of the rhythm, giving rise to
a visualization of rhythmic space, here, on the contrary, the visual aspect of space invaded by silence is reduced to this sole "property," that
is, to this "situation" of the soul of the boat tensed to listen.

The remembering of the rhythm and its break is therefore going to
play a role in this conflict of foam and laces or cambric [*batistes*] which
circumscribe the listening place with a mysterious boundary, or, who
knows, the birthplace of the artifice of that boundary.

"In the doubt of the final game,"[18] one could say with Mallarmé, the
notion of baptism (which the word "batistes" evokes here) is linked with
that of blasphemy (p. 74), provoking this combat of whiteness and black-
ness, of innocence and ruse, which is the same combat as that of writing.
Worked like a black lace by the white of Verse, or negatively defined as a
white lace on a night background, writing is above all this game of a "gar-
land with the same" (p. 74), a compromise of ingenuity and calculation.

These interchangeable doubles, frequent in Mallarmean poetry,
take on in the "Nénuphar blanc," a little before the reabsorption of the

---

17. " 'As well any woman' . . . I was going to conclude. When an imperceptible noise
made me doubt whether the inhabitant of the bank haunted my leisure or, beyond all
hope the pond.

The step ceased, why?"

18. "Une dentelle s'abolit," p. 74. Cf. also "Pour un baptême," p. 177.

extent of the word into its point of silence, the figure, both confused
and inverted by the play of the mirror, of a skirt that, while brushing
the ground, seems to emerge from the water. For the back and forth oscillation of the boat is substituted here the more secret oscillation of
feet:

> Subtil secret des pieds qui vont, viennent, conduisent l'esprit où le veut
> la chère ombre enfouie en de la batiste et les dentelles d'une jupe afflu-
> ant sur le sol comme pour circonvenir du talon à l'orteil, dans une flot-
> taison, cette initiative par quoi la marche s'ouvre, tout au bas et les plis
> rejetés en traîne, une échapée, de sa double flèche savante (p. 285).[19]

But the rhythmic coming and going is more a march in place which resembles immobility. The *initiative* of the walk is hidden from perception and only leaves to view the "path" of a division of "worldly" *initials*, only vestige, one could say, of the imaginary wake of the *yole* and
of the way it is written.

Again the rippling of the source could open up into trails, in seams,
in intervals between two banks or between two points, but these are
going to situate themselves now on the vertical axis.

One might observe that the closed space of the rippled pond, where
the spreading out of the stream came to be reabsorbed, was at the origin of the divergence of the hedges. By an opposite movement, the watermark which circumscribes the walk tightens the circle of the new
image of the source whose ripples will be, on the contrary, thrown behind in a double arrow. This image, one might say, announces the end
of the poem, the return trip seen as a double possibility. Before reaching that, it must be pointed out that this mixture of foam and lace hides
a superposition of images: that of the skirt masking the step of the
"stranger" linked with the image of the boat concealing the shoe of the
rower.

Gradually the closed space (pond, boat, skirt, straps attaching the
shoe) tends to tighten itself around an invisible point that the *buckle*
of the "belt" [*ceinture*][20] now closes.

In its upward projection, this "belt buckle" suggests the image of
the female waist [*taille*] or of a clump [*taillis*] of reeds, whereas from its

19. "Subtle secret of feet which go, come, lead the mind where desires the dear
shadow hidden in the cambric and the laces of a skirt flowing down on the ground as if
to surround from the heel to the toe, in a watermark, this initiative by which the gait
opens for itself, right beneath and the folds held back in a train, a path, by its double knowing arrow."

20. *Ceintures* also contains the sense of "enceinte", enclosure.

reflection in the water the image of a diamond buckle seems to be born, closing even "more authentically" the space of the "belts."

Whatever the space reduction might be, its *place* escapes view, except that in spite of all these vertically superimposed screens, the rower, whose glance was first "fixed inwardly," after having "bent [himself] into a sportive stance," not only has almost identified himself with the instrument, but receives now all its vibrations in a sort of unison. "With [his] ear at the level of the mahogany," the poet will have no need of vision to detect the presence which he will capture solely in the "rustling of an arrival." This is why he can ignore the features of Madame which might tend to distract him from that "charm of something underneath," which resounds in the rower's ear in all its folds and grooves. All the preceding images of enclosed space are concentrated here in this new image of the buckle (= ear) which hangs over the rhythmic site.

> A quel type s'ajustent vos traits, je sens leur précision, Madame, interrompre chose installée ici par le bruissement d'une venue, oui! ce charme instinctif d'en dessous que ne défend pas contre l'explorateur la plus authentiquement nouée, avec une boucle en diamant, des ceintures (p. 285).[21]

Strange hero of the mirror, this Narcissus who refuses to see himself in the features of his "feminine possibility" and thus defers his own death!

> Si vague concept se suffit: et ne transgressera le délice empreint de généralité qui permet et ordonne d'exclure tous visages, au point que la révélation d'un (n'allez point le pencher, avéré, sur le furtif seuil où je règne) chasserait mon trouble, avec lequel il n'a que faire (p. 285).[22]

To preserve the music of the poem means therefore keeping the *suspense* which destroys all consistency of the image of *Echo* to only retain the *echo* of a "rustling."

Such, summarized here, is the entire poetics of the "Nénuphar," whose title, as we have suggested, "as something other than the known

---

21. "To whatever type your features conform, I sense that their precision, Madame, interrupts something fixed here by the rustling of an arrival, yes! this instinctive charm of something underneath which is not defended against the explorer by the most authentically closed, with a diamond buckle, of belts."

22. "Such a vague concept suffices: and will not transgress the delight marked with generality which permits and orders the exclusion of all faces, to the extent that the revelation of one (do not tilt it, well-established, over the stealthy threshold where I reign) would chase away my emotion, with which it has no connection."

calyxes," is a receptacle of musical virtualities, in the same way the *yole,* more than a boat, becomes by its name the instrument of the poet's enchantments.

Seen thus, the fiction of the trip is an aggregate of projections and rejections of meanings found in the "creux néant musicien," of words, in the folds of their immemorial source. Oscillations, then sparklings, or vibration gathered by the ear at this point of "crisis of verse" where, as Mallarmé again says: "All becomes suspense, fragmentary disposition with alternation and opposition, uniting in the total rhythm, which would be the unspoken poem, at the blank spaces" (*Crise de vers,* p. 367).

After that, how can one know if this "exquisite emptiness" with which the poem regales us, is a trip of *relaxation* [*détente*],[23] where one goes at the behest of adventure, or rather the site of a *waiting* [*attente*] or an *understanding* [*entente*], even of a "perfect harmony"?

It remains that the poem sparkles with all these meanings combined, as the games of calculation and chance are combined in the image of the vagabond watcher and as the anagrams of the words *rameur* and *dérameur* are entwined in the word *maraudeur.*

It is thus that through the fortuitousness of adventure now appears the calculation of the marauder who measures his gestures, watches and spies. It then seems that chance was only an excuse and this casual "dress" a disguise designed to reinforce the effect of verisimilitude:

Ma présentation, en cette tenue de maraudeur aquatique, je la peux tenter, avec l'excuse du hasard (*Nénuphar,* p. 285).[24]

One notices simultaneously that the turns and twists of this trip are merely ways of shaping a discourse spoken not to be heard:

Que de discours oiseux en comparaison de celui que je tins pour n'être pas entendu, faudra-t-il, avant de retrouver aussi instinctif accord que maintenant . . . (pp. 285–286).[25]

The maneuver of the well-calculated watch can thus take the appearance of a wandering. Even the spontaneity of the improvised greeting is *foreseen* in case the watcher of signs is surprised in his hid-

23. See note 4.
24. "I can attempt my introduction, in this dress of an aquatic marauder, with the excuse of chance."
25. "How many discourses, idle in comparison to that which I uttered in order to be unheard, will be necessary, before finding a harmony as intuitive as this one."

ing place. This effect of surprise would give to his "introduction" a remarkable naturalness, all the more credible if it is compared to a polite "phrase" pronounced on the occasion of a visit. This is what would authorize the poet to proffer a greeting in a movement of "inspiration":

> . . . mieux que visite, suivie d'autres, l'autorisera (p. 285).[26]

But, *inspiration* being equally the act by which one takes in one's breath, it follows that these two contrary movements are neutralized at the boundaries of silence and speech, at this positive and negative limit of a nothing [*rien*], of a not [*pas*], and of a nobody [*personne*], all made of "intact dreams" and "breath withheld"

> dans la peur d'une apparition (p. 286).[27]

From this "moving limit" alone can the question, which allows the alternative, loom up:

> Conseille, ô mon rêve, que faire?

The first alternative aims at the total erasure of the poem, the other concludes the "maneuver" of which it was the object.

If the trip proceeded at the beginning as the remembering of a dream, here the poet rewinds the thread of the dreamy silkworm (verse) [*ver(s) rêveur*] with the sole object of keeping intact the memory of this non-trip, of which the water lily [*né-nu-phar*] is the hidden sign:

> Résumer d'un regard la vierge absence éparse en cette solitude et comme on cueille, en mémoire d'un site, l'un de ces magiques nénuphars clos qui y surgissent tout à coup, enveloppant de leur creuse blancheur un rien fait de songes intacts, du bonheur qui n'aura pas lieu et de mon souffle ici retenu dans la peur d'une apparition, partir avec: tacitement, en déramant peu à peu sans du heurt briser l'illusion ni que le clapotis de la bulle visible d'écume enroulée à ma fuite ne jette aux pieds survenus de personne la ressemblance transparente du rapt de mon idéale fleur (p. 286).[28]

26. ". . . better than a visit, followed by others, would authorize."
27. "In fear of an appearance."
28. "To resume in a glance the virgin absence sprinkled in this solitude, and as one plucks, in memory of a place, one of those magical closed lilies which suddenly rise up, enveloping with their hollow whiteness a nothing, made of intact dreams, of happiness which will not take place and of my breath held here in the fear of an appearance, to leave with it: silently . . ." [Translation continues in note 5]

Here indeed is what is meant in the proper sense of the word
déramer, by "the action of removing a cocoon." As for the other sense
of *déramer,* which designates the backwards maneuver and thus the
rhythm of erasing, Mallarmé invents it by this ingenious "coup de *dé*"
which creates the opposition to the sense of *ramer.*

Everything that could denounce the "abduction" or even better the
theft [*vol*]²⁹ of this rhythmic beat must disappear, including even the
least seam of the idle discourse. Only the closed lily remains, with
petals folded in like the useless wings which anticipate the image of a
swan's egg whose "flights have not flown."

Such is the maneuver which has the *idle* discourse veer off toward
a discourse of birds [*oiseux/oiseaux*] in the second alternative: the
"quest of water flowers" changes into a quest for *swans* [*cygnes*] or for
signs [*signes*] which brings to light another aspect of the marauder or of
the writer. These latter only follow the opening out of the flight or the
writing to discover the nest or the rhythmic source:

> Si, attiré par un sentiment d'insolite, elle a paru, la Méditative ou la
> Hautaine, la Farouche, la Gaie, tant pis pour cette indicible mine que
> j'ignore à jamais! car j'accomplis selon les règles la manœuvre: je dé-
> gageai, virai et je contournais déjà une ondulation du ruisseau, empor-
> tant comme un noble œuf de cygne, tel que n'en jaillira le vol, mon ima-
> ginaire trophée, qui ne se gonfle d'autre chose sinon de la vacance
> exquise de soi qu'aime l'été à poursuivre, dans les allées de son parc,
> toute dame, arrêtée parfois et longtemps, comme au bord d'une source
> à franchir ou de quelque pièce d'eau (p. 286).³⁰

Certainly, the intention remains the same in spite of the divergence of
the arrows, but do not the contours of the idle discourse run the risk of
stiffening in allowing to be seen, in this non-erased poem, the face of
"some friend or other": the Meditative, Haughty, Fierce or the Gay.
Four faces to which correspond respectively four moments of the poem
which can be detailed in the following manner: fixation of the inward

29. *Voler,* of course, is both "to steal" and "to fly."
30. "If, drawn by a feeling of something unusual, she appeared, the Meditative or the
Haughty, the Fierce, the Gay lady, so much the worse for that inexpressible face that I
shall never know! for I completed the maneuver according to the rules: I pushed off,
turned and was already rounding a curve in the stream, carrying away like a noble swan's
egg, such as from which no flight will spring, my imaginary trophy, which does not swell
from anything except the exquisite emptiness of itself which every woman, in summer,
loves to pursue, in the avenues of her park, halting sometimes and for a long time, as if
on the edge of a spring to be crossed or of some pond."

glance, resurgence of the watery copse, stopping of the step, enjoyment of the confused intimacy.

There lies the risk that occurs in following the outline of the composition, whose established meanings Mallarmé has tried to destroy to preserve this "Figure que nul n'est" (*Richard Wagner, rêverie,* p. 1592), joined to the incognito of this "inexpressible face which he will never know." We realize that any "ordinary" appearance would thus cancel this "feminine possibility" of Self that the poet attempts to throw back into the scope of the text's virtualities.

This "exquisite emptiness of [it]self" which figures in the conclusion of the poem, as a common pursuit of the poet and the friend, can only be understood if one sees that it is a game of doubles, which the surface of the mirror would limit in their "confused intimacy."

It remains that if a too-great precision of features could endanger the oscillations of the writing, it is to conjure away this peril that the poet invents this double ending where the everything and the nothing of the appearance of the poem remain the two possibilities of an alternative whose oscillation should suffice to neutralize the precision and thus to safeguard the essential indetermination.

Rather than claiming to formulate any essence of Mallarmean poetics, my analysis aimed rather to pick up this game of "fragmentary disposition with alternation and opposition" in the poem.

If I have happened to play with words, it is because the "prose poem" requires this particular attitude of observation and of illumination to see what makes a *critical* poem of the prose poem:

> The breaks in the text, rest assured, take pains to concur with sense and only inscribe blank space as far as their points of illumination: a form, perhaps, emerges, present, permitting that which for a long time was the prose poem and our study, to end up as a critical poem, if one joins the words better. (*Notes,* p. 1576).

I have also gone so far in my exploration as to scrutinize the figure of letters in words such as *yole* for example. To *yole* we could add the word "joli" (pretty) which presents in the alternation of descending (j) and ascending (l) rhythms, hollows (o) and fullnesses (i), of its letters, a condensed figuration of the poem, which presents itself as a quest not of *beauty,* but of its *surroundings,* admirably expressed by the form and the meaning of "joli."

However, we did not want to venture farther on the paths of this cabbalistic science which Mallarmé himself considers as chimerical:

Such a magisterial effort of the imagination touches one of the sacred
or perilous mysteries of Language; and which it will be prudent to analyze only on the day when Science, possessing the vast repertoire of idioms ever spoken on earth, will write the history of the letters of the
alphabet through all the ages and what was almost their absolute meaning, sometimes guessed, sometimes misapprehended by man, creators
of words: but there will no longer be, in this time, either Science to sum
this up, or some one to say it. Chimera, let us be satisfied, for now, of
the light which magnificent writers throw on this subject (*Mots anglais*,
p. 921).

It is really in the spirit of this last sentence that we have conducted
our analysis! All the more that in this game of chance and calculations
where the poet, as Poe says, is also a mathematician, we would have
little chance of succeeding. For, not only does the poet foresee the calculations of *others* but he speculates on the intuition of the *other* and
goes beyond by a divining whose mark is unique. Evidently, we are referring to the three characters of the *Purloined Letter*, the inspector, the
minister and Dupin, whose leaps beyond the respective ruses culmi-
nate in the figure par excellence of the Poet who is reborn indefinitely
in the game of his inventions.

Thus every reader who tries to guess the poem is always and more
astutely guessed by it.

—Translated by Kathryn Crecelius

JACQUES EHRMANN

The Tragic/Utopian Meaning
of History*

Attempting to make a theoretical and concrete test of the relationships
which obtain *historically* (that is, in a particular phase of Western history) between areas such as "history" and "literature" amounts to
showing how certain forms of so-called "literary" imagination may be
found in certain forms of so-called "historical" imagination. Each
would then serve to illuminate the other and to make its critique possible. One need only recall that history and literature were originally
indistinguishable, each one being *stories* (*récits*) or *histories* which
only gradually became distinguishable one from the other.

Thus, whatever its level of abstraction, or more precisely, at its high-
est level of abstraction, the problem of history encounters the problem
of the story, and *vice versa.* Those involved in it, actors or characters
(may the words indeed be separated?) are the subject-objects of the action, of which the organization which they propose and to which they
testify simultaneously constitutes the story [*récit*], the chronology, the
chronicle, the logic and, of course, their meaning [*sens*].[1] Their meaning, that is, a particular way of telling time.

From which this temporary conclusion may be drawn: both history
and literature invent themselves. I deliberately retreat behind this re-
flexive which leaves the verb no other subjects but history and literature themselves.

Without fearing to belabour the obvious, let us say that history
changes, or more exactly, that the way it is *recounted* changes.
Voltaire's history is not Bossuet's; Hegel's is not Voltaire's; Marx's . . . ;

---

*From *Yale French Studies* 58 (1979): *In Memory of Jacques Ehrmann: Inside Play
Outside Game.*

1. The French text continually plays upon two meanings of the word *sens*—"meaning" and "direction,"—and occasionally upon a third meaning, "sense." [tr.]

YFS 96, *50 Years of Yale French Studies: A Commemorative Anthology,* eds.
Porter and Waters, © 1999 by Yale University.

Freud's . . . ; and so on until ours, which is not the last. This obvious point allows us to unmask the cliché hidden in the metaphor of the *thread* of history. As if history developed like a thread unwinding! Here, the most elementary analysis of any literary (or of any kind of) story demonstrates the fallacy of this metaphor and suffices to place into question, along with the concept of history, the concept of causality which gives meaning [*sens*] to history: in fact, it is *we* (!) who impose upon causality both its direction and its meaning.

This is then the history to be questioned through the experience of literature, through which is written and in which is built both our individual and our collective history, the story[2] which literary critics read and interpret in the history of its tellers.

Involved here is the combined union of two forms of temporal sequence: the individual, which bears the mark of temporality; and the collective, which bears the mark of historicity. Individual destiny on the one hand, marked by individual birth and death; collective destiny on the other, marked by the origin and the end of humanity.[3]

Thus history is lived and apprehended *alternately* (and not simultaneously) along the double perspective [*optique*] of temporality and historicity, as in the *optical play* of Necker's cube, whose front and back sides continuously alternate and cannot be held in place for more than a few fractions of a second, since each side needs to play itself off against the others. It is therefore necessary to make a kind of (retinal) accommodation, according to whether one is playing time or history in one or another of its forms.

In accordance with the structure which we shall discover in these complementary and mutually-exclusive forms, through which our civilization has heretofore deciphered [*déchiffré*] and invented its (hi)story, we may give them names: tragic and utopian.

But why the word "form?" Because history as game and as calling-into-play of destiny is played in a certain area, according to a design [*découpage*] which gives it form and meaning, in a certain *space* where history and destiny take *place*. This history's, this destiny's place—that is, their expression, the place therefore where the thought of destiny becomes concrete and is formed into the destiny of thought—this history's place is *literature*, in its deepest and most extended sense: the

2. The French *histoire* has been translated sometimes as "story," sometimes as "history," depending upon the context. [tr.]

3. Although separated in order to facilitate the analysis, these two forms of destiny are clearly linked, in fact, dialectically.

language of history, of story, the language of the place where and through which man sets forth, articulates and draws the figure of his historical destiny.

Therefore literature,—this speculation (and here the economic and philosophical senses of the word fuse and join that of *play* which has already been touched upon and which all speculation implies),—this speculation is located upon the two levels which I have just mentioned: the tragic and the utopian; one referring to an *arche*, the other to a *telos*.

The utopian and the tragic therefore are the two irreducible and indissociable sides of thought bent upon its completion: aiming on the one hand toward its origin as if toward its own end, on the other hand aiming at its end as projection of its "true origin," each one bearing another life, and thereby its own death.

So history is built into this double form, whose complementary nature I shall now describe.

I shall begin by analyzing tragic structure, and then utopian structure, with due apologies for the necessarily schematic nature of these remarks. It should be kept in mind that the examples discussed have a primarily illustrative value, that other examples may be substituted for them, and that in each case a concrete analysis (which cannot be undertaken here) should modify and add needed details to the theoretical suppositions proposed here. I should also like to emphasize that the forms which I am proposing are by no means archetypes—they are empty forms to be filled in. Furthermore, what I here call "tragic" and "utopian" thought cannot be limited to the "genres" with which these terms are conventionally associated. One final remark: we shall be considering extreme examples, between which exist countless intermediary cases, in which a mixture of the two forms may be observed.

THE TRAGIC MODE

Oedipus Rex

What better way to illustrate the mode of this speculation, the mode of tragic play, than to take the example of the story of Oedipus, as told by Sophocles.

Where is it located? In other words, what is the tragic place? It is Thebes, the place of Oedipus' birth as well as of his downfall. The very same place, or rather the place of this repeated downfall:

1) his first birth itself;

2) his second birth: that is, the birth of Oedipus unto his truth. Thus, in the first place, the place where Jocasta and Laius live. Hence the place (following the oracle) from which Oedipus has initially been rejected; the place of his exclusion. But also the place of his return and of his new exclusion. Oedipus is the stranger *par excellence:* stranger to the city, but also stranger to his own (hi)story, for it is completely enclosed in the brackets of his double exclusion.

Oedipus quite literally lives his story in the outer regions of *another* world, and not as his own. The best proof of this story's incriminating misplacement is the following: Oedipus kills his father in the interval separating Corinth from Thebes, "at the crossing of two roads,"—a *no place par excellence.*

Hence the tragic rests upon a spatial misreading [*méconnaissance spatiale*] on the part of the tragic hero or, to call him by another name which now appears more appropriate: the tragic voyager.

At first, the other world is Corinth to which Oedipus has been exiled. But for him it is the world itself, until the moment when the oracle causes him to flee from it and to seek another world (of innocence) which will turn out to be the world (of his guilt) itself.

The tragic voyager is thus simultaneously haunted, drawn and driven toward another world which he falsely thinks he can make his own and which, ironically because unknown to him, will end up by indeed becoming his. As I have said, this spatial misreading always places Oedipus *outside* of his own history, of his own destiny, until the moment when—but then it is already too late—he realizes that his own destiny has already been *played out.*

And yet, that is his destiny itself.

Tragedy begins at the moment when the tragic voyager sets out *en route* to his destiny. His story, his history consists of this progression toward the tragic place, this elsewhere to which he turns his back at the same time that he draws near to it, which he finally surrounds and which at the same time finally surrounds him.

The tragic story—the tragedy of history—is thus that very hollow, that absence which places itself in the lag, the dis-location of elsewhere and here (or on a temporal level, of *ante* and *nunc*). And it is precisely at the moment when he finds himself in the center of this place that he finds himself expelled from it.

After the tragic place has once again closed upon the tragic voyager, it ejects him from it. The circle is closed: death is repetition and recognition; it is rebirth unto birth, unto the truth of the end in the beginning. The voyager leaves the tragic place or dies.

But this is not all that should be said. A reading of *Oedipus* shows us something else: this work possesses *en abyme* (that is, like a kind of inverted and miniaturized reflection of the main form) the utopian form which I have yet to describe.

The principal elements are these: Oedipus, to whom Thebes owes its welfare, may be identified with this city. Its fate is as important to him as his own (as we know, they really are connected). At the very beginning of the play, the priest addresses Oedipus in these terms:

> King, you yourself
> have seen our city reeling like a wreck
> already; it can scarcely lift its prow
> out of the depths, out of the bloody surf.
> A blight is on the fruitful plants of the earth,
> A blight is on the cattle in the fields,
> a blight is on our women that no children
> are born to them. . . .

And later on, he again speaks to Oedipus:

> So, let us never speak about your reign
> as of a time when first our feet were set
> secure on high, but later fell to ruin.
> Raise up our city, save it and raise it up.
> Once you have brought us luck with happy omen;
> be no less now in fortune.
> If you will rule this land, as now you rule it,
> better to rule it full than empty. . . .

In these remarks are both a doubling and an inversion: the city was dying, Oedipus gave it life; the city is dying, Oedipus is killing it. But Oedipus does desire the city's welfare and makes it his own:

> Your sorrow has one object only: everyone for himself. My own heart
> mourns for Thebes, and for you and for me, all together.

Oedipus is thus a sort of philosopher-king, as in Plato's *Republic*.

Did he not answer the Sphinx? He "knows" and through his knowledge he has saved the city. However, this is just what Tiresias reproaches him for; and Oedipus replies: "If I have saved the city, what does the rest matter?" This "rest" to which he turns his back is of course his individual and tragic destiny. But how could he know, since he has been living on a different level: the utopian level of knowledge founded upon a particular form of ignorance.

Can one then not say that the question which the Sphinx asked Oedipus was really not for him but for the city or, if you will: the Sphinx was a question for the city, for which Oedipus was but the mediator. So by answering the Sphinx's question for the city, Oedipus' knowledge enables him to solve the city's problem, but not his own. And he thereby fails, since through his ignorance, he himself becomes the stain of which the city must rid itself in order to live. The city in turn becomes the mediator through which Oedipus learns of his own ignorance. Individual and collective destiny become one.

Phèdre

Lucien Goldmann perceptively saw that the main theme of Racine's *Phèdre* is flight,[4] but he saw in it only a theme. Without finding fault with Goldmann, whose main concerns were elsewhere, I should point out that, in our attempt to locate a common tragic structure in rather diverse works, flight appears to be an element of this structure. An essential element, since it points out—whether neutrally called "displacement" or, more emphatically, "*dis*-location"—that passage from one place to another, an example of which we have just observed in *Oedipus Rex.*

That we are dealing here with something more than a theme, even more than the main theme of *Phèdre,* was seen by Roland Barthes who, when discussing Racine's theater as a whole, considers flight as one of the elements of a Racinian topography. Let us then utilize these very pertinent remarks to pursue our analysis still further.[5]

The tragic place in *Phèdre* is clearly Trézène. But this place does not at first appear as an *inside.* Quite to the contrary, Trézène is in the first place the outside, to which Phedra exiles Hippolytus. The inside is Athens, from which she exiles him. Thus we may say that Thebes is to Oedipus, at the moment when he is exiled from Corinth, what Trézène is to Phedra/Hippolytus, when Phedra exiles Hippolytus from Athens.

Thus when Barthes defines the tragic hero as the man enclosed, he fails to account for that which leads the hero into his tragic situation and which can only be understood in terms of the dialectics of inside

4. *The Hidden God.*
5. Roland Barthes, *Sur Racine,* pp. 15–20.

and outside. For whoever flees, flees both *toward* and *from.* The tragic hero is both exiled *in* and locked *out.*[6]

The double-exiled Hippolytus tries to end his exile. For he is exiled not only from Athens, but also from himself, since (a common seventeenth-century theme) he is in love with Aricia and no longer possesses himself:

> Maintenant je me cherche et ne me trouve plus
>
> . . .
>
> Je ne me souviens plus des leçons de Neptune   (lines 547 and 550)

Phedra, too, is the exiler exiled:

> J'adorais Hippolyte; et le voyant sans cesse
>
> . . .
>
> Je l'évitais partout   (lines 286 and 289)

And calling him to mind on his "fleeing chariot," she realizes that she has lost her self-possession:

> Insensée, où suis-je? et qu'ai-je dit?
> Où laissé-je égarer mes voeux et mon esprit?
> Je l'ai perdu . . . (lines 179–181)

Here madness, amorous or tragic, is expressed in a double question, setting up a contradictory equivalency: that is, an error on the level of the *forgotten* place which he should have kept in mind, present ("Where am I?") and on that of the words he has uttered and which are therefore present, but which he should have *forgotten* ("What have I said?").[7]

Precisely the same kind of error regarding one's interlocutor—although the signs are inverted, since this time absence is taken for presence—precisely this error is made by Phedra who sees in Hippolytus a younger Theseus: "What am I saying? He is not dead at all, since he breathes in you."

This "What am I saying?" allows us to return to the problem, referred to already, of the present, spoken word. On this topic, Barthes writes: "the order of language is the only tragic order" and "all conduct which suspends language makes life cease."[8]

---

6. A more sustained analysis of the *"actants"* in these tragedies would enable us to show the structural differences from one play to another.

7. That present which is absence and nostalgia of a peaceful past was also expressed by Hippolytus in the opposition between "now" and "I no longer remember" in the lines quoted above.

8. *Sur Racine,* p. 18.

These remarks are quite true, but they do not account for the non-voluntary, fatal side of the tragic language. For it is not only conduct which determines language . . . and life (*cf.* the "Sortez!" of Roxanne to Bajazet, a veritable death sentence), but language which, because without the characters' knowledge, determines their conduct . . . and their lives. If the characters die of other people's words, they also die of having themselves spoken; since to speak is to express, to make present that which should have remained absent, to make known what should have remained unknown. The words having escaped from the characters, having fled (from their mouths), flight becomes as increasingly urgent as it is vain.

Alienated in the very words they speak, it is when they are the most foreign to themselves that they are struck by the truth.

Through words knowledge makes its murderous way. The words outstrip the characters, pulling and attracting them against their own will, toward the Place, the center where Truth becomes manifest, unbearable . . . simply *present.* Then, in the moment when the past converges on the present, the future cancels itself out. In the structure of tragic imagination, truth has no future. More precisely put, its only future is in the past conditional mood, in the "would have been."

The past conditional of an absence dreamed as presence, inhabited by the small-scale utopia which our discussion of Oedipus has already uncovered in tragic structure. Past conditional of the impossible identification to which Phedra desperately gives herself: identifying Hippolytus with Theseus, and herself with Ariadne. Need we recall these famous lines:

> Ma soeur du fil fatal eût armé votre main.
> Mais non, dans ce dessein je l'aurais devancée;
> L'amour m'en eût d'abord inspiré la pensée.
> C'est moi, prince, c'est moi, dont l'utile secours
> Vous eût du labyrinthe enseigné les détours.   [lines 649–656]

The labyrinth, utopian place *par excellence,* where Phedra shuts herself up with Hippolytus in thought:

> Moi-même devant vous j'aurais voulu marcher;
> Et Phèdre au labyrinthe avec vous descendue
> Se serait avec vous retrouvée, ou perdue.   [lines 660–662]

The labyrinth is the utopian *elsewhere,* that monstrous elsewhere whose walls close once more upon the couple who have become *other,* in order to protect and to isolate them from the rest of the world. The labyrinth is literally the place of error dreamed, where finding oneself and losing oneself become synonymous.

But the utopia to which Phedra momentarily seeks to flee cannot endure, for it is located in the past, a past that is *experienced*, but differently experienced. And so this utopia is nothing but the fantasm of a non-existent past (is this not characteristic of the past?)—of a past-perfect happiness which never took *place.*

If we now try to see what these two works (*Oedipus Rex* and *Phèdre*), chosen as examples of a certain mode of imagination, have in common, we realize that their overall structure is identical. It is this structure which I propose to call the structure of tragic thought.

Therefore I may now try to define it as the spatio-temporal figure described by the lag, the dis-location of one place relative to another, by the sliding of one place to another, connected and separated by a consciousness which cannot live and think them together, as inside and outside, without exploding them, thus disintegrating both them and itself. Or differently put: it is the sliding of one place to another, connected and separated by a consciousness which, *in order to* live and think them together, as inside and outside, must explode them, thus disintegrating both them and itself. For at the very moment when knowledge becomes *inside*, when it finally is integrated as knowledge, this accumulation of a finally-recovered past causes it to be lost.

THE UTOPIAN MODE

The analysis of tragic form has already enabled us to make some progress in analyzing the area of utopia. Thus we may limit ourselves to sketching the main lines of this second figure. The inverted (*en abyme*) image of the utopian figure, which is framed within the tragic figure, has allowed us to discover the reversal of the signs of ignorance and knowledge that operates from one form to the other. For this reason I feel justified in affirming that each of these forms contains the other as its contrary.

Utopia

To illustrate this topic one hardly knows which of the countless possible examples to choose; but it seems appropriate to begin by turning to Thomas More. Let us once again ask ourselves what the relationship is between the hero and the utopian place. Who is the hero of More's Utopia? More tells us that, having caught sight of the man who is about to recount his travels, he had taken him for a sailor. But before introducing the men to each other, More's friend explains to him his error: "But you are quite mistaken, for his sailing has not been like that of Palinurus, but that of Ulysses, or rather, of Plato." And he goes on to praise the man's learning—his knowledge of Latin and Greek, his interest in philosophy—in a word, he paints the portrait of a humanist. He also reveals the man's name: it is Raphael Hythloday, formed from the Greek *hythlos*, meaning nonsense, vain chatter, and *daios*, meaning knowledge.

Asked to relate his experiences, Raphael begins his account, not with a description of the imaginary place from which he has purportedly just returned, but with a critique of English institutions. Like someone who pulls out a thread and ends up by pulling apart the entire fabric, Raphael starts by criticizing the practice of inflicting capital punishment upon simple thieves, in order to show that it poses the vaster and more fundamental problem of property. Then property is shown to be connected with all other problems: war, the idleness of the nobility, farming and agriculture, the prices of commodities, prostitution, gambling, etc. . . . .

Only after this systematic critique will a response be given to the problems raised: by the description, in the Second Book, of Utopia.

We have observed that utopian form is marked by two contradictory places, England and Utopia, connected and separated by the experience of the utopian voyager. One after the other, these worlds are dismissed: the utopian world is the Other World, which, as the name says, is located "noplace," "U-topos." But it is also the place of happiness, "Eu-topos." I do not think that it is this world, our world, which gives its meaning to the other world, to utopia, but rather it is our possibility of imagining another world which gives meaning to our own. Our world is thus but the reverse side of the other world, that world of happiness, the only world worth living, the only *real* world.

And so the text endlessly oscillates between inside and outside, each world being at once the inside and the outside of the other.

The Romance of the Rose

"In the twentieth year of my life, at that time when Love demands his tribute from the young, I went to bed as usual, and was sleeping deeply, when I dreamed a dream most beautiful and pleasing." It was in May, "a time of love and full of joy."

The narrator dreams that he is walking, that he strolls along a river bank and . . .

> After a while I found myself before a great, enclosed orchard of crenu-
> late walls, richly decorated on the outside with pictures and figures . . .
> I closely examined the figures painted in gold and blue all along the wall.
> It was high and square: it served as fencing for the orchard, instead of
> hedges.

The orchard is magnificent:

> For my part, I was so delighted by it that, if the passage had been clear,
> I should not for a treasure have foregone seeing their assembly [that of
> the people inside] . . . Upon hearing such gladness, I took to grieving,
> asking myself through what stratagem I might penetrate into the gar-
> den. I could find no passageway, and knew not if there were some open-
> ing or way of entry. . . . Finally it occurred to me that it was impossible
> that in so beautiful an orchard there not be a door, a ladder, or an open-
> ing. I therefore hastened to go around the fortress, and came upon a nar-
> row, firmly-closed door.

And once he has been admitted, he remarks: "I thought myself in the Earthly Paradise; the place was so delightful that it seemed supernat-ural."

What follows is well-known: Guillaume de Lorris writes an Art of Loving; Jean de Meung continues by assembling a kind of *summa* of contemporary knowledge. I shall jump immediately to the end of the romance. The narrator, in love with the Rose, finally overcomes her af-ter a strenuous battle:

> If it were given to me to come into port, I wanted to make my armor
> touch the relics. . . . I thought my first throw [of the staff] was good, but
> I could not make it. My staff came out, I threw it back in, but in vain: I
> felt a palisade inside which I did not see. . . . And trying so hard to break
> through the palisade that I sweated great beads . . . I nonetheless man-
> aged to catch sight of a narrow way through which I could pass; but I
> had to break the fence. . . .

The story ends with these remarks:

> Before leaving these grounds where I should willingly have stayed
> longer, I gathered to my great joy the flower of the fair, leafy rosebush,
> and I got the red rose. Then it was day, and I awoke.

Let us see how this work is organized according to our system of opposition between *inside* and *outside:*
1.   This dream contrasts implicitly with a state of wakefulness. Thus,
     everything happens in the brackets of this erotic dream, until the
     moment when the narrator ends his erotic dream with a nocturnal
     emission.
2.   But there is another set of brackets:
     —At the beginning, the entry into the garden, with the wall and the
     little opening.
     —At the end, the deflowering of the Rose, the breaking-down of the
     palisade.
3.   Inside these double brackets:
     —the Art of Love (Guillaume de Lorris' first part)
     —knowledge (Jean de Meung's second part)
     That is, the two answers which our civilization has invented to the
problem posed by death or, in other words, the problem of *desire.*
4.   It is not unimportant to recall that this dream of love and knowl-
     edge is located in an idyllic place, described as an Earthly Paradise.
     The future proposed by the dream reflects back upon an earlier
     state, a state inhabited by a perfection not to be discovered or in-
     vented, but to be *re*-discovered, *re*-invented. This first place—par-
     adise lost—is explicitly or implicitly at the root of all myths of the
     ideal city, and even of all *thought* about the ideal city. Of Thomas
     More's thought in particular; for in posing the problem of property,
     he implicitly poses the problem of the origin of society, which
     amounts to saying: the problem of the *law.*
     Just as the examples of the tragic were each only a particular exam-
ple of the tragic structure, so each of these examples of utopian thought
is a variation of the same structure. This structure is made up of the
juxtaposition of two places, of an inside and an outside, connected and
separated by a consciousness which makes them at once present and
absent to each other.

History and Meaning

In attempting to discuss tragic and utopian figures, I have emphasized
their spatial character, the role that these places (and their dis-location)
play in locating tragic and utopian stories. I have only alluded in passing to those "stories" built into the roads which separate and connect

these places: or more precisely, I have only alluded in passing to the type of knowledge which these stories offer of History.

But since it is not my goal to grant more importance to space or to structure rather than to history, it now becomes appropriate to play off the spatial dimension against the temporal and/or historical, and to suggest the meaning of this play. Indeed, the interplay of *here* and *elsewhere* corresponds to the interplay of *now* and *then* (past or future), and both play together with the other two terms. In other words, tragic and utopian space refer to a tragic and utopian time, that is, to a past and to a future of history, to an *arche* and to a *telos*, where it finally finds its meaning.

In the case of the tragic voyager, experience is *lived* in chronology (from past to present), but is only *understood* after the event by an inversion of chronology that forces the tragic voyager to stem the current of time. Such a step places him outside of himself, outside of his own story, literally eccentric to his own history.

One may also say that the present, initially empty of meaning, cannot be understood as the future of the past (as a simple chronology of events might lead one to believe). On the contrary, it is the past that, once interpreted, makes up the future (however ephemeral) of the present. Think of Oedipus!

The past, as *arche,* thus enables the tragic hero to reconquer his own history by the discovery of his origin. Through this detour, this return, the present is filled with meaning, the center filled in—even at the price of death.

In the case of the utopian voyager, the situation is inverted; experience is *understood* through a reversal of chronology. It is the *future*, the *elsewhere* which explains the *present*, the *here*, and gives them their meaning. But this experience is *lived* only as a project unfulfilled. Consequently, the utopian voyager is also uprooted from his own history, from the present, eccentric to himself.

From him the present (empty of meaning) is not given as the past of the future; it is the future which is given as past (although elusive, or perhaps because elusive) of the present. To be sure of this, one need only remember that the utopia described by More is a society without property or, to put it like the *philosophes,* a society where "one does not distinguish between thine and mine"; More's Utopia refers us to a transparent past located at the origin of society. This very origin is then projected upon the screen of the future.

The future (although elusive or because elusive) is the *telos* which enables utopian consciousness, the utopian hero to set out to conquer his history, thanks to the discovery of his end. It is therefore only after this back-and-forth motion that the present recovers its center, even if it is literally given "no place."

We may thus conclude, after having taken a look back at the history of meaning in our civilization, that the decentering of structure corresponds to the decentering of history, as well as to their *recentering*.

But this is not all. However reassuring the words of such a conclusion may be, by no means may they mark the end of our inquiry. On the contrary, they are barely adequate to indicate its beginning. Hence all the preceding has been but a preamble to what it remains for me to say—although rest assured, it will be brief.

Indeed, what would be the use of pointing out the structurality of the history of meaning, its archaeoteleological nature, without adopting a position regarding this discovery? But as of now such a position can only be stated in the interrogative mode of discourse which is waiting to be invented.

—If this has been our history, must it indefinitely so remain? Dependent upon an archaeology and an eschatology?

—If we wish to go beyond the forms imposed by tragic-utopian thought, must we not at the same time break away, rid ourselves of the absent-present center of tragic-utopian consciousness?

—And if we wish, without flinching, to observe the play of meaning as it is revealed to us in its decentering, have we any solution but to break away from the moorings which hold down play in an origin and in an end?

Then it would not be enough to travel again from meaninglessness to meaning, from nonsense to sense. It would not suffice to embark upon this journey through the language of history, at whose origin or end we would finally reach the truth. In other words, it would not be enough to repeat, paraphrasing Strabo, that all language is a lie, since it offers meaning where meaning is not to be found—for that would be but another way of once again granting it truth.

No. We must try to imagine [*penser*] language and, *a fortiori*, literature at the level of its dislocation, in the very brackets that we have seen open between each of the terms marking time and space.

We must try to imagine the world's play at the level of its decentering.

In a word—and here I shall conclude—having broken adrift from meaning, it remains for us only, with all the discipline required by such an undertaking, to drift along with meaning. Our timidity, our perplexity, our fear or our furor to dare it would only be justified by our experience in making our way.

—Translated by Jay Caplan

Contributors' Notes

(Notes from the original issue from which an article is reprinted here appear in italics. Updated information appears in roman.)

ORA AVNI is a Professor in the Department of French at Yale University. She has recently published *D'un passé à l'autre. Aux portes de l'histoire avec Patrick Modiano* (1997) and *The Resistance of Reference: Linguistics, Philosophy, and the Literary Text* (1990).

JACQUES DERRIDA *is a Visiting Professor in the Yale French Department. His most recent book is* Glas *(Paris: Galilee, 1974).* Professor at the Ecole des hautes études en sciences sociales in Paris, Derrida's most recent publications include *Demeure. Maurice Blanchot* (1998) and *Cosmopolites de tous les pays* (1997).

ROGER DRAGONETTI, *Professor of Medieval French Literature at the University of Geneva, has written on Mallarmé in recent articles and in his* Aux fontières du langage poétique *(Romanica Gadensia, 1961).* His later publications include *Mallarmé et l'esthétique du quotidien* (1992) and *Le gai savoir dans la rhétorique courtoise. Flamenca et Jourfroi de Poitiers* (1982).

JACQUES EHRMANN came to teach at Yale in 1962. He died in 1972, at the age of 41. His influence on students and readers was considerable. His passion and originality can be clearly seen in the volumes of *Yale French Studies* that he edited, and in his book *Un paradis désespéré. L'amour et l'illusion dans L'Astrée* (1962).

JACQUES GUICHARNAUD, *whose short stories,* Entre chien et loup *appeared with the Gallimard imprint during those "gala years," is at work on a study of Molière.* Currently Professor Emeritus in the Yale French Department, Guicharnaud was a popular and charismatic teacher during his forty-seven years at Yale. He was a leading

YFS 96, *50 Years of Yale French Studies: A Commemorative Anthology,* eds. Porter and Waters, © 1999 by Yale University.

figure in the Theater Studies program and, in the French Department, often taught courses on the seventeenth-century moralists and dramatists.

MICHAEL HOLQUIST, *Yale slavicist, is currently on leave in Leningrad.* Professor of Slavic and Comparative Literature at Yale, and Chair of the Department of Comparative Literature, he is currently working on a book devoted to philology and history.

FRANÇOISE JAOUËN is Associate Professor of French at Yale University and the author of *De l'art de plaire. Pascal, La Rochefoucauld, La Bruyère* (1996).

MARIO MAURIN, *of Bryn Mawr, has written a study of André Suarès.* He has taught modern French literature at Bryn Mawr college since 1953 and has also written about Henri de Régnier, Leopardi, Nerval, Hugo, Sand, Zola, Loti, Frost, Henri Peyre, and many others.

GEORGES MAY, *Assistant Professor at Yale, has published Tragédie cornelienne, tragédie racinienne and D'Ovide à Racine.* May taught at Yale for almost forty-five years, retiring in 1991. He was also Dean of Yale College for eight years and Provost of the University for two. His former students are among the major "dix-septiémistes" and "dix-huitiémistes" in the United States today.

JEREMY MITCHELL, *an Oxford graduate, is with the Consumers Union in England.*

HENRI PEYRE *has concluded his study of the contemporary French novel, which will appear under the aegis of the Oxford University Press.* He chaired the Yale French Department from 1939 to 1962. After retiring from Yale in 1969, he went on to a new career at the City University of New York. During the 1940s and 1950s this prolific writer and popular lecturer represented France for many Americans. He died in 1988.

CHARLES A. PORTER, Professor of French at Yale University, has written on Restif de la Bretonne, Chateaubriand, and Renaud Camus, among others.

ALYSON WATERS is the Managing Editor of *Yale French Studies* and a translator. She teaches translation and translation theory in the Yale French Department and has translated Louis Aragon, Eric Chevillard, Assia Djebar, Margot Kerlidou, and Henri Michaux, among others.

KURT WEINBERG taught for many years at the University of British Columbia and the University of Rochester. He was the author of books on Heine, Kafka, Gide's *Prométhée,* and of *The Figure of Faust in Valéry and Goethe* (1976). He died in 1996.

The following issues are available through **Yale University Press,** Customer Service Department, P.O. Box 209040, New Haven, CT 06520-9040.

69 The Lesson of Paul de Man (1985) $17.00
73 Everyday Life (1987) $17.00
75 The Politics of Tradition: Placing Women in French Literature (1988) $17.00
Special Issue: After the Age of Suspicion: The French Novel Today (1989) $17.00
76 Autour de Racine: Studies in Intertextuality (1989) $17.00
77 Reading the Archive: On Texts and Institutions (1990) $17.00
78 On Bataille (1990) $17.00
79 Literature and the Ethical Question (1991) $17.00

Special Issue: Contexts: Style and Value in Medieval Art and Literature (1991) $17.00
80 Baroque Topographies: Literature/History/ Philosophy (1992) $17.00
81 On Leiris (1992) $17.00
82 Post/Colonial Conditions Vol. 1 (1993) $17.00
83 Post/Colonial Conditions Vol. 2 (1993) $17.00
84 Boundaries: Writing and Drawing (1993) $17.00
85 Discourses of Jewish Identity in 20th-Century France (1994) $17.00
86 Corps Mystique, Corps Sacré (1994) $17.00
87 Another Look, Another

Woman (1995) $17.00
88 Depositions: Althusser, Balibar, Macherey (1995) $17.00
89 Drafts (1996) $17.00
90 Same Sex / Different Text? Gay and Lesbian Writing in French (1996) $17.00
91 Genet: In the Language of the Enemy (1997) $17.00
92 Exploring the Conversible World (1997) $17.00
93 The Place of Maurice Blanchot (1998) $17.00
94 Libertinage and Modernity (1999) $17.00
95 Rereading Allegory: Essays in Memory of Daniel Poirion (1999) $17.00

Special subscription rates are available on a calendar-year basis (2 issues per year):
Individual subscriptions $26.00
Institutional subscriptions $30.00

ORDER FORM   **Yale University Press,** P.O. Box 209040, New Haven, CT 06520-9040
I would like to purchase the following individual issues:

_____

_____

For individual issues, please add postage and handling:
Single issue, United States $2.75   Each additional issue $.50
Single issue, foreign countries $5.00   Each additional issue $1.00
Connecticut residents please add sales tax of 6%.

Payment of $_____ is enclosed (including sales tax if applicable).

MasterCard no. _____ Expiration date _____

VISA no. _____ Expiration date _____

Signature _____

SHIP TO _____

_____

_____

See the next page for ordering other back issues. Yale French Studies is also available through Xerox University Microfilms, 300 North Zeeb Road, Ann Arbor, MI 48106.

The following issues are still available through the **Yale French Studies Office**, P.O. Box 208251, New Haven, CT 06520-8251.

19/20 Contemporary Art $3.50	42 Zola $5.00	54 Mallarmé $5.00
33 Shakespeare $3.50	43 The Child's Part $5.00	61 Toward a Theory of Description $6.00
35 Sade $3.50	45 Language as Action $5.00	
39 Literature and Revolution $3.50	46 From Stage to Street $3.50	
	52 Graphesis $5.00	

Add for postage & handling

Single issue, United States $3.00 (Priority Mail)   Each additional issue $1.25
Single issue, United States $1.80 (Third Class)   Each additional issue $ .50
Single issue, foreign countries $2.50 (Book Rate)   Each additional issue $1.50

YALE FRENCH STUDIES, P.O. Box 208251, New Haven, Connecticut 06520-8251
A check made payable to YFS is enclosed. Please send me the following issue(s):

Issue no.   Title   Price

_____

_____

                                              Postage & handling _____

                                                        Total _____

Name _____

Number/Street _____

City _____ State _____ Zip _____

The following issues are now available through Periodicals Service Company, 11 Main Street, Germantown,N.Y. 12526, Phone: (518) 537-4700. Fax: (518) 537-5899.

1 Critical Bibliography of Existentialism	19/20 Contempoary Art
2 Modern Poets	21 Poetry Since the Liberation
3 Criticism & Creation	22 French Education
4 Literature & Ideas	23 Humor
5 The Modern Theatre	24 Midnight Novelists
6 France and World Literature	25 Albert Camus
7 André Gide	26 The Myth of Napoleon
8 What's Novel in the Novel	27 Women Writers
9 Symbolism	28 Rousseau
10 French-American Literature Relationships	29 The New Dramatists
11 Eros, Variations...	30 Sartre
12 God & the Writer	31 Surrealism
13 Romanticism Revisited	32 Paris in Literature
14 Motley: Today's French Theater	33 Shakespeare in France
15 Social & Political France	34 Proust
16 Foray through Existentialism	48 French Freud
17 The Art of the Cinema	51 Approaches to Medieval Romance
18 Passion & the Intellect, or Malraux	

36/37 Structuralism has been reprinted by Doubleday as an Anchor Book.
55/56 Literature and Psychoanalysis has been reprinted by Johns Hopkins University Press, and can be ordered through Customer Service, Johns Hopkins University Press, Baltimore, MD 21218.